Modern Language Association of America

Approaches to Teaching
World Literature

Joseph Gibaldi, Series Editor

1. Joseph Gibaldi, ed. *Approaches to Teaching Chaucer's* Canterbury Tales. 1980.
2. Carole Slade, ed. *Approaches to Teaching Dante's* Divine Comedy. 1982.
3. Richard Bjornson, ed. *Approaches to Teaching Cervantes'* Don Quixote. 1984.
4. Jess B. Bessinger, Jr., and Robert F. Yeager, eds. *Approaches to Teaching* Beowulf. 1984.
5. Richard J. Dunn, ed. *Approaches to Teaching Dickens'* David Copperfield. 1984.
6. Steven G. Kellman, ed. *Approaches to Teaching Camus's* The Plague. 1985.
7. Yvonne Shafer, ed. *Approaches to Teaching Ibsen's* A Doll House. 1985.
8. Martin Bickman, ed. *Approaches to Teaching Melville's* Moby-Dick. 1985.
9. Miriam Youngerman Miller and Jane Chance, eds. *Approaches to Teaching* Sir Gawain and the Green Knight. 1986.
10. Galbraith M. Crump, ed. *Approaches to Teaching Milton's* Paradise Lost. 1986.
11. Spencer Hall, with Jonathan Ramsey, eds. *Approaches to Teaching Wordsworth's Poetry.* 1986.
12. Robert H. Ray, ed. *Approaches to Teaching Shakespeare's* King Lear. 1986.
13. Kostas Myrsiades, ed. *Approaches to Teaching Homer's* Iliad *and* Odyssey. 1987.
14. Douglas J. McMillan, ed. *Approaches to Teaching Goethe's* Faust. 1987.
15. Renée Waldinger, ed. *Approaches to Teaching Voltaire's* Candide. 1987.
16. Bernard Koloski, ed. *Approaches to Teaching Chopin's* The Awakening. 1988.
17. Kenneth M. Roemer, ed. *Approaches to Teaching Momaday's* The Way to Rainy Mountain. 1988.
18. Edward J. Rielly, ed. *Approaches to Teaching Swift's* Gulliver's Travels. 1988.
19. Jewel Spears Brooker, ed. *Approaches to Teaching Eliot's Poetry and Plays.* 1988.
20. Melvyn New, ed. *Approaches to Teaching Sterne's* Tristram Shandy. 1989.
21. Robert F. Gleckner and Mark L. Greenberg, eds. *Approaches to Teaching Blake's* Songs of Innocence and of Experience. 1989.
22. Susan J. Rosowski, ed. *Approaches to Teaching Cather's* My Ántonia. 1989.
23. Carey Kaplan and Ellen Cronan Rose, eds. *Approaches to Teaching Lessing's* The Golden Notebook. 1989.
24. Susan Resneck Parr and Pancho Savery, eds. *Approaches to Teaching Ellison's* Invisible Man. 1989.
25. Barry N. Olshen and Yael S. Feldman, eds. *Approaches to Teaching the Hebrew Bible as Literature in Translation.* 1989.
26. Robin Riley Fast and Christine Mack Gordon, eds. *Approaches to Teaching Dickinson's Poetry.* 1989.

27. Spencer Hall, ed. *Approaches to Teaching Shelley's Poetry.* 1990.
28. Sidney Gottlieb, ed. *Approaches to Teaching the Metaphysical Poets.* 1990.
29. Richard K. Emmerson, ed. *Approaches to Teaching Medieval English Drama.* 1990.
30. Kathleen Blake, ed. *Approaches to Teaching Eliot's* Middlemarch. 1990.
31. María Elena de Valdés and Mario J. Valdés, eds. *Approaches to Teaching García Márquez's* One Hundred Years of Solitude. 1990.
32. Donald D. Kummings, ed. *Approaches to Teaching Whitman's* Leaves of Grass. 1990.
33. Stephen C. Behrendt, ed. *Approaches to Teaching Shelley's* Frankenstein. 1990.
34. June Schlueter and Enoch Brater, eds. *Approaches to Teaching Beckett's* Waiting for Godot. 1991.
35. Walter H. Evert and Jack W. Rhodes, eds. *Approaches to Teaching Keats's Poetry.* 1991.
36. Frederick W. Shilstone, ed. *Approaches to Teaching Byron's Poetry.* 1991.
37. Bernth Lindfors, ed. *Approaches to Teaching Achebe's* Things Fall Apart. 1991.
38. Richard E. Matlak, ed. *Approaches to Teaching Coleridge's Poetry and Prose.* 1991.
39. Shirley Geok-lin Lim, ed. *Approaches to Teaching Kingston's* The Woman Warrior. 1991.
40. Maureen Fries and Jeanie Watson, eds. *Approaches to Teaching the Arthurian Tradition.* 1992.
41. Maurice Hunt, ed. *Approaches to Teaching Shakespeare's* The Tempest *and Other Late Romances.* 1992.
42. Diane Long Hoeveler and Beth Lau, eds. *Approaches to Teaching Brontë's* Jane Eyre. 1993.
43. Jeffrey B. Berlin, ed. *Approaches to Teaching Mann's* Death in Venice *and Other Short Fiction.* 1992.

Approaches to Teaching Whitman's *Leaves of Grass*

Edited by

Donald D. Kummings

The Modern Language Association of America
New York   1990

Donald Barlow Stauffer, "Teaching Whitman's Old-Age Poems," copyright ©
1976, Case Western Reserve University, Human Values and Aging project.
Reprinted by permission.

Library of Congress Cataloging-in-Publication Data

Approaches to teaching Whitman's Leaves of Grass / edited by Donald D.
   Kummings.
      p.   cm.—(Approaches to teaching world literature ; 32)
   Includes bibliographical references and index.
   ISBN 0-87352-537-X   ISBN 0-87352-538-8 (pbk.)
      1. Whitman, Walt, 1819–1892. Leaves of grass.   2. Whitman, Walt,
   1819–1892—Study and teaching.   I. Kummings, Donald D.   II. Series.
   PS3238.A6   1990
   811'.3—dc20   90-44456

Cover illustration of the paperback edition: detail from Alexander Schilling,
Country Road [Long Island], c. 1890, etching.

Second printing 1992

Published by The Modern Language Association of America
10 Astor Place, New York, New York 10003-6981

CONTENTS

PREFACE TO THE SERIES

In *The Art of Teaching* Gilbert Highet wrote, "Bad teaching wastes a great deal of effort, and spoils many lives which might have been full of energy and happiness." All too many teachers have failed in their work, Highet argued, simply "because they have not thought about it." We hope that the Approaches to Teaching World Literature series, sponsored by the Modern Language Association's Publications Committee, will not only improve the craft—as well as the art—of teaching but also encourage serious and continuing discussion of the aims and methods of teaching literature.

The principal objective of the series is to collect within each volume different points of view on teaching a specific literary work, a literary tradition, or a writer widely taught at the undergraduate level. The preparation of each volume begins with a wide-ranging survey of instructors, thus enabling us to include in the volume the philosophies and approaches, thoughts and methods of scores of experienced teachers. The result is a sourcebook of material, information, and ideas on teaching the subject of the volume to undergraduates.

The series is intended to serve nonspecialists as well as specialists, inexperienced as well as experienced teachers, graduate students who wish to learn effective ways of teaching as well as senior professors who wish to compare their own approaches with the approaches of colleagues in other schools. Of course, no volume in the series can ever substitute for erudition, intelligence, creativity, and sensitivity in teaching. We hope merely that each book will point readers in useful directions; at most each will offer only a first step in the long journey to successful teaching.

Joseph Gibaldi
Series Editor

PREFACE TO THE VOLUME

In 1943, Max Eastman asserted that just as Shakespeare, Goethe, Pushkin, Dante, Hugo, and Li Po are the great poets of their countries, so Whitman is the great poet of America. Eastman's view was not widely shared by the men and women then teaching in America's colleges and universities. Indeed, years would go by before Whitman would be generally accepted, in the words of Galway Kinnell, "as our greatest native master, the bearer of the American tradition" (216). Whitman's rise began in the 1950s, signaled by a provocative essay by Randall Jarrell, "Walt Whitman: He Had His Nerve"; by an outpouring of major biographies and critical studies during the centennial of the first *Leaves of Grass*, celebrated 1955; and by the publication of Allen Ginsberg's *Howl*. Also important in Whitman's ascent was the gradually diminishing influence of the New Criticism, a formalist approach that dominated literary study for decades and tended to disparage Whitman and other writers whose work "placed a premium on simplicity, transparency, and emotional directness" (Lauter xviii). Nowadays, Whitman's reputation is secure, his place in the literary canon largely unchallenged. However, he often suffers from the treatment accorded many another major author—that is, readers approach him dutifully, reverentially, as an exhibit in a wax museum rather than as a poet of living relevance. This volume attempts to suggest ways in which teachers may vitalize Whitman and his *Leaves* for present and future generations of students.

This volume, like its predecessors in the MLA's Approaches to Teaching World Literature series, is addressed to the beginning or nonspecialist teacher at the undergraduate level. Parts of the book, however, are also directed to senior professors and Whitman specialists, graduate students, and advanced undergraduates who need for their research projects the guidance provided by an evaluative review of Whitman and Whitman-related studies.

The volume is divided into two parts: "Materials" and "Approaches." The first part, written by the editor, discusses such topics as preferred editions of *Leaves of Grass*, required and recommended student readings, essential secondary materials, and useful teaching aids, such as tapes, records, and films. Restrictions on space here require a limited yet representative listing of titles, with an emphasis on book-length studies and significant audiovisual resources. Much of the information in "Materials" is derived from the more than one hundred responses to the survey of Whitman teachers that preceded work on this volume.

The second part consists of essays written by invited contributors. Nineteen experienced instructors here describe their approaches to teaching Whitman's poetry and prose. The editor has made an effort to strike a balance between innovative and traditional methods and to include approaches that are broadly representative of pedagogical philosophy and method. For particulars on the essays, see the introduction at the beginning of part 2. Completing the book are a list of contributors and survey participants, a Works Cited list, and an index of proper names.

Many individuals have contributed to the creation of this volume. Especially deserving of thanks are the participants in the Modern Language Association survey and the members of the Association's Committee on Teaching and Related Professional Activities (now the Publications Committee). The former generously shared with me their knowledge and experience; the latter endorsed this Whitman project. Also entitled to a special thanks is the series editor, Joseph Gibaldi. From beginning to end, he offered encouragement and sound counsel.

I am profoundly indebted to my friend Earle Labor—not only for his meticulous criticism of parts of the manuscript but also for his inspirational commitment to life and letters. I am much obliged to Ed Folsom, who gave freely of his time and expertise at several stages of this undertaking. For informed and useful suggestions, I am grateful to John Buenker, Ronald Gottesman, Andrew McLean, and Alan Shucard. And for the sabbatical during which I wrote the prospectus for this volume, I am pleased to acknowledge the Parkside Campus of the University of Wisconsin.

Finally, I wish to express my gratitude to Trudy Rivest, who produced a thoroughly professional typescript; to Lynn Gorecki, who served as my research assistant for two semesters; to my son Jeremy, who read proof; and to my wife, Patricia, who provided—in the midst of her own demanding career—unfailing support.

The deepest source of inspiration during the course of my work has been the cherished remembrance of my son Kevin S. Kummings, 1963–1981. It is to his memory that this book is dedicated.

DDK

Part One

MATERIALS

Donald D. Kummings

Editions and Anthologies

As revealed by the survey of Whitman teachers that preceded preparation of this book, *Leaves of Grass* is taught, either wholly or in part, in a rich assortment of undergraduate courses. Prominent in this mélange are Composition and Literature, Introduction to Poetry, American Literature to 1865 (or American Literature 1855–1920), Survey of American Poetry, Literature and Culture of Nineteenth-Century America, The American Renaissance (or American Romanticism), Writers of the Gilded Age, American Literary Classics, Major Authors (Blake and Whitman; Emerson and Whitman; Whitman and Dickinson; Whitman, Williams, and Ginsberg; etc.), Literary Theory, Masterpieces of World Literature, Literature across Two Continents, and Seminar on Whitman. The uses made of Whitman's poems (and prose writings) vary from class to class and from teacher to teacher. Fortunately, the undergraduate instructor finds relatively easy the task of choosing a textbook, for there are many fine editions of *Leaves of Grass* as well as several anthologies featuring ample and judicious selections.

Among the nearly two dozen editions of *Leaves of Grass* currently in print one is especially popular with Whitman teachers: the *Norton Critical Edition*, edited by Sculley Bradley and Harold W. Blodgett. The Norton presents the edition preferred by the poet himself, the deathbed edition of 1891–92. Because the Norton reproduces the contents of the standard scholarly edition of *Leaves* (the *Comprehensive Reader's Edition*), its text is authoritative. Along with *Leaves* proper, the Norton includes "Old Age Echoes" (a group of thirteen poems assembled by Whitman's executors), sixty-seven poems and passages excluded from *Leaves*, forty-three poems posthumously published and here collected for the first time, twenty-two poems never before published, and a selection of manuscript fragments. It also includes key prose writings: the prefaces, "A Backward Glance o'er Travel'd Roads," and eight pages of informal comments arranged under the title "Whitman on His Art." Finally, it contains an introduction (to the growth of *Leaves of Grass*), an album of Whitman photographs, a chronology of the poet's life, and a selection of essays by thirty critics. Most teachers have high praise for the Norton's extensive footnotes, which are variously bibliographical, exegetical, and interpretive, and for its line numbers, which are provided for both poetry and prose. There are two aspects of the Norton about which survey respondents complained: its exclusion of *Democratic Vistas* and its price. As one remarked, "The edition's cost restricts its use to graduate and certain advanced undergraduate classes. It is too expensive for a class in which students are required to purchase a number of other books or in which limited time is spent on Whitman."

While most respondents admired the authoritativeness of the *Norton Critical Edition*, quite a few preferred either *Walt Whitman's* Leaves of Grass:

The First (1855) Edition, edited by Malcolm Cowley, or Leaves of Grass *by Walt Whitman: Facsimile Edition of the 1860 Text,* edited by Roy Harvey Pearce. Such a preference reflects the common view that the best Whitman is early Whitman. Many teachers agree with Cowley that certain Whitman poems, notably "Song of Myself" and "The Sleepers," are most effectively realized in their original versions and that all twelve poems of the 1855 *Leaves* are in the author's "boldest and freshest style." And many agree with Pearce that the 1860 *Leaves* is the product of Whitman's most fecund period and the only edition that can be called an "articulated whole." The texts honored by Cowley and Pearce, however, are far less inclusive than the one honored by Bradley and Blodgett. Moreover, neither the 1855 nor the 1860 text is the *Leaves* that Whitman himself approved and recommended to future generations. Thus the Cowley and Pearce editions, which both contain excellent introductions, would seem to have limited and specialized uses. They are probably most appropriate in courses that study the evolution of *Leaves of Grass.*

An edition rapidly gaining favor among undergraduate as well as graduate instructors is Justin Kaplan's *Walt Whitman: Complete Poetry and Collected Prose*—one of the inaugural volumes in the Library of America series. The Kaplan edition is the most comprehensive one-volume collection of Whitman ever published. It includes, in facsimile, the 1855 *Leaves of Grass* (complete), the 1891–92 "authorized" *Leaves* (complete), the 1892 *Complete Prose Works* (*Specimen Days, Collect, Notes Left Over, Pieces in Early Youth, November Boughs, Good-Bye My Fancy,* and *Memoranda*) and a supplementary group of "fugitive prose pieces which, in the editor's opinion, clearly belong with the rest" ("The Eighteenth Presidency!," Emerson's 1855 letter to Whitman, Whitman's 1856 response to his "dear Friend and Master," and a handful of Whitman notes to various editions of *Leaves*). Though the Library of America edition omits some work—for example, "Old Age Echoes" and the excluded and uncollected poems printed in the Norton—it nevertheless makes available about as much material as any teacher could want. Even if relatively expensive, this edition has to be considered a prime candidate for adoption in the Whitman seminar or other advanced courses.

Five other editions of *Leaves of Grass* were strongly recommended by various respondents: *Walt Whitman: Complete Poetry and Selected Prose,* edited by James E. Miller, Jr.; Leaves of Grass *and Selected Prose,* edited by Lawrence Buell; *The Portable Walt Whitman,* edited by Mark Van Doren and revised by Malcolm Cowley; *Walt Whitman:* Leaves of Grass, edited by Gay Wilson Allen; and *Walt Whitman: The Complete Poems,* edited by Francis Murphy. The Miller, Buell, Allen, and Murphy editions reprint the complete 1891–92 *Leaves of Grass;* the Van Doren reprints selections from the first and last *Leaves*—seven poems from the 1855, ninety-three from the 1891–92 edition. Extra poems appear in the collections by Miller ("Rejected Poems") and Murphy ("Old Age Echoes," "Poems Excluded from

Leaves of Grass," "Early Poems," and the 1855 text of "Song of Myself"). Whitman's prose is particularly well represented in the Miller, Buell, and Van Doren editions: all three include the 1855 preface, "A Backward Glance o'er Travel'd Roads," and *Democratic Vistas;* and two of them (Buell and Van Doren) provide *Specimen Days* complete. All five editions have reliable texts and informative introductions. Three have special features: in Miller, the "Glossary of Difficult Terms"; in Buell, "Documents"—a sampling of letters, reviews, journal excerpts, .and so on, pertinent to *Leaves;* and in Murphy, seventy-six pages of first-rate notes on the poems. Because the five editions are available in paperback and modestly priced, they can be used in a wide range of courses.

Along with their observations on "teaching editions" of *Leaves of Grass,* respondents provided remarks on anthologies in which Whitman is represented. Their comments tended to focus on collections suitable for introductory surveys of American literature, those classes students take either for general education credit or as part of the English major. The textbook most widely adopted in the lower-division survey is volume 1 of *The Norton Anthology of American Literature* (3rd ed.), edited by Nina Baym et al.; the section in which Whitman appears is edited by Hershel Parker. By and large, teachers were satisfied with the Norton's Whitman selections. They praised Parker's "substantial and lively introduction," the "terse but full textual notes" at the bottom of the page, and the "reliable, up-to-date bibliographical notes" at the back of the book. However, some teachers complained because the Whitman material is not duplicated in volume 2 of the *Norton Anthology.* One said, "Members of my department like the option of presenting Whitman in either the first or the second semester of a two-semester course." Two other collections were frequently mentioned: *Anthology of American Literature,* two volumes (4th ed.), whose general editor is George McMichael, and *The American Tradition in Literature,* two volumes (7th ed.), edited by George Perkins et al. While less enthusiastically endorsed than the Norton, these anthologies offer copious selections and helpful editorial materials. Both include Whitman in the first and second volumes.

Required and Recommended Student Reading

Most of those who teach Whitman's poetry at the undergraduate level do not require secondary readings, and some instructors do not even recommend them, except in upper-division classes. One respondent summed up the view of many when he said, "I don't find the time for supplementary works. So many poems to look at!" There are indeed numerous poems in *Leaves of Grass* that merit a look in the undergraduate classroom. Most teachers regard as musts "Song of Myself," "Out of the Cradle Endlessly Rocking," "When Lilacs Last in the Dooryard Bloom'd," "Crossing Brooklyn Ferry," and "Passage to India." Other poems frequently assigned include selections from (or, in advanced courses, all of) the *Drum-Taps, Calamus*, and *Children of Adam* groups. Still others are "The Sleepers," "There Was a Child Went Forth," "As I Ebb'd with the Ocean of Life," "A Noiseless Patient Spider," "When I Heard the Learn'd Astronomer," "The Dalliance of the Eagles," "To a Locomotive in Winter," "This Compost," "Chanting the Square Deific," "Prayer of Columbus," "Starting from Paumanok," "Salut au Monde!," "Song of the Open Road," "A Song of the Rolling Earth," and "So Long!" Nevertheless, undaunted by the sheer bulk of Whitman's poetry or by constraints on time, some instructors do require or recommend secondary readings.

The works teachers most often ask their students to read in conjunction with the poetry of *Leaves of Grass* are Whitman's prose writings. Esteemed among these are five essays—declarations of literary intentions—that the poet published in various editions of his masterwork: the prefaces of 1855, 1856, 1872, and 1876, and "A Backward Glance o'er Travel'd Roads" (1888). A particular favorite in the classroom is the 1855 preface, a seminal statement of American poetic theory that is serviceable as an introduction to, and gloss on, "Song of Myself." Worth noting here is that a few teachers reported using William Everson's version of the 1855 preface. In *American Bard* (1982), Everson—without altering Whitman's words or word order—recast the preface's prose into lines of verse. Everson's "arrangement" prompted James E. Miller, Jr., to say, "Now [the 1855 preface] can be seen and read for what it is, one of the great poems of *Leaves of Grass*."

Three other prose works by Whitman—*Democratic Vistas, Specimen Days*, and *An American Primer*—are also valued, especially by teachers of upper-level classes. Harold W. Blodgett has called the first work "the most remarkable single pronouncement upon American democracy in American literature" (114). Teachers assign all or parts of it for different reasons, but mainly, perhaps, to show Whitman as a severe, penetrating critic of political and social realities of nineteenth-century America, thus qualifying students' impressions of the poet as an utter optimist or idealist. *Specimen Days*, as Whitman himself said, is "a way-ward book": it is a grab bag of reminiscences and autobiographical material, war memorandums, nature notes, and miscellaneous sketches. Still, it contains fine writing that teachers can profitably assign in connection with the poetry of *Leaves*, as one respondent indicated: "I often use the Civil War sections of [*Specimen Days*] at all levels in order to discuss *Drum-Taps*; [Whitman's] prose brings those poems immediately alive and contextualizes them effectively." Like *Specimen Days*, *An American Primer* is an odd and improvised work, one that consists of some 110 miscellaneous notes on the English language. Yet teachers find it provocative and helpful in certain courses. One respondent said, "I have used *An American Primer* successfully in my seminar on Whitman. His views on the vitality and wellsprings of American English form an excellent context for studying his poetic diction."

Some instructors believe that *Leaves of Grass* is best considered in its relation to New England Transcendentalism or Emersonianism. Accordingly, they highlight the Walt Whitman–Ralph Waldo Emerson nexus and require students to read, along with Whitman's poetry, one or more of Emerson's lectures or essays. The Emerson work they most often use is "The Poet." Presented initially as a lecture (which Whitman heard in New York in 1842) and then published in *Essays: Second Series* (1844), eleven years before the appearance of *Leaves of Grass*, "The Poet" describes the as-yet-unseen ideal poet and the incomparable American materials awaiting the poet's "tyrannous eye." Critics now generally agree that this essay strongly influenced the development of Whitman's theory and practice as an "American bard." Other Emerson works sometimes employed in connection with *Leaves* include "Self-Reliance," "The American Scholar," "The Over-Soul," "The Divinity School Address," "Experience," and *Nature*.

Occasionally required or recommended at the undergraduate level are various critical essays that tend to take the form of a broad overview or general assessment. The two most often mentioned by survey respondents were D. H. Lawrence's "Whitman" and Randall Jarrell's "Walt Whitman: He Had His Nerve." First published as a chapter in *Studies in Classic American Literature* in 1923, Lawrence's essay is a brilliant tour de force on Whitman's "mentalizing tendencies" and "American heroic message." Jarrell's article, originally published in the *Kenyon Review* in 1952, is a wonderfully persuasive demonstration of Whitman's skill and power as a poet. Other essays noted by respondents include Pablo Neruda's "We Live in a Whitmanesque Age," James Wright's "Delicacy of Walt Whitman," Robert Bly's "What Whitman Did Not Give Us," Kenneth Rexroth's "Walt Whitman," James E. Miller's "Walt Whitman's Omnisexual Vision," Floyd Stovall's "Main Drifts in Whitman's Poetry," and Helen Vendler's "Body Language: *Leaves of Grass* and the Articulation of Sexual Awareness." Most of these essays can be found in the standard collections of Whitman criticism.

Few teachers seem to require undergraduates to read full-length biographies, critical works, background studies, or anthologies of criticism. For advanced classes, however, many do put such books on library reserve, there to be consulted for oral reports, term projects, or critical papers. According to the survey, the Whitman monographs most frequently placed on the reserve shelf are these: (1) biographies: Gay Wilson Allen's *Solitary Singer*, Justin Kaplan's *Walt Whitman: A Life*, Paul Zweig's *Walt Whitman: The Making of the Poet*, and Roger Asselineau's *Evolution of Walt Whitman: The Creation of a Personality*; (2) critical works: Allen's *New Walt Whitman Handbook* and *A Reader's Guide to Walt Whitman*, James E. Miller's *Critical Guide to* Leaves of Grass, Edwin Haviland Miller's *Walt Whitman's Poetry: A Psychological Journey*, Asselineau's *Evolution of Walt Whitman: The Creation of a Book*, C. Carroll Hollis's *Language and Style in* Leaves of Grass, and Howard J. Waskow's *Whitman: Explorations in Form*; (3) background studies: F. O. Matthiessen's *American Renaissance*, Lawrence Buell's *Literary Transcendentalism*, Roy Harvey Pearce's *Continuity of American Poetry*, and Robert K. Martin's *Homosexual Tradition in American Poetry*; (4) anthologies of criticism: Jim Perlman, Ed Folsom, and Dan Campion, editors, *Walt Whitman: The Measure of His Song*; Francis Murphy, editor, *Walt Whitman: A Critical Anthology*; and Pearce, editor, *Whitman: A Collection of Critical Essays*. A landmark book—David S. Reynolds's *Beneath the American Renaissance*—appeared in print after Whitman teachers returned their responses to the survey; it undoubtedly belongs on the list of background studies.

The Instructor's Library

Reference Tools

If any reference on Whitman may be described as indispensable, it is Gay Wilson Allen's encyclopedic *New Walt Whitman Handbook*. The first of its five chapters recounts the development of Whitman biography, beginning with the hagiography of the poet's personal friends and culminating in the scholarly, "objective" biography of the present era. The second traces the complex evolution of Whitman's poetry through the six editions of *Leaves of Grass*, those of 1855, 1856, 1860, 1867, 1871, and 1881. Chapter 3 reviews Whitman's social, political, and philosophical ideas. Chapter 4 discusses the poet's prosodic techniques and artistry. The last chapter surveys Whitman's reception and influence in foreign countries. Rounding out the volume are selected bibliographies, a chronological table, and an introduction that comments on Whitman scholarship from 1975 to 1985. The book is now available in paperback.

As recently as 1980, bibliographic resources on Whitman were scattered and fragmentary. Teachers and scholars had to rummage among at least half a dozen different sources, each with limitations, in order to piece together anything like a complete bibliography. Then appeared *Walt Whitman, 1838–1939: A Reference Guide*, by Scott Giantvalley, and *Walt Whitman, 1940–1975: A Reference Guide*, by Donald D. Kummings, now generally regarded as the standard bibliographies of writings about Whitman. These two comprehensive volumes provide fully annotated year-by-year lists of nearly 8,200 items—book-length studies, monographs, dissertations, articles, chapters or passages in books, notes, reviews, and significant incidental references. Easy access to entries is ensured by author, title, and subject indexes. For a supplement to Giantvalley's book, see his "*Walt Whitman, 1838–1939: A Reference Guide*: Additional Annotations." For bibliographies of secondary writings published after 1975, see the *Walt Whitman Quarterly Review* (which contains the most complete listings), the *MLA International Bibliography* (published annually), and *American Literature*, each issue of which features "A Selected, Annotated List of Current Articles on American Literature."

Instructors interested in critical or evaluative bibliographies should consult the annual surveys in *American Literary Scholarship* (1963–). Far from inclusive, these overviews nevertheless assay the best of a given year's production. Clearly in need of updating but still helpful are Roger Asselineau's chapter on Whitman in *Eight American Authors* and the bibliographical assessments in *Literary History of the United States: Bibliography*, by Robert E. Spiller et al. Ed Folsom's "Whitman Project: A Review Essay" is narrow in scope but illuminating in its judgments of recent textual, bibliographical, biographical, and critical work on the poet. Also deserving mention is the American literature section in the annual volumes of *The Year's Work in English*.

Other useful bibliographies include four brief ones that list poems dealing in some essential way with Whitman: Roberts W. French's "Whitman as Poetic Subject," Ed Folsom's "Poets Respond: A Bibliographic Chronology," Edward A. Malone's "Whitman as Poetic Subject: Additional Citations," and Folsom's "Poets Continue to Respond: More Citations of Whitman as Poetic Subject." There are two reasonably complete bibliographies of Whitman bibliographies: James T. F. Tanner's for the years 1902–64 and Donald D. Kummings's for 1897–1982. Finally, there is *American Studies: An Annotated Bibliography* (1986), edited by Jack Salzman. This three-volume compilation lists and synopsizes more than 7,600 books that fall into eleven distinct fields of American studies: anthropology and folklore; art and architecture; history; literature; music; political science; popular culture; psychology; religion; sociology; and science, technology, and medicine. Although *American Studies* is not directly concerned with Whitman, it cites dozens of relevant scholarly works.

A valuable resource for anyone wishing to explore Whitman's language or style is Edwin Harold Eby's *Concordance of Walt Whitman's Leaves of Grass and Selected Prose Writings* (1949–54). Originally published in five fascicles, this reference work was reprinted in 1969 in a one-volume edition. Unfortunately, Eby's concordance is keyed to outdated editions of Whitman's poetry and prose.

Not to be overlooked as reference tools are the twenty-two volumes of *The Collected Writings of Walt Whitman*, whose general editors are Gay Wilson Allen and Sculley Bradley. This massive edition, still in progress, includes *The Early Poems and the Fiction*, edited by Thomas L. Brasher; *Prose Works 1892*, two volumes, edited by Floyd Stovall; *The Correspondence*, six volumes, edited by Edwin Haviland Miller; *Leaves of Grass: Comprehensive Reader's Edition*, edited by Harold W. Blodgett and Sculley Bradley; *Daybooks and Notebooks*, three volumes, edited by William White; *Leaves of Grass: A Textual Variorum of the Printed Poems*, three volumes, edited by Bradley, Blodgett, Arthur Golden, and White; and *Notebooks and Unpublished Prose Manuscripts*, six volumes, edited by Edward F. Grier. *The Collected Writings* provides not only definitive texts but also informative introductions, elaborate accounts of textual variants, and abundant notes (biographical, bibliographical, historical, and critical).

Biographical and Critical Works

The biographies most frequently recommended by veteran teachers of Whitman are Gay Wilson Allen's *Solitary Singer*, Justin Kaplan's *Walt Whitman: A Life*, Paul Zweig's *Walt Whitman: The Making of the Poet*, and Roger

Asselineau's *Evolution of Walt Whitman: The Creation of a Personality.* Many respondents called Allen's the definitive biography, praising its objectivity, reliability, and thoroughness: "It contains information not easily found elsewhere." Nevertheless, a few teachers did complain of its plodding manner, one contending that the book "is 'exhaustive' not only in the best but in the worst sense of the word." Teachers referred to Kaplan's biography as fresh, fetching, highly readable—"a biography for the eighties." However, several respondents disagreed. One said, "I've yet to understand why Kaplan's biography has earned so much praise. He drew only on secondary materials for most of his work, and he didn't question those materials. His quotations from the poetry are particularly gratuitous; I get no sense that he understands the poetry or has even read it very carefully." There were numerous accolades for Zweig's book. One instructor characterized it as "tremendously suggestive, especially for teaching Whitman, and [it's] particularly good with the Civil War material (the place I think Allen's is weakest)." Another instructor, though, dismissed Zweig's account as a "masterwork of histrionics." Finally, many admired what one respondent called the "solid scholarship" of Asselineau's biography, although some instructors found it weak on the poet's social and cultural background.

Three other biographies often received laudatory notices: *Walt Whitman Reconsidered*, by Richard Chase; *The Foreground of* Leaves of Grass, by Floyd Stovall; and *The Historic Whitman*, by Joseph Jay Rubin. Of Chase's study a respondent said, it is "one of those 'old-fashioned' critical works that remains more valuable than most contemporary writing on Whitman." Stovall's biography elicited a comment that applies equally well to Rubin's: "Maybe more than a beginning teacher would want to tackle, but the book is surprisingly easy to read, and it's full of useful information on Whitman's early career and sources."

Respondents now and then called attention to older biographies that they considered "still of value" or "still worth looking into": Newton Arvin's *Whitman*, Frederik Schyberg's *Walt Whitman*, Henry Seidel Canby's *Walt Whitman: An American*, Emory Holloway's *Whitman: An Interpretation in Narrative*, and Bliss Perry's *Walt Whitman: His Life and Work*. They also referred on occasion to works "of real biographical value." These include the six volumes of Horace Traubel's *With Walt Whitman in Camden* (which provide "literal transcriptions" of Whitman's casual talks with the author and with others during the last years of the poet's life) and five collections of letters written by Whitman's relatives and close associates: *Civil War Letters of George Washington Whitman*, edited by Jerome M. Loving; *Mattie: The Letters of Martha Mitchell Whitman*, edited by Randall H. Waldron; *The Letters of Dr. Richard Maurice Bucke to Walt Whitman*, edited by Artem Lozynsky; *Dear Brother Walt: The Letters of Thomas Jefferson Whitman*, edited by Dennis Berthold and Kenneth M. Price; and *Calamus Lovers: Walt Whitman's Working-Class Camerados*, edited by Charley Shively.

Full-length critical works on Whitman are plentiful, and once again survey respondents have proved helpful in identifying those most likely to benefit the teacher. The principal critical works tend to fall, albeit roughly in some cases, into six categories: general introductions to the poet's life and works; discussions of interrelations between Whitman and other poets; psychological, philosophical, and religious studies; analyses of literary technique; sociocultural investigations; and studies of reception and influence.

Regarded as the best of the general introductions are Gay Wilson Allen's *New Walt Whitman Handbook*, James E. Miller's *Critical Guide to* Leaves of Grass, and Roger Asselineau's *Evolution of Walt Whitman: The Creation of a Book*. Allen's *Handbook* discusses biographical studies of Whitman, the growth of *Leaves of Grass*, and the poet's thought, art, and international influence. According to one respondent, Allen's summary evaluation is "certainly the most useful tool available for the new teacher of Whitman— comprehensive, direct, balanced." (For additional remarks on the *Handbook*, see the section "Reference Tools.") Miller's *Critical Guide* provides close readings of Whitman's major poems and a structural analysis of *Leaves of Grass* as a whole. Asselineau's *Creation of a Book* examines Whitman's main themes—mysticism, metaphysics, ethics, aesthetics, sexuality, patriotism, democracy, slavery, industrialism—and certain of his poetic techniques—style, language, prosody. Other worthwhile introductions are Allen's *Reader's Guide to Walt Whitman* and Miller's *Walt Whitman*, a volume produced for the Twayne series.

Notable among studies exploring relationships or correspondences between Whitman and other writers are *Emerson, Whitman, and the American Muse*, by Jerome Loving, and *Walt Whitman and Emily Dickinson: Poetry of the Central Consciousness*, by Agnieszka Salska. Loving investigates in detail the personal and literary connections of Emerson and Whitman. One respondent considered his book especially useful for the survey teacher. Salska develops an extended comparison of two poets who drew on a common source—Emersonian transcendentalism—and yet produced markedly contrasting styles of poetry. Other helpful comparative studies include *Walt Whitman and Wallace Stevens*, by Diane Middlebrook; *American Beauty: William Carlos Williams and the Modernist Whitman*, by Stephen Tapscott; and *T. S. Eliot and Walt Whitman*, by Sydney Musgrove.

Provocative criticism of Whitman and his poetry can be found in books whose orientation is psychological, philosophical, or religious, notably Edwin Haviland Miller's *Walt Whitman's Poetry: A Psychological Journey*, Stephen A. Black's *Whitman's Journeys into Chaos: A Psychoanalytic Study of the Poetic Process*, David Cavitch's *My Soul and I: The Inner Life of Walt Whitman*, V. K. Chari's *Whitman in the Light of Vedantic Mysticism*, George B. Hutchinson's *Ecstatic Whitman: Literary Shamanism and the Crisis of the Union*, and David Kuebrich's *Minor Prophecy: Walt Whitman's New*

American Religion. The most celebrated of these analyses is Miller's. One instructor called his book "the best of the psychological studies and, in addition, a good introduction to the psychological study of literature." Another pronounced it "the best book on Whitman." Miller's thesis is that Whitman's major poems take the form of regressive psychic journeys that constitute a search for a womblike condition.

Informative discussions of Whitman's literary techniques can be found in *Language and Style in* Leaves of Grass, by C. Carroll Hollis; *Whitman: Explorations in Form,* by Howard J. Waskow; *The Structure of* Leaves of Grass, by Thomas Edward Crawley; and *The Trial of the Poet: An Interpretation of the First Edition of* Leaves of Grass, by Ivan Marki. Hollis demonstrates that the revolutionary linguistic and stylistic features of the 1855, 1856, and 1860 editions of *Leaves of Grass* derive from the oratorical tradition in mid-nineteenth-century America. One respondent declared that Hollis's study "would be illuminating for anyone teaching [Whitman] at any level." Waskow maintains that Whitman views reality as a "bipolar unity" and that his vision generates different kinds of poetic forms: didactic, imagistic, narrative, dramatic, and "reader engagement." Crawley argues that a unifying principle runs through *Leaves of Grass* and culminates—in the edition of 1881—in a significant structural pattern. Emphasizing structural analysis and explication, Marki highlights the virtues (as well as several flaws) of the 1855 *Leaves.* Other books that comment on Whitman's artistry are *Walt Whitman's "Song of Myself": A Mosaic of Interpretations,* by Edwin Haviland Miller; *The Uncertain Self: Whitman's Drama of Identity,* by E. Fred Carlisle; *The Dear Love of Man: Tragic and Lyric Communion in Walt Whitman,* by John Snyder; and *Walt Whitman's Poetry and the Evolution of Rhythmic Forms,* by Pasquale Jannacone.

Among the studies that emphasize the social and cultural context of Whitman's writings four stand out: *Walt Whitman and the Body Beautiful,* by Harold Aspiz; *The Lunar Light of Whitman's Poetry,* by M. Wynn Thomas; *Whitman the Political Poet,* by Betsy Erkkila; and *Whitman's Poetry of the Body: Sexuality, Politics, and the Text,* by Myrth Jimmie Killingsworth. Aspiz demonstrates that *Leaves of Grass* was shaped in fundamental ways by Whitman's obsession with the human body and with the scientific and quasi-scientific medical lore of his day. Thomas shows how changes in Whitman's poetry reflected the evolution of nineteenth-century American capitalism from an artisanal to an urban-monopolistic phase. Erkkila reveals that Whitman's poems engage—through language, symbol, and myth—the power struggles of his time, involving not only the issue of state governance but also the issues of race, gender, class, capital, technology, western expansion, and war. Killingsworth points out the profound social and political implications of Whitman's revolutionary sexual themes and of his "radical use of idiosyncratic tropes" (46). Additional studies with a sociocultural dimension are *Walt Whitman: Poet of Science*, by Joseph Beaver; *Walt Whitman and Opera*, by Robert D. Faner; and *Whitman as Editor of the* Brooklyn Daily Eagle, by Thomas L. Brasher.

For an enlightening account of Whitman's reception and influence in foreign countries the novice teacher should turn initially to the last chapter of Allen's *New Walt Whitman Handbook*: "Walt Whitman and World Literature." Also instructive are Allen's *Walt Whitman Abroad*, a gathering of essays by various authors on Whitman's influence in Germany, France, Scandinavia, Russia, Italy, Spain and Latin America, Israel, Japan, and India; and Roger Asselineau and William White's *Walt Whitman in Europe Today*, which contains essays, again by various authors, on Whitman's "presence" in Spain, Germany, Belgium, France, Italy, Czechoslovakia, Yugoslavia, Denmark, Sweden, Iceland, and Russia. Providing expanded coverage of certain countries are Betsy Erkkila's *Walt Whitman among the French*, Harold W. Blodgett's *Walt Whitman in England*, and Fernando Alegría's *Walt Whitman en Hispanòamérica*. For information on Whitman's reputation in his own country the most helpful sources are Charles B. Willard's *Whitman's American Fame: The Growth of His Reputation in America after 1892* and Jay B. Hubbell's *Who Are the Major American Writers? A Study of the Changing Literary Canon*.

Along with the biographical and analytical works surveyed here, teachers may wish to consult anthologies of criticism, for these make readily accessible many of the best or most suggestive of the briefer assessments of Whitman—chapters from books, scholarly articles, conference papers, review essays, poetic tributes. Of the numerous collections available, the one most widely admired is *Walt Whitman: The Measure of His Song*, edited by Jim Perlman, Ed Folsom, and Dan Campion. One respondent judged it "the best compilation of appreciative and contagious comment." Another declared, "If I had to rely on a single volume of critical assessments, appreciations, etc., this would be it." Devoted wholly to nonacademic responses to Whitman, *Measure* consists of some ninety-three essays, letters, and poems by writers such as Emerson, Thoreau, Swinburne, Hopkins, Pound, D. H. Lawrence, Hart Crane, Lorca, Neruda, Henry Miller, Borges, Ginsberg, Berryman, Creeley, Levertov, Kinnell, June Jordan, and Bly. Somewhat comparable collections include *Start with the Sun: Studies in Cosmic Poetry*, by James E. Miller, Jr., Karl Shapiro, and Bernice Slote, and *The Artistic Legacy of Walt Whitman*, edited by Edwin Haviland Miller.

More academic or scholarly are *Walt Whitman: A Critical Anthology*, edited by Francis Murphy; *A Century of Whitman Criticism*, edited by Edwin Haviland Miller; *Walt Whitman: The Critical Heritage*, edited by Milton Hindus; and *Critical Essays on Walt Whitman*, edited by James Woodress. Like the volume edited by Perlman, Folsom, and Campion, these four compilations include selections dating from the mid-1850s to the early

1980s and thus encourage a historical overview of critical reactions to Whitman.

Some anthologies are notable for their generous samplings of modern and contemporary criticism. Those most utilized are *Whitman: A Collection of Critical Essays*, edited by Roy Harvey Pearce; *The Presence of Walt Whitman*, edited by R. W. B. Lewis; *Leaves of Grass One Hundred Years After*, edited by Hindus; *Walt Whitman: A Collection of Criticism*, edited by Arthur Golden; *Walt Whitman: Here and Now*, edited by Joann P. Krieg; and *On Whitman: The Best from American Literature*, edited by Edwin H. Cady and Louis J. Budd.

Finally, special mention should be made of chapters on Whitman in the following books: Randall Jarrell's *Poetry and the Age*, D. H. Lawrence's *Studies in Classic American Literature*, Tony Tanner's *Reign of Wonder*, Charles Feidelson's *Symbolism and American Literature*, Albert Gelpi's *Tenth Muse: The Psyche of the American Poet*, Martin Bickman's *Unsounded Centre: Jungian Studies in American Romanticism*, Edwin S. Fussell's *Lucifer in Harness: American Meter, Metaphor, and Diction*, Gay Wilson Allen's *American Prosody*, John F. Lynen's *Design of the Present: Essays on Time and Form in American Literature*, and Robert Shulman's *Social Criticism and Nineteenth-Century American Fictions*. Widely applauded among these contributions is Jarrell's, with one respondent describing it as "*the* exemplary introduction to the poet. Would that all of us could do in two weeks in a survey course what Jarrell does in fifteen pages, that is, give students a sense of what a magnificent poet Whitman is."

Background Studies

Among works illuminating the literary, historical, political, and social backgrounds of *Leaves of Grass*, F. O. Matthiessen's *American Renaissance: Art and Expression in the Age of Emerson and Whitman* heads the list for many teachers. Although outdated in certain respects, Matthiessen's study contains stimulating remarks on the language and style of *Leaves* and on the interrelations of Whitman and four of his contemporaries—Emerson, Thoreau, Hawthorne, and Melville. Comparable to Matthiessen's volume and arguably just as significant are *Literary Transcendentalism: Style and Vision in the American Renaissance*, by Lawrence Buell, and *Beneath the American Renaissance*, by David S. Reynolds. Buell examines Whitman and other writers (minor as well as major) in terms of their own aims and approaches rather than in terms of modern standards of literary sophistication. Reynolds demonstrates that Whitman, Emerson, Thoreau, Hawthorne, Melville, Poe, and Dickinson were profoundly indebted not only to the devices and themes of classical literature but also to the ephemeral, shapeless, crude, but nonetheless rich, materials of nineteenth-century popular culture.

Other important works on the American renaissance period include *Myth and Literature in the American Renaissance*, by Robert D. Richardson; *Visionary Compacts: American Renaissance Writings in Cultural Context*, by Donald E. Pease; *American Hieroglyphics*, by John T. Irwin; *European Revolutions and the American Literary Renaissance*, by Larry J. Reynolds; *The Times of Melville and Whitman*, by Van Wyck Brooks; *The American Newness: Culture and Politics in the Age of Emerson*, by Irving Howe; *The Representation of the Self in the American Renaissance*, by Jeffrey Steele; and *The American Renaissance Reconsidered*, edited by Walter Benn Michaels and Pease.

A key feature of the American renaissance is the transcendentalist movement, and the Whitman instructor should have a firm grasp of its philosophical principles and literary productions. This objective is no doubt best achieved by reading the transcendentalist writers themselves. The essential works are *Nature*, "The Poet," "Self-Reliance," "The American Scholar," "The Divinity School Address," "The Over-Soul," "Experience," and "The Transcendentalist," by Emerson; and *Walden*, "Civil Disobedience," and "Life without Principle," by Thoreau. These writings can be illuminated by several of the books mentioned above, particularly Buell's and Matthiessen's, and by the following secondary sources: Alexander Kern, "The Rise of Transcendentalism, 1815–1860," in *Transitions in American Literary History*, edited by Harry Hayden Clark; Jerome Loving, "Walt Whitman," in *The Transcendentalists: A Review of Research and Criticism*, edited by Joel Myerson; Philip F. Gura and Joel Myerson, editors, *Critical Essays on American Transcendentalism*; and Myerson, editor, *The American Renaissance in New England*.

Like studies of the American renaissance, literary histories situate the poet and his writings in a cultural context. The following histories discuss Whitman's relation to various traditions in American poetry: Roy Harvey Pearce's *Continuity of American Poetry*, Robert K. Martin's *Homosexual Tradition in American Poetry*, James E. Miller's *American Quest for a Supreme Fiction*, Hyatt H. Waggoner's *American Poets: From the Puritans to the Present*, Bernard Duffey's *Poetry in America*, Donald Barlow Stauffer's *Short History of American Poetry*, and Alan Shucard's *American Poetry: The Puritans through Walt Whitman*. The work most acclaimed in this group is Pearce's, which views Whitman as the inheritor of New England antinomianism and places him (along with Taylor, Emerson, Dickinson, Robinson, Frost, and Stevens) in the mainstream or Adamic tradition.

Other literary histories provide commentary on Whitman and the fitful growth of an indigenous literature in the United States. The most perceptive and engaging of these are Larzer Ziff's *Literary Democracy: The Declaration of Cultural Independence in America*, Benjamin T. Spencer's *Quest For Nationality: An American Literary Campaign*, Robert Weisbuch's *Atlantic Double-Cross: American Literature and British Influence in the Age of Emer-*

son, and Benjamin Lease's *Anglo-American Encounters: England and the Rise of American Literature*. Also pertinent is a collection of essays edited by Margaret Denny and William H. Gilman, *The American Writer and the European Tradition*.

Requiring at least brief notice are two literary histories that focus on American authors and the Civil War: Daniel Aaron's *Unwritten War* and Edmund Wilson's *Patriotic Gore*. Aaron argues that for Whitman the war validated the basic messages of *Leaves of Grass*—the nobility of the common individual and the ultimate grandeur of democracy. More historical than literary but important to the instructor concerned with Whitman and the national catastrophe are George M. Fredrickson's *Inner Civil War: Northern Intellectuals and the Crisis of the Union* and George B. Forgie's *Patricide in the House Divided: A Psychological Interpretation of Lincoln and His Age*. "Fredrickson's book," commented one respondent, "offers a remarkable reading of the various mind-sets leading up to and through the war and puts Whitman's nursing into an interesting historical perspective."

The nonspecialist or beginning teacher of Whitman should keep in mind the value not only of specialized but also of general literary histories. In the monumental *Columbia Literary History of the United States*, Jerome Loving presents a concise and up-to-date overview of the poet's life and work. In the *Literary History of the United States*, Henry Seidel Canby's chapter on Whitman, while exhibiting signs of age, remains instructive. Worthy of attention, too, are the treatments of Whitman in Alfred Kazin's *American Procession: The Major Writers from 1830 to 1930—the Crucial Century*, Jay Martin's *Harvests of Change: American Literature, 1865–1914*, and Brian Harding's *American Literature in Context, II: 1830–1865*.

Some of the boldest and most challenging assessments of Whitman and his cultural milieu are to be found in books that employ methodologies commonly associated with the field of American studies. Wide-ranging, such books aspire to pull together and to generate interpretive theses on many aspects of American experience. Works of this kind cited repeatedly by survey respondents include *The American Adam*, by R. W. B. Lewis; *The American Jeremiad* and *The Puritan Origins of the American Self*, by Sacvan Bercovitch; *The Machine in the Garden: Technology and the Pastoral Ideal in America*, by Leo Marx; and *The Imperial Self*, by Quentin Anderson. Works cited just once or twice include Mason I. Lowance's *Language of Canaan*, Ann Douglas's *Feminization of American Culture*, Marx's *Pilot and the Passenger: Essays on Literature, Technology, and Culture in the United States*, Henry Nash Smith's *Virgin Land: The American West as Symbol and Myth*, Edwin S. Fussell's *Frontier: American Literature and the American West*, Roderick Nash's *Wilderness and the American Mind*, and Cecilia Tichi's *New World, New Earth: Environmental Reform in American Literature from the Puritans through Whitman*.

For a panoramic view of the social and cultural features of Whitman's time and place, one can draw on a number of outstanding histories of nineteenth-century American life. The accounts most frequently recommended by seasoned instructors are Russel Blaine Nye's *Society and Culture in America, 1830–1860* and Alan Trachtenberg's *Incorporation of America: Culture and Society in the Gilded Age*. Strongly endorsed as well are Sean Wilentz's *Chants Democratic: New York City and the Rise of the American Working Class, 1788–1850* and Edward K. Spann's *New Metropolis: New York City, 1840–1857*. Others that merit perusal include Herbert G. Gutman's *Work, Culture, and Society in Industrializing America: Essays in American Working-Class and Social History*, John F. Kasson's *Civilizing the Machine: Technology and Republican Values in America, 1776–1900*, Douglas T. Miller's *Birth of Modern America, 1820–1850*, Robert H. Wiebe's *Opening of American Society: From the Adoption of the Constitution to the Eve of Disunion*, Alice Felt Tyler's *Freedom's Ferment: Phases of American Social History to 1860*, Ronald G. Walters's *American Reformers, 1815–1860*, John D'Emilio and Estelle B. Freedman's *Intimate Matters: A History of Sexuality in America*, and Peter Gay's *Bourgeois Experience: Victoria to Freud*, volumes 1 (*Education of the Senses*) and 2 (*The Tender Passion*). Related to such works and still basic is *Democracy in America*, the remarkable study by Alexis de Tocqueville.

Insights into the intellectual life of Whitman's era can be gleaned from what long has been viewed as a standard source: Vernon L. Parrington's three-volume *Main Currents in American Thought*. In volume 3, *The Beginnings of Critical Realism in America*, Parrington includes a chapter entitled "Walt Whitman: The Afterglow of the Enlightenment." Additional intellectual histories of the first rank are William Charvat's *Origins of American Critical Thought, 1810–1835*, Rush Welter's *Mind of America, 1820–1860*, Irving H. Bartlett's *American Mind in the Mid-Nineteenth Century*, Ralph Henry Gabriel's *Course of American Democratic Thought* (2nd ed.), and Merle Curti's *Growth of American Thought* (3rd ed.). About Charvat's work a respondent remarked, "If we think Whitman was a rebel, we'd do well to know what he was rebelling against. This little book is a gold mine of information on early nineteenth-century thought."

Remaining for consideration are works with a religious orientation. Convinced that *Leaves of Grass* (a book Whitman himself once called "the New Bible") is most meaningfully interpreted in the context of religion, several respondents urged the following as basic background studies: *American Civil Religion*, edited by Russell E. Richey and Donald G. Jones (see especially Robert N. Bellah's essay "Civil Religion in America"); *Redeemer Nation: The Idea of America's Millennial Role*, by Ernest Lee Tuveson; *God's New Israel: Religious Interpretations of American Destiny*, edited by Conrad Cherry; *This Sacred Trust: American Nationality, 1798–1898*, by Paul C. Nagel; *The Oriental Religions and American Thought: Nineteenth-Century Explorations*, by Carl T. Jackson; and *The Varieties of Religious Experience*, by William James (see especially the chapter entitled "Mysticism").

Pedagogical Studies

There is no book that deals directly with the classroom presentation of
Whitman and his writings; however, some volumes at least marginally per-
tain. Of value are casebooks, handy compilations of primary and secondary
materials, such as Whitman's "Song of Myself": Origin, Growth, Meaning,
edited by James E. Miller, Jr.; The Poet and the President: Whitman's
Lincoln Poems, edited by William Coyle; Walt Whitman: "Out of the Cradle
Endlessly Rocking," edited by Dominick P. Consolo; and Whitman the Poet:
Materials for Study, edited by John C. Broderick. Perhaps even more bene-
ficial is Gay Wilson Allen and Charles T. Davis's anthology Walt Whitman's
Poems, which provides what one respondent called "model explications"—
readings that lend themselves to a variety of pedagogical purposes. Finally,
almost everyone can profit from books such as Reconstructing American
Literature: Courses, Syllabi, Issues, edited by Paul Lauter, and Teaching
Literature: What Is Needed Now, edited by James Engell and David Perkins.
Although neither of these is concerned primarily with Whitman, the Lauter
collection includes numerous references to the poet among its recommendations for revamping college and university offerings in American literature,
and the Engell-Perkins collection offers provocative statements on the teaching of poetry.

In addition to these sources, instructors have at their disposal more than
a dozen essays that squarely address practical and philosophical issues con-
nected with teaching Walt Whitman. The best of these include the following:
Harold W. Blodgett's "Teaching 'Song of Myself,' " John C. Gerber's "Varied
Approaches to 'When Lilacs Last in the Dooryard Bloom'd' " (written for
high school teaching but easily adapted for use on the undergraduate level),
Leo Marx's "Democratic Vistas: Notes for a Discussion," James E. Miller,
Jr.'s "Mysticism of Whitman: Suggestions for a Seminar Discussion," Harry
R. Warfel's "Seminar in Leaves of Grass," Sculley Bradley's "Teaching of
Whitman," J. M. Armistead's "Ending With Whitman," Richard Freed's
"Teaching Whitman to College Freshmen," and Sandra L. Katz's "Recon-
sideration of Walt Whitman: A Teaching Approach."

Other contributions of note are Robert D. Faner's "Use of Primary Source
Materials in Whitman Study," Andrew Schiller's "Approach to Whitman's
Metrics," Arthur Schwartz's "Each and All of Whitman's Verse," Sister M.
Judine's "Whitman and Dickinson: Implications for School Programs," My-
ron Simon's " 'Self' in Whitman and Dickinson," Merton M. Sealts's "Mel-
ville and Whitman," Robert M. Muccigrosso's "Whitman and the Adolescent
Mind," and John Ditsky's " 'Retrievements Out of the Night': Approaching
Whitman through the 'Lilacs' Elegy."

Aids to Teaching

Not everyone is inclined to use audiovisual aids. Some teachers grumble about the hassle they occasionally entail; others complain that certain media deemphasize the written word or encourage a passive learning environment. Such views notwithstanding, most questionnaire respondents reported that they fairly regularly use facsimile editions, original nineteenth-century materials, photographs, slide programs, illustrations, reproductions of paintings, audiocassettes and records, and films, filmstrips, and videocassettes.

High on the list of stimulating visuals are facsimiles of the first (1855) and third (1860) editions of *Leaves of Grass*. Clearly among the best facsimiles of the first edition is the one edited by Richard Bridgman and issued by the Chandler Publishing Company: it photographically reproduces the copy of the 1855 *Leaves* housed in the Department of Rare Books and Special Collections of the General Library of the University of California at Berkeley. An outstanding facsimile of the third edition is that in volume 1 of *Walt Whitman's Blue Book*, edited by Arthur Golden; also good is the text reprinted in 1961 by Cornell University Press (ed. Pearce). Similarly helpful in engendering a ground sense of Whitman and his era are originals (or, if these are unavailable, reprints) of nineteenth-century materials: newspapers, works of popular literature, political pamphlets, reform tracts, physiology and sex manuals, and the like.

Photographs, too, can enhance the teaching of *Leaves of Grass*. As one respondent pointed out, "the photographs of Whitman [can be used] to comment on how his changing appearance from the 1840s to the 1890s corresponds to the changes in his understanding of the poet's role." The single most visually arresting collection of photographs of Whitman is that in the large-format edition of *Specimen Days* published by David R. Godine. Another excellent gallery of portraits—accompanied by detailed notes—can be found in a special double issue of the *Walt Whitman Quarterly Review* (Folsom, "*This Heart's Geography's Map*"). A handy (though relatively small) album of pictures is included in the *Norton Critical Edition* of *Leaves of Grass*. Just as serviceable as the portraits of Whitman, at least when one is teaching *Drum-Taps* or *Specimen Days*, are the Civil War photographs of Mathew Brady and Alexander Gardner. An ample selection of Brady's work appears in William C. Davis, editor, *Shadows of the Storm*, which is volume 1 of *The Image of War, 1861–1865*. Gardner's work is reproduced in his *Photographic Sketch Book of the Civil War*. Additional photographic resources include *Walt Whitman*, a popularized biography by Gay Wilson Allen, and *The Illustrated* Leaves of Grass, edited by Howard Chapnick.

Some instructors develop their own slide programs. One said, "I show slides of contemporary engravings and lithographs depicting certain of Whitman's subjects." Another remarked, "I present my own slide collection of

Whitman's birthplace in West Hills, New York, his house in Camden, New Jersey, and his gravesite in Harleigh Cemetery." A third used slides of paintings by Jean-François Millet, Thomas Eakins, William Sidney Mount, and the American luminists Fitz Hugh Lane, Martin Johnson Heade, and John F. Kensett.

Although some instructors develop tapes of their own readings and lectures, many more use professionally produced audiocassettes and records. Among the readings currently in circulation are *Orson Welles Reads "Song of Myself"* (a cassette of a reading originally broadcast on BBC radio); *Treasury of Walt Whitman* (2 cassettes), by Alexander Scourby; *Walt Whitman's Leaves of Grass* (2 cassettes) and *Walt Whitman: Eyewitness to the Civil War* (2 cassettes), by Ed Begley; *Walt Whitman's Leaves of Grass* (2 cassettes), by Dan O'Herlihy; *Walt Whitman's Leaves of Grass* (1 disc), by David Allen; and *In the Soul* (1 disc, with selections accompanied by original synthesizer music), by Anita Kerr. (Consult the Works Cited list for further information about these tapes and records.) Among lectures currently in distribution are *Walt Whitman*, by Gay Wilson Allen and Arthur Golden; *Whitman as a Disciple of Emerson, Drum-Taps,* and *Leaves of Grass,* all by William Pierce Randel; *Works of Walt Whitman* (2 cassettes), by Charles T. Davis; and *Walt Whitman and the Democratic Epic* (a discussion of "Song of Myself"), by Edwin Cady and Louis Budd. The audiocassettes by Allen and Golden, Randel, and Davis can be purchased from Gould Media, Inc., 44 Parkway West, Mount Vernon, NY 10552. The Cady and Budd audiocassette can be acquired from the Annenberg/CPB Audio-Print Collection, WHA Radio, University of Wisconsin-Extension, 821 University Avenue, Madison, WI 53706.

There are numerous musical compositions—easily accessible on record, tape, and compact disc—that can deepen students' understanding and appreciation of Whitman. One instructor illuminates the Romanticism of Whitman (and of others in the nineteenth century) with selections from Beethoven's Ninth Symphony. Another illustrates the recitative-aria form in Whitman's poetry with the "Casta Diva" from Vincenzo Bellini's *Norma.* Still others put to a variety of uses compositions by one or more of the artists who have produced music based on, or inspired by, the poetry of *Leaves of Grass.* These composers include Frederick Delius, Paul Hindemith, Kurt Weill, Dmitri Shostakovich, Ralph Vaughan Williams, Gustav Holst, Howard Hanson, Roy Harris, and Charles Ives. For specific information on composers and their work, see Kenneth P. Neilson, *The World of Walt Whitman Music: A Bibliographical Study.*

Probably the best of the currently available film treatments of the poet is *Walt Whitman,* a one-hour video program that is part of a biographical and critical series entitled *Voices and Visions: Modern American Poetry.* Featured in this program are striking visual images, texts on screen, music, and computer graphics; eminent poets and critics—Allen Ginsberg, Donald Hall,

Galway Kinnell, Harold Bloom, and Justin Kaplan—provide readings and commentary. Also commendable is *The Living Tradition*. Though short (20 min.), this film effectively combines readings—by Ginsberg—of Whitman's poetry with visuals that exemplify Whitman's view of America. Meriting some attention are two filmstrips: *Walt Whitman: Poet for a New Age* (29 min.) and *Walt Whitman's Civil War* (23 min.). In the latter, Whitman is portrayed by Will Geer. Finally, there is *Song of Myself* (36 min.), a CBS-TV production (air date: 9 Mar. 1976) that casts Rip Torn as Walt Whitman and explores, among other subjects, Whitman's relationship with Peter Doyle (played by Brad Davis). Quite a few respondents expressed reservations about this film, citing "lacunae" and "distortions." However, one instructor argued that "while *Song of Myself* has flaws and inaccuracies (which can be pointed out) it is nonetheless valuable as a biographical dramatization and especially as a visual, speaking image of the poet."

Part Two

APPROACHES

INTRODUCTION

Written by experienced teachers of *Leaves of Grass*, the nineteen essays that follow explore a broad range of subjects and issues central to Whitman studies—narrative techniques, elements of language and style, prosodic innovations, biographical concerns, literary relations, cultural backgrounds, philosophical perspectives, and strategies for interpreting individual poems and prose works. Nearly all the approaches suggested have been classroom-tested. The collection as a whole reflects a variety of critical methodologies (formal, biographical, linguistic, contextual, archetypal, political, interdisciplinary, etc.) and addresses a variety of teaching situations (e.g., introductory courses in writing, required surveys, specialized upper-division courses). Although the collection stresses pedagogy rather than criticism, the orientation of some of the essays is more theoretical than practical. Only about a third of them delineate models ready-made for classroom application. At times, therefore, nonspecialist or beginning teachers of Whitman will find it necessary to adapt an essay's suggestions to their own purposes. Unless otherwise indicated, the text of *Leaves of Grass* referred to throughout these essays is that of the *Comprehensive Reader's Edition* edited by Harold W. Blodgett and Sculley Bradley, abbreviated *LG*.

"Approaches" begins with five essays on "Song of Myself"—the main poem in the history and development of *Leaves of Grass* and the work commonly regarded as Whitman's greatest achievement. In the first essay M. Jimmie Killingsworth illuminates a problem that confronts the reader not only in "Song of Myself" but in many other Whitman poems as well—distinguishing between literal person and literary persona. The essay by John B. Mason considers the pedagogical implications of Whitman's call for a cooperative and yet "gymnastic" reader, providing along the way thoughts on teaching the poet's daunting catalogs. Drawing on his years of language study, C. Carroll Hollis illustrates the value of focusing on several distinctive style markers in "Song of Myself." Betsy Erkkila demonstrates a way to place "Song of Myself" within the context of American political turmoil in the 1850s. Finally, Roger Asselineau sketches several contexts for "Song of Myself" (including one that uses the writings of Gaston Bachelard); he insists in the end that Whitman's "multitudes" preclude the exclusive use of one approach for teaching.

The next group of essays considers other major works, including "Out of the Cradle Endlessly Rocking," "Crossing Brooklyn Ferry," "The Sleepers," "When Lilacs Last in the Dooryard Bloom'd," "There Was a Child Went Forth," "Passage to India," *Children of Adam, Calamus, Drum-Taps*, selected poems of Whitman's Camden years, the prefaces (of 1855, 1856, 1872, 1876) to *Leaves of Grass*, "A Backward Glance o'er Travel'd Roads," *Democratic Vistas*, and *Specimen Days*. Dennis K. Renner applies various approaches (psychoanalytic, generic, historical) to "Out of the Cradle," identifying tensions or conflicts between them and indicating where they may be reconciled. Robert K. Martin writes on *Enfans d'Adam* and *Calamus*, bringing to bear on these clusters a combination of approaches: deconstructive, feminist, gay, political. Using Jungian psychology, Lorelei Cederstrom traces archetypal patterns and symbols in poems such as "Crossing Brooklyn Ferry," "The Sleepers," and "Song of the Open Road." Martin Bidney ranges freely over a number of the major poems. He draws fascinating comparisons between musical effects in Whitman's poems and those of Ezra Pound, William Blake, Paul Claudel, and Velimir Khlebnikov. Maintaining that "Whitman perfected the technique of reader seduction long before Roland Barthes wrote the theoretical text on it," William H. Shurr finds reader seduction the key to Whitman's poetry. In the belief that too little attention is paid to work written after "Passage to India," Donald Barlow Stauffer reviews the poetry of Whitman's later years, assessing its quality and pointing out those poems still worth teaching. Susan Day Dean rounds out this group of essays with an examination of Whitman's major prose works, which are, she claims, "indispensable to the study of his verse."

In the third group of essays, Robin Riley Fast, Kenneth M. Price, and Sherry Southard propose ideas for teaching Whitman in lower-division classes such as the American literature survey, introduction to literature, basic or advanced composition, and technical writing. Mindful of the advantages and, in particular, the disadvantages of teaching a major figure in an undergraduate survey, Fast outlines a plan for the instructor who devotes only three or four class sessions to Whitman's poetry. Price, too, comments on the American literature survey, demonstrating that Whitman can be effectively presented there in terms of connections with his American predecessors, and these include not just Emerson but Longfellow, Poe, and Bryant as well. Southard explains—in a systematic and detailed way—how students who specialize in scientific, technical, or other nonhumanistic fields can profit from a research project based on the language of *Leaves of Grass*.

The approaches in the last group of essays are useful mainly to teachers of advanced courses. Ed Folsom insists that if we "come at Whitman's work armed with systematic training and a formal approach [we will] miss him." He therefore recommends the scope and flexibility of an interdisciplinary approach, in which Whitman's concerns and those of the particular students determine the instructor's focus and modus operandi. Alan Helms presents a vivid, class-by-class account of his experiences—bad as well as good—in teaching a semester-long seminar on Whitman's poetry and prose. Propounded in his essay are insights relevant for the Whitman instructor on the lower as well as the upper level of the undergraduate curriculum. Noting that traditional scholarship and pedagogy have minimized—with deleterious results—the importance of women in Whitman's life, Sherry Ceniza situates the poet and his work in the context of nineteenth-century feminism. Doris Sommer concludes the section with an essay expounding the value of a comparative literature approach, revealing fascinating links between Whitman and Latin American writers (e.g., Octavio Paz, Jorge Luis Borges, and Pablo Neruda).

An instructor may find among these essays an approach that can be adopted in toto. Much more likely is that he or she will discover certain ideas and procedures that can be incorporated into an approach previously contemplated or into one already in use. At the very least, instructors should encounter a challenge—feel a need to consider and to clarify their own pedagogical principles or, better yet, give thought to approaches as yet untried. No one has to worry that the essays in this volume exhaust the approaches to *Leaves of Grass*. "There are millions of suns left," as Whitman reminded us back in the middle of the nineteenth century.

TEACHING "SONG OF MYSELF"

Whitman's I:
Person, Persona, Self, Sign

M. Jimmie Killingsworth

Whitman's unconscious ambivalence toward himself is
manifest in the ambiguity of the third line [of "Song of
Myself": "For every atom belonging to me as good
belongs to you"]. If the atoms that belong "as good" to
others as to himself comprise his body, it is fair to ask
who is the *me* to whom the atoms belong? The *me*
must be separate from the body, but if the *me* is the
soul, the soul must dominate the body. If Whitman
intends a mystical assertion of faith, he must soon run
afoul of his own conviction that body and soul are
equally important. What begins as a celebration of the
self becomes a troublesome question: who and what
am I?

Stephen A. Black,
Whitman's Journeys into Chaos

The Critical Problem of "Myself" in the Classroom

Who is "myself"? Some undergraduate readers of "Song of Myself" will tell
you it is Walt Whitman, the author of the poem, writing in his own person
about life in the nineteenth century. Other students, more advanced in their

studies, will view this perspective as that of the uninitiated and will substitute for the personalist approach a rhetorical view: the "I" of the poem is a persona, a character or a set of characters the poet invents in order to achieve his purposes. But, as Stephen Black suggests, these purposes are far from clear in the poem itself.

If you do not initiate this debate in your class, you will be expected, at the very least, to mediate. Your options will be to choose one or the other of the positions (person or persona); to show how the two positions are in fact closely related and to work toward a synthesis or a substitute position; or to avoid the question altogether. The last option is unsatisfactory to most teachers because all readers admit that the problem of the "I" is central to the poem. But I do not want automatically to discount that choice, for you could approach "Song of Myself" with a poststructuralist methodology, "de-centering" the question of "myself" and beginning your discussion from the "margins."

The following material is offered as a help for whichever option you choose. I begin by identifying four possible ways of viewing "myself": (1) the (auto)biographical I, in which the speaker is identified as Walt Whitman, poet and person; (2) the rhetorical I, in which the speaker is identified as a persona or set of personas; (3) the ideological I, in which the speaker is represented as the result of the social and political forces of the poet's day; and (4) the semiotic I, in which the self celebrated in the poem is understood as a collection of social and linguistic effects.

Under each of these heads I situate a series of quotations that you may use in any of several ways: as a set of notes to help you prepare your presentation in class, as points for discussion to be offered to the class, or as points of departure for student papers. Students may choose one of the four perspectives and use it to give a reading; attack one of the perspectives using one or more of the others; or make a single quotation the focal point for a short paper on one section of "Song of Myself." I also offer students a bibliography, which, though not exhaustive, serves as a good start toward any research paper. Students who go to the library empty-handed may be daunted by the quantity and variety of the literature dealing with this important critical question in the study of Whitman's most celebrated poem.

For each of the four perspectives, I offer a short commentary on the quotations, a set of notes that you may find useful in your own reading of the quotations. These comments explain my reasons for selecting and arranging the quotations as I have.

Critical History

The best entrance into the quotations is perhaps the historical path provided by Robert C. Elliott. He locates a shift in critical theory that we might associate with the New Criticism. By denying the existence of an authorial, and thereby authoritative, voice through such doctrines as the intentional fallacy, the New Critics were able to declare their independence from biographical and historical studies and from what Michel Foucault has called the "sovereignty of the author" (126). Now they could turn their attention to the rhetorical analysis of the text.

Yet the New Critics retained the essential humanism of the nineteenth century and therefore required a human subject or subjects around which to unify their analyses. Enter the persona, a weakened substitute for the banished author. With the advent of French structuralism, as Elliott notes, the subject itself, the self as a transcendental signified, is decentered, and the notions of person and persona are theoretically replaced with the idea of the *text*, whose systems of signification themselves give rise to the properties that we read as persons or personas. The text writes the author. In practice, however, this theoretical position is rarely realized, and the notion of voice or persona is retained though weakened (see Foucault 129). Still reeling from the effects of Jacques Derrida's critique of the metaphysics of "presence" (see Derrida, *Of Grammatology* xxi–xxxv, 97–100, 141–64), literary criticism seems to be still in search of a concept that will supersede the notions of person and persona. "What can we mean," asks Harold Bloom, "when we speak of the voice of the poet . . . ? Is there a pragmatic sense of voice . . . that does not depend upon the illusions of metaphysics?" (*Agon* 184).

Several crosscurrents modify this historical tide. In particular, Freud's and Marx's theories have weakened the concept of self considerably by asserting the presence of factors outside the control of the conscious, writing subject—the forces of the unconscious and those of ideology. But, in Whitman criticism, the Freudians have tended to take a rather purely biographical approach, with an admixture of the New Criticism. In favoring Eriksonian and ego psychology, they have ignored the structuralist implications of Freud's work. It is in the field of ideological criticism that Whitman scholars have shifted toward a decentering of the subject. Little of the work in this area is typically Marxist, however; most of it deals with some aspect of sexual politics, the major concern of feminist and gay critics.

My divisions, then, are not purely historical, though there is in my arrangement a hint of a movement away from the humanistic tradition of the nineteenth and early twentieth centuries. I cannot trace the complete movement in Whitman scholarship because it begins to thin once we reach the division of ideological criticism, and, except for the ground-breaking work of C. Carroll Hollis, it stops short of semiotics. These last two categories, then, represent interesting opportunities for the ambitious student researcher.

The (Auto)Biographical I

1

After continued personal ambition and effort, as a young fellow, to enter with the rest into competition for the usual rewards, business, political, literary, &c—to take part in the great *mêlée*, both for victory's prize itself and to do some good—After years of those aims and pursuits, I found myself remaining possess'd, at the age of thirty-one to thirty-three, with a special desire and conviction. Or rather, to be quite exact, a desire that had been flitting through my previous life, or hovering on the flanks, mostly indefinite hitherto, had steadily advanced to the front, defined itself, and finally dominated everything else. This was a feeling or ambition to articulate and faithfully express in literary or poetic form, and uncompromisingly, my own physical, emotional, moral, intellectual, and aesthetic Personality, in the midst of, and tallying, the momentous spirit and facts of its immediate days, and of current America—and to exploit that Personality, identified with place and date, in a far more candid and comprehensive sense than any hitherto poem or book.

Perhaps this is in brief, or suggests, all I have sought to do. Given the Nineteenth Century, with the United States, and what they furnish as area and points of view, "Leaves of Grass" is, or seeks to be, simply a faithful and doubtless self-will'd record. In the midst of all, it gives one man's—the author's—identity, ardors, observations, faiths, and thoughts, color'd hardly at all with any decided coloring from other faiths or other identities. (Whitman, "A Backward Glance o'er Travel'd Roads," 1888; Bradley and Blodgett 563)

2

Even for the treatment of the universal, in politics, metaphysics, or anything, sooner or later we come down to one single, solitary soul.

There is, in sanest hours, a consciousness, a thought that rises, independent, lifted out from all else, calm, like the stars, shining eternal. This is the thought of identity—yours for you, whoever you are, as mine for me. . . . In such devout hours, in the midst of the significant wonders of heaven and earth, (significant only because of the Me in the centre,) creeds, conventions, fall away and become of no account before this simple idea. Under the luminousness of real vision, it alone takes possession, takes value. Like the shadowy dwarf in the fable, once liberated and look'd upon, it expands over the whole earth, and spreads to the roof of heaven. (Whitman, *Democratic Vistas*, 1871; *Prose Works* 2: 393–94)

3

Thus we clearly see what is the subject of *Leaves of Grass*. It is the personality of Whitman; it is a self-analysis, a self-portraiture. The main figure in the painting is Walt Whitman himself; while America, American civilisation, and nineteenth-century progress furnish the setting, the environment, the background to that figure.   (Smuts 60)

4

"Song of Myself" . . . is the reverie of the outsider, the isolate, the perennial American Protestant, who struggles to reassert the collective dream, only to end, as Whitman does, in a retreat into the self that copes with, or, perhaps more precisely, evades, reality through imaginative transcendence into the timelessness and harmony of art. The serio-comic tone serves as a protective mechanism to disguise the poet's uncertainty and disenchantment from his audience and probably from himself. . . .

. . . In the second line Whitman employs another characteristic device when he attempts to establish a kind of amorous dialogue with his audience—"And what I assume you shall assume." The trickery of the device, however, is self-evident and reveals not only society's failure but Whitman's too: although many people appear in the poem, no one converses with the protagonist, who is, in final analysis, as thwarted as the old maid who in her fantasy caresses the bodies of twenty-eight swimmers.   (E. H. Miller, *Whitman's Poetry* 86–87)

Commentary

Whitman himself, in the documents quoted and elsewhere, was the leading purveyor of the view that the poem was autobiographical. His earliest critics and biographers followed suit. John Addington Symonds, before writing a critical analysis of the poems, asked Whitman to clarify the meaning of the word *Calamus*. The passage from Jan Smuts, which was written in 1895, typifies this tradition.

The excerpts from Whitman's prose, when read carefully, however, point to the true complexity of his views. In quotations 1 and 2, the self is portrayed as a becoming, not a being, as that which is molded by society and language and then unmolded and re-formed by inner and cosmic forces. To say at any one moment that the figure represented is Walt Whitman is to be wrong the next. Keep these passages in mind as you read the denial in section 4 of "Song of Myself"—"These come to me days and nights and go from me again, / But they are not the Me myself"—and then ask who *is* the me myself, and you will learn that to freeze that person in time is to lose him. Edwin Haviland Miller denies the reality of the poem as person and uses psychoanalysis to locate signs or symptoms of what person lies behind the tissue of illusions in "Song of Myself." What the poet says he is, the lover of himself and the world, becomes in this reading a fantasy of what ought to be. In truth, the "merge" with himself and with others is impossible. In a reversal of the common designation of "outsider," this isolated self, like the twenty-ninth bather of section 11, observes the world from the inside out.

The Rhetorical I

1

Dear friend, let me warn you somewhat about myself—& yourself also. You must not construct such an unauthorized & imaginary ideal Figure, & call it W. W. and so devotedly invest your loving nature in it. The actual W. W. is a very plain personage, & entirely unworthy such devotion. (Whitman to Anne Gilchrist, 20 Mar. 1872; *Correspondence* 2: 170)

2

Are you the new person drawn toward me?
  To begin with take warning, I am surely far different from what you suppose;
  Do you suppose you will find in me your ideal?
  . . . .
  Do you suppose yourself advancing on real ground toward a real heroic man?
  Have you no thought O dreamer that it may be all maya, illusion? (*Calamus*, 1860; Bradley and Blodgett 123)

3

[A] massive shift in literary opinion . . . had been going on since the early years of the [twentieth] century—a shift away from nineteenth-century orthodoxies and centering on the proposition that literature is, or ought to be, impersonal—as far as possible from the confessional style of much nineteenth-century writing.
  Popularized by Ezra Pound, given impetus by Yeats, institutionalized by Eliot in his poetry and criticism, the notion of the persona is at the center of that phase of modernism which holds that the "I" of a poem is a dramatized "I," no more to be identified with the actual poet living in history than the Bishop ordering his tomb is to be identified with Robert Browning. (R. C. Elliott 13, 16)

4

In one sense, it can be said that in any poem there is not one persona but several. Coexistent and almost inextricably entangled with one another are several points of view each of which qualifies and complicates the autonomy of the others, and none of which is ever quite identical with the poet.   (G. T. Wright 23)

5

The idea that a poet may adopt various personae or masks in poems that appear to be expressions of direct author experience is now widely accepted. . . . This essay is an attempt to distinguish the various voices used by Whitman, particularly in the volumes of 1855 and 1860, shifting our attention from Whitman's ideas, and from vexing biographical and bibliographical problems, to the verse itself. In the early Whitman I believe we can distinguish five personae: the orator, the bard, the realistic observer, the personal Walt Whitman, and the lyrist.   (McElderry 25)

6

One of the salient features of the poetry [in *Leaves of Grass*] is a fascinating interplay of voices. Now the poet speaks from one side of his mind, now from another; now he speaks in his own person, now he is a prophet or God.

"Myself" in Whitman's poetry becomes, by turns, a demiurge or oversoul; an epitome of America; a proteus of various shapes and moods; the book or poem itself; and lastly you, the reader.   (Buell 312, 326)

7

The predominant attitude or stance [in the poem] is controlled, almost detached, bemusement. The poet observes from it rather than lives the experiences of his consciousness and displays its powers by describing them, as if he were giving an outsider's account of not himself but his self. This "contemplative" angle of vision seems to put into rhetorical practice one of Whitman's most cherished insights: "I cannot understand the mystery, but I am always conscious of myself as two —as my soul and I: and I reckon it is the same with all men and women."   (Marki 115; Whitman quotation from *Uncollected Poetry and Prose* 2: 66)

8

There are at least three Whitmans in the poem, and it is problematic which of the three is the proper reference of the . . . title. We can call these Whitmans (following their author) my self, my soul and the real Me or Me myself. I would translate these respectively as: my masculine *persona*, Walt Whitman, one of the roughs, an American; the American soul (largely as expounded by Emerson); my more ambiguous *persona*, somewhat feminine, somewhat boyish. Freudian translations will not work: the rough Whitman is not wholly an id; the quasi-Emersonian soul does not operate like a superego; the real Me is hardly an ego, not even the narcissistic, partly conscious ego of Freud's later thought. All three of these Whitmanian visions or fictions participate in all three of the Freudian notions, and it is one of Whitman's uncanny powers that he cuts across all available maps of the mind.   (Bloom, *Agon* 26)

9

Literature exists in the context of one presence calling to another. . . . There is a kind of dialectic at work here. In so far as the work is objectified, set apart from the existent writer who gives it being as a kind of well wrought urn is detached from its creator, its evocative effect becomes more poignant. . . . Joyce's progress from *Stephen Hero* through *A Portrait of the Artist* to *Ulysses* and *Finnegans Wake* is progress from personal involvement to artistic detachment, and, as the masklike detachment grows, the evocative quality of the work, its pull on the sensibilities of the reader, grows. Because Poe can never achieve so great a detachment, because his personal problems and neuroses show through . . . the evocative quality of his work remains less poignant than that of Joyce. . . .   (Ong 59)

10

To change the book—go over the whole with great care—to make it more intensely the poem of *Individuality*—addressed more *distinctly to the single personality listening to it*—ruling out, perhaps, some parts that stand in the way of this—cull out the egot[istic] somewhat. (Whitman, undated ms. scrap, c. 1856; Bradley and Blodgett 763)

Commentary

Whitman's assertions of himself as hero were more than once taken seriously by his readers, one of whom, Anne Gilchrist, offered to become the woman he waited for and to bear his child. Whitman recoiled from this proposal and fell back on the claim that the "I" of "Song of Myself" is an invented character. This critical position, modeled here by Whitman himself, would be taken up with vigor a century later by the New Critics. But notice that in his letter in the first quotation he puts the responsibility on the reader, who is charged with constructing an "imaginary ideal Figure," which is "unauthorized," that is, devoid of his authorship and his authority. A similar passage appears in the *Calamus* poems. This reader response has nothing to do with the "me myself," the poet warns, and, in anticipation of the semiotic I, he suggests that all selfhood is illusory, nothing more substantial than a figure of speech.

To seek a single unifying voice in "Song of Myself" must be the final frustration of the biographical critic. But the rhetorical critic can avoid such rigor. George T. Wright argues that the poetic persona is rarely singular but is instead a vehicle for the poetic traits beloved by the New Critics— ambiguity and tension. A common approach is to read multiple voices in "Song of Myself," an approach sanctioned by the poem itself, especially section 24. Bruce R. McElderry, Jr.'s identification of personae is based largely on a recognition of poetic functions—oratorical, bardic, reportorial, and lyric—with a rude interruption by "the personal Walt Whitman." McElderry uses this classification, notable for the overlapping and uncertainty of the categories, to demonstrate the development of the poet, from the "bardic inflation" of "Song of Myself" to the "lyric perfection" of the later poems (31). Lawrence Buell offers his identification of personae as a testimony to Whitman's poetic range. Ivan Marki admits the existence of multiple voices but argues for the dominance of the "contemplative" I, which, nevertheless, insists on dividing itself in two—"my soul and I." Combining the Freudian with the rhetorical approach—in a typical move that shows a conviction about the relation of rhetoric and repression—Bloom sees three Whitmans, not just three personae in the typical New Critical sense. He believes he has caught the "me myself" in what I would argue is one pose among many—the "ambiguous *persona*, somewhat feminine."

All these classifications of the personae retain as one voice (or, for Bloom, as all voices) that of the person Walt Whitman. Walter J. Ong gives us a scheme for relating the degree of personality and impersonality in a poem. Person and persona may be situated at two poles of a continuum, one invocative, the other evocative. The invocative poem *calls to* the reader and puts the person of the poet on display. The evocative poem *calls forth* the reader, encouraging participation in the play of voices that constitute the poem. Miller's and Bloom's Whitman is invocative, Buell's is mainly evocative, and McElderry's scampers this way and that along the continuum. In the manuscript note (quotation 10), Whitman promises himself to revise the poem to make it less invocative and more evocative.

The Ideological I

1

The body is not a self, as such; it becomes a self only when it has developed a mind within the context of social experience.   (Mead 50)

2

As the values of the middle class become dominant [as in the late eighteenth century], sincerity is widely endorsed as a standard to which poets are expected to conform, readers evince increasing interest in the persons and personalities of poets, and poets themselves turn inward, exploring their own beings and making poetry of the exploration. The speakers of their poems, who once enjoyed conventional life only, came to be more and more closely identified with actual authors, to the point where in some cases speaker and poet seem, and are intended to seem, identical.   (R. C. Elliott 86)

3

If we look . . . at the lives and works of Emily Dickinson and Walt Whitman, two American poets who are roughly contemporary with each other and who are both iconoclastic in analogous ways, we find the . . . pattern of female self-effacement and male self-assertion . . . strikingly formulated.   (Gilbert and Gubar 554)

4

Granted . . . the contemporary argument that all literature is to some degree a form of indirection, it is nevertheless true that Whitman's homosexuality gave him an additional reason for employing a mode which for a century and a quarter has thrown most readers off the track of his most intimate meanings. Unable to speak directly of his homosexuality, this extremely sexual poet must employ an elaborate system of disguises . . . to convey his meaning; in order to become "undisguised and naked," he must first disguise himself.   (Helms 63)

5

The Author himself—that somewhat decrepit deity of the old criticism—can or could some day become a text like any other: he has only to avoid making his person the subject, the impulse, the origin, the authority, the Father, whence his work would proceed, by a channel of *expression*; he has only to see himself as a being on paper and his life as a *bio-graphy* (in the etymological sense of the word), a writing without referent, substance of a *connection* and not a *filiation*: The critical undertaking . . . will then consist in returning the documentary figure of the author into a novelistic, irretrievable, irresponsible figure, caught up in the plural of its own text. . . .   (Barthes, S/Z 211–12)

6

If there exists a "discourse" which is not a mere depository of thin linguistic layers, an archive of structures, or the testimony of a withdrawn body, and is, instead, the essential element of a practice involving the sum of unconscious, subjective, and social relations in gestures of confrontation and appropriation, destruction and construction—productive violence, in short—it is "literature," or, more specifically, the *text*.   (Kristeva 16–17)

Commentary

What determines the self? This question perhaps precedes "who is myself?" Social philosophers like George H. Mead, a forerunner of the contemporary "social constructionists" (see Bruffee), suggest that the self is more or less the sum of relationships that the person (or "individual" or "life form") is expected to carry on within a society. The various personae of Whitman's poem would thus correspond to a series of social roles. Though Whitman recognized role-playing as an aspect of the self in section 4 of "Song of Myself" and in passages like those quoted under the heading "The (Auto)Biographical I" above, he usually tried to distance himself from this activity, but in so doing he merely stepped into another role, that of the romantic rebel or the ironic observer. "To touch my person to some one else's is about as much as I can stand," we read at the end of section 27, and section 28 begins, "Is this then a touch? quivering me to a new identity. . . ." Contact with others overwhelms and transforms the self. The passivity expressed throughout the poem points to the self's lack of control in the face of social demands. This lack of control corresponds to the poet's lack of intentionality. Any personal aims of Walt Whitman the man (if they are even possible) fall prey to the conditioning forces of ideology.

Ideology—the partly conscious constellation of forces that governs heart, mind, and body—asserts itself in a number of ways in the portrayal of "myself." Though Whitman was ostensibly a radical in his approach to topics like sexuality and slavery, he was, we must remember, adopting the values of the rising bourgeoisie in shaping his personalistic ideals and in embracing the aesthetic of sincerity outlined by Robert C. Elliott. "Song of Myself" is the hymn of the "self-made man." Sandra Gilbert and Susan Gubar would have us emphasize the masculinity of this formula. They cite Whitman as one of the leading practitioners of phallic poetics. "This day," he claims in section 40, "I am jetting the stuff of far more arrogant republics." But from the perspective of gay criticism Alan Helms suggests that this machismo was one of Whitman's many "disguises" and argues that the poem's characteristic mode of revealing and concealing is a typical behavior of the homosexual living in a predominantly heterosexual world. (See also H. Beaver 103–05.)

Though the placement of the quotation from Elliott may suggest that ideological criticism is a throwback to the biographical and historical approach, in fact it subsumes the biographical and rhetorical approaches and shows the way beyond. Whitman scholars have yet to pursue the leads of the contemporary brand of feminist and political criticism that flourishes in the poststructuralist world of French letters. Roland Barthes and Julia Kristeva, the two most notable figures of the radical *Tel Quel* group, trace the concepts of author and self to the masculinist singularity of the bourgeoisie. The replacement concept, the text, posits a plural world where meaning is gathered in relationships rather than injected by the phallic author as father of his "work." At this point the ideological I merges with the semiotic I.

The Semiotic I

1

I sometimes think the Leaves is only a language experiment—that it is an attempt to give the spirit, the body, the man, new words, new potentialities of speech.   (Whitman, *American Primer* viii–ix)

2

Recent structuralist and poststructuralist theory in France goes even beyond the social scientists in abolishing traditional notions of the self. The linguistic "I," [Roland Barthes] says . . . , must be thought of in a completely apsychological way. "I" is nothing other than (he quotes the linguist Emile Benveniste) "the persona who utters the present instance of discourse containing the linguistic instance *I*." Similarly, Lévi-Strauss, Lacan, Foucault, Derrida contribute in their various ways to the "decentering" of the subject. The self, personal identity, is as much an illusion to them as it was to David Hume.   (R. C. Elliott 95)

3

We all acknowledge that Whitman is not the persona of *Leaves* but we do so against Whitman's continual insistence (except in that one letter to Mrs. Gilchrist) that he is the "I" of the poetry. But it is a moot point as far as this study goes, for the only concern is with the persona's speech acts as a stylistic feature of the poetry.   (Hollis, *Language* 78)

4

Indeed, we might well take the vague journeyings [of the mystic] as but the verbal equivalent of a universalized first person pronoun. The kind of super-person thus envisaged *beyond* language but *through* language may be *generically* human rather than *individually* human insofar as language is a *collective* product and the capacity of complex symbolic action is distinctive of the human race. Hence, the Self we encounter at the outer limits of language would be a *transcendent* Self, an individual "collectively redeemed" by being apprehended through a medium itself essentially collective. (The matter is further complicated, however, by the fact that the individual himself is largely a function of this collective medium.)   (Burke, *Grammar of Motives* 300)

5

There is no element of man's consciousness which has not something corresponding to it in the word. . . . Thus my language is the sum total of myself. . . .   (Peirce 189)

Commentary

"What is the reality to which *I* or *you* refers?" asks Emile Benveniste; "It is solely a 'reality of discourse,' and this is a very strange thing." *I* and *you* are part of a class of " 'empty' signs" that "become 'full' as soon as a speaker introduces them into . . . his discourse" (218, 219). In spoken language the references of these pronouns are usually clear, but in written discourse they remain vague, ambiguous, or "free." Hence, "every atom belonging to me as good belongs to you." You and I may be freely identified because either of us is potentially "myself." Buell's suggestion that the persona of the poem is ultimately identified with "you, the reader" takes on a new significance in this light. Persona making, the semiosis of the self, in fact becomes the theme of the poem. As Whitman came to acknowledge, the poem is a "language experiment" concerned with giving "new potentialities of speech" to "the spirit, the body, the man" by testing the range of meanings attributable to signs like *I* and *you*.

Though poststructuralist ideological criticism provides a means of reconciling the political themes with this reading, the overt "mysticism" of the poem, such as that of section 5, may be seen as a hindrance. But Kenneth Burke's definition of the mystical journey as "the verbal equivalent of a universalized first person pronoun" provides support on this front. What better characterization of the Whitmanian hero could we want? Myself is "generically" rather than "individually" human. The division of the self and its re-mergence in section 5 and elsewhere describe the poetic experience of one who is " 'collectively redeemed' by being apprehended through a medium itself essentially collective"—language.

The central question of the poem thus becomes not *who is myself?* but *what is myself or the process by which meaning is assigned to myself?* "My language," as Charles Sanders Peirce has written, "is the sum total of myself."

The Poet-Reader Relationship in "Song of Myself"

John B. Mason

Throughout his career as a poet, Whitman was fond of speaking of the "suggestiveness" of his verse, and at the close of his career he settled on the term as the best index to his poems. In "A Backward Glance o'er Travel'd Roads," he wrote, "The word I myself put primarily for the description of them as they stand at last, is the word Suggestiveness. I round and finish little, if anything; and could not, consistently with my scheme. The reader will always have his or her part to do, just as much as I have had mine" (*Prose Works* 2: 724–25). Whitman was never to be explicit about his conception of the reader's "part," but he came as close as he would to a definite explanation in an eloquent passage in *Democratic Vistas*:

> Books are to be call'd for, and supplied, on the assumption that the process of reading is not a half-sleep, but, in the highest sense, an exercise, a gymnast's struggle; that the reader is to do something for himself, must be on the alert, must himself or herself construct indeed the poem, argument, history, metaphysical essay—the text furnishing the hints, the clue, the start or frame-work. Not the book needs so much to be the complete thing, but the reader of the book does. (*Prose Works* 2: 424–25)

For Whitman the suggestiveness of a poem exists to prompt readers to construct the very poem they are reading. This was a radical and ambitious conception of poetry in the mid-nineteenth century, and it presents a challenge yet today for those first reading and studying Whitman's poems.

To explain to students what Whitman is asking of them, one should help them first to understand that Whitman's suggestiveness is not merely symbolization. Students will assume that reader activity means interpretation, wherein the reader works to make clear what the poet has made obscure. And with the help of their professor they will surely note that Whitman's poems are rich in symbolization. They need to understand, however, that Whitman asks for much more than symbolic interpretation. In the first place, he undercuts symbolic interpretation by creating a persona just as puzzled by a symbol as is the reader:

> A child said *What is the grass?* fetching it to me with full hands;
> How could I answer the child? I do not know what it is any more
>   than he. (*LG* 33; sec. 5)

The speaker in this famous section of "Song of Myself" goes on to offer a list of speculations about the meaning of the grass, but no one meaning is designated; the speaker is not an authority. In addition to being too elitist, symbolic interpretation for Whitman is too linear and too slow. The act of interpreting a symbol must necessarily follow the act of beholding the symbol. Whitman seeks not reflection but discovery, as when the reader at the end of "Song of Myself" discovers that the poet has merged with the symbol of the grass and is beneath the reader's "boot-soles." The reader's saying that the grass means "the essence of existence" (which it does) does not bring the reader and poet into the immediate and intimate relationship that Whitman seeks. Whitman does not use the poem to record the relationship; he uses the poem to realize it. He offers a "gymnast's struggle," a wrestling match between equals, the object of which is not the taking away of meaning but the mutual creation of meaning.

For new readers of "Song of Myself," a more fruitful approach than symbolic interpretation lies in an analysis of Whitman's rhetorical devices, which, ironically for us teachers of the poem, present these readers with major stumbling blocks. When students are free to criticize Whitman after they first read "Song of Myself," they are likely to complain about its length, Whitman's diction, the speaker's forms of addressing the audience, and especially the catalogs. Yet Whitman uses those very features to engage his readers in a "gymnast's struggle."

Often the first problem students have with "Song of Myself" results from their hearing only Whitman's public voice. They assume they have before them fifty pages or so of declamation *about* Whitman's self. The poem, of course, is also a song coming *from* the self and directed to another. The presence of a listener is assumed throughout much of the poem, particularly in its opening and closing sections. The poem is both oratorical and conversational; it presents a public speech and a private, even intimate, conversation. When students focus exclusively on the persona's public display, they miss much of the poem's conversation and they fail to take their part.

The length of "Song of Myself" makes it atypical of a conversation, and it is no wonder that students may be reluctant to take their part. After all, what sort of conversation goes on that long? Perhaps students have experienced one sort of conversation that does last that long—what we students of a generation back called a rap session. The rap session, unlike other conversations, has no set boundaries, proceeds by no rules other than the association of ideas, and can last as long as the stamina of the participants. It is not so exhaustive as it is exhausting, and by the end of the rap session, the conversants achieve the intimacy that occurs among fellow travelers at the close of a long journey. The very length of "Song of Myself" contributes to the intimacy that Whitman seeks, and to read only portions of the poem works against the possibility of such an intimacy. In fact, to read the poem in installments works against Whitman's rhetoric. At least the first reading of the poem should be done at a single sitting, which most assuredly will prove to be perplexing, irritating, and exhausting. Those responses are natural consequences of the poem's rushing its reader from beginning to end. Whitman's reluctance to abandon the physical format of the first edition, with its lines stretched across an oversized page and with no sectional divisions, could have reflected his desire to project the reader through the poem. Most of my undergraduates report that their first reading of the poem straight through takes them about three hours. I urge them in advance not to pause, not to reread, and not to worry about places where they become confused (for example, when they hit abrupt transitions).

As students quickly discover, the trip through "Song of Myself" is sometimes bumpy. Even as they feel they are being propelled, they feel the ups and downs of Whitman's diverse diction, what Edwin Fussell calls a "psychedelic eclecticism of vocabularies" (*Lucifer* 123). I like to have students diagram Whitman's registers in some of the lines from the poem. For example, the speaker describes a "butcher-boy":

High ("poetic")		repartee	
Middle (neutral)	I loiter enjoying his		and his
Lower (colloquial)			shuffle and
Lowest (slang)			break-down.

(*LG* 39; sec. 12)

Whitman himself would probably object to having slang labeled as the lowest level of usage, but the diagram nevertheless makes clear to students the roller-coaster effect produced by Whitman's diction. When asked to account for such a varied diction, students generally argue that Whitman seeks to be all-inclusive, and I see merit in the argument. Even so, I like to challenge them, presenting the possibility that Whitman was simply ignorant of what he was doing. Randall Jarrell insisted that "only a man with the most extraordinary feel for language, or none whatsoever, could have cooked up Whitman's worst messes" (67). Could it be that Whitman in fact had no feel for language, that he was as ignorant as some of his most severe critics, such as Amy Lowell, have contended? Could he not tell one part of speech from another? What sort of poet writes, "What blurt is this about virtue and about vice?" (*LG* 50; sec. 22). My hope, of course, is that students will come to believe that Whitman did know what he was doing and that his "language experiment" is a means of establishing rapport with the reader. Gay Wilson Allen and Charles T. Davis propose that Whitman mixes high and low levels of diction in order to project two voices, the interplay of which suggests the unrestrained, the unconfined, and the undefinable (48–49). According to this interpretation, Whitman can simultaneously present himself as the common person and still the bard, the readers' equal and still their leader. The mixed diction in section 16 of "Song of Myself" certainly serves such ends by illustrating the speaker's diversity and by proving that he is indeed "Stuff'd with the stuff that is coarse and stuff'd with the stuff that is fine" (LG 44). The same speaker who can say of himself, "And am not stuck up, and am in my place," can say of the universe, "The palpable is in its place and the impalpable is in its place" (LG 45; sec. 16).

The diversity of Whitman's diction is not merely a display of the poet's pliancy and his rapport with the reader; it actually seeks to establish that rapport. In complaining about Whitman's more outrageous experiments with language, F. O. Matthiessen unintentionally justified them: "In its curious amalgamation of homely and simple usage with half-remembered terms he read once somewhere, and with casual inventions of the moment, he often gives the impression of using a language not quite his own" (531). Whitman sought a language that was not his but was shared with the reader. The effect is that of language coming into being, rather than language conceptualized before its appearance on the page. Whitman's experiments with words dramatize the creative, often bumbling, efforts of people in conversation, and a good way to illustrate this quality of the poem is to have students read the poem aloud in class, working from a "script" they have prepared. The script contains not only the words that are on the page but also the words that the students imagine Whitman hopes to "hear" from his reader.

"Song of Myself" is conversational owing to several rhetorical features in addition to the poet's diction. Students learn much by working together in groups, generating lists of the characteristics of conversation, as opposed to other forms of discourse. They can then be asked to identify which of those conversational features appear in the poem. They are quickest to cite the speaker's direct addresses to the reader and the speaker's questions.

Most of my students have expressed at least some dissatisfaction with the way Whitman begins "Song of Myself." They voice the irritation we all feel when someone approaches us and says, "I know just how you feel." It is important for students to express this feeling and to understand that their response is perfectly natural and appropriate. All of us fail to appreciate someone who gets too chummy too quickly. We do not like to be crowded, and the speaker of "Song of Myself" begins by crowding us:

> I celebrate myself, and sing myself,
> And what I assume you shall assume,
> For every atom belonging to me as good belongs to you.   (LG 28)

Students may naturally feel repelled by this apparent egotism, but before they decide just what their relationship is to the speaker of the poem, they should contrast those first three lines with three lines near the poem's end:

> You will hardly know who I am or what I mean,
> But I shall be good health to you nevertheless,
> And filter and fibre your blood.   (LG 89; sec. 52)

Clearly a different sort of voice is speaking at the end of the poem, even though the meanings are much the same. Declamation has been replaced by a quiet and intimate rhetoric. To understand how this change has come about, students can attempt to trace through the poem Whitman's shifting uses of the second-person pronoun. The "you" is often the reader, but not always. In section 5 it is the speaker's soul. Frequently it is one of the many people with whom the speaker has empathized: "Where are you off to, lady? for I see you" (*LG* 38; sec. 11). Sometimes the understood "you" is ambiguous, as it is at the beginning of section 38, where the speaker shouts, "Enough! enough! enough! / Somehow I have been stunn'd. Stand back!" (*LG* 72). Is he shouting to his readers? To the "mockers and insults" that he says have brought him to his "crucifixion"? To the physical phenomena that have bombarded him in the preceding sections? At times there is no "you" at all; when the speaker launches into the great catalog that forms section 33, all sense of otherness is lost as he undertakes a mesmerizing inventory of the universe. Students will likely decide there is no absolute pattern to Whitman's use of the second-person pronoun, but they will probably recognize that the second person frames the poem. The poem begins with a good deal of second person as the speaker lounges in his self-satisfaction and *assumed* intimacy with the reader. In the middle sections, wherein the speaker has left the lounging pose to confront life, both past and present, in its varied forms, the use of the second person diminishes. It returns in the late sections as the speaker again approaches the reader, but without the smugness of the opening sections.

The questions in "Song of Myself" also occur in a general pattern. In the early sections, questions are often rhetorical, or the speaker often answers his own questions:

What do you think has become of the young and old men?
And what do you think has become of the women and children?
They are alive and well somewhere. . . . (*LG* 34; sec. 6)

Has any one supposed it lucky to be born?
I hasten to inform him or her it is just as lucky to die, and
I know it. (*LG* 35; sec. 7)

Those last two lines are especially bothersome to students. If asked why, they are likely to argue against the notion that death can be a "lucky" occurrence. But if you have them leave off the last four words, they are surprised to find that they do not mind the lines so much; it is that self-congratulatory tag that grates on their sensibilities. As the poem progresses, the self-contained, self-satisfied speaker gives way to the loving comrade and to the more genuine question. In fact, it is at the beginning of section

20 that genuine questions begin to occur, and this is just after the speaker, closing section 19, has whispered to his reader:

> This hour I tell things in confidence,
> I might not tell everybody, but I will tell you.   (*LG* 47)

Actually, he does not go on to tell anything at all. Rather, he asks:

> Who goes there? hankering, gross, mystical, nude;
> How is it I extract strength from the beef I eat?
>
> What is a man anyhow? what am I? what are you?   (*LG* 47)

Students might be asked to describe each of these questions. The first is closest to a rhetorical question: the answer, "Walt Whitman," is obvious. The next is one that can be both answered and not answered: a scientific explanation of ingestion would hardly suffice. The last three questions are entirely unanswerable, or, rather, their answers require that readers look to themselves for answers. The very last question in "Song of Myself" is the question toward which the entire poem moves: "Will you speak before I am gone? will you prove already too late?" (*LG* 89; sec. 51). Whitman's questions in "Song of Myself," like his forms of address to the reader, are working paradoxically to merge poet and reader and to free the reader from the poet—to cause readers to become their own questioners, their own speakers, their own poets. Students may misunderstand Whitman's rhetoric and think of it as coercion (several critics have). As I have argued elsewhere, Whitman is not a trickster with his questions but a teacher ("Questions"). Whitman's sort of teaching is far from coercion. As he says in section 47, "He most honors my style who learns under it to destroy the teacher" (*LG* 84; this line may be my students' consistent favorite). In a sense, "Song of Myself" does enable the reader to destroy the poet. The poet and reader merge, not to lose individual identities but to become fellow travelers and conversants. But just as the pupil becomes a full-fledged speaker, the poet disappears, to merge with the elements that will nourish the reader, the newly born poet. Many of my students are future teachers, and they seem to delight in discussing this aspect of Whitman's aesthetics, especially after we have spent some time talking about Whitman's experiences as a teacher and about his views on education (*I sit* 51–57).

Despite the students' interest in Whitman's aesthetics of liberation and their appreciation of the conversational qualities of "Song of Myself," they have severe difficulties with the poem's most notorious feature—its catalogs. Unless students can come to appreciate or at least tolerate the catalogs, they have no chance of becoming the readers that Whitman seeks. Rather than have students simmer in their anger, I encourage them to express their abhorrence. The catalogs, after all, have the quality that students today hold in greatest contempt: they are boring. But I want my students to reflect carefully on their responses. When pressed to describe their reading accurately, students—and just about everyone, I would guess—admit that they skim the catalogs. In understanding why Whitman adopted the catalog technique, students should first accept skimming as a legitimate reading strategy. In fact, they can be asked to look at the catalogs for features that encourage skimming: in particular, syntactical parallelism and anaphora.

Students can now be asked if Whitman might have any reason for wanting his readers to skim. Examples of discourse intended for skimming—telephone books, college catalogs, portions of the Bible—can be examined. Are the rhetorical purposes the same? Not always, of course. We skim the telephone book to get to a particular place. We skim a Whitman catalog to get an overview, a single image of a varied, polychromatic universe. I sometimes take to class a turn-of-the-century "flipbook" made to simulate the effect of a motion picture. When the reader flips the corners of the pages, a motion picture results, but if the reader flips too slowly, the illusion is lost. Like the single pictures in this book, each item in a Whitman catalog is fully realized, but for there to be motion, there must be speed.

Students need to accept their impulse to skim, but they should realize that the catalogs—at least those in "Song of Myself"—are not haphazardly constructed. The best way for students to discover Whitman's great craft is for them to write catalogs of their own. They can also learn much by contrasting Whitman's catalogs with those in the parodies that have been written (see, e.g., Saunders). Whitman is surprisingly difficult to parody; substituting a mere list for a Whitman catalog does not work, except, perhaps, for the catalogs in some of Whitman's disasters, such as "Song of the Broad-Axe." In those inferior attempts at cataloging, there is little principle of organization. Lines are movable and removable. When Whitman is at his best, as in "Song of Myself" and "Crossing Brooklyn Ferry," the catalogs are structured in ways to help the reader move from the particular to the enlarged vision, and from stasis to activity. (For discussions of some of these structural techniques see articles by Coffman; Warren; Mason.)

Again, having students work in groups to discover the structural principles in some of the shorter catalogs is worth the effort. However, readers do not sense those structural patterns as they read, and it is a mistake to overemphasize the formal qualities of Whitman's poetry. Whitman, perhaps more than any poet before or since, placed great faith in his readers. He trusted them to be competent readers, and we teachers of Whitman's poetry have as our first responsibility guiding our students to trust their reading. There is always the danger of solipsism, but Whitman was not so fearful that readers' individual needs might cause them to misread his poetry. By encouraging students to recognize Whitman's desire for active readers, examine themselves as readers, describe their reading and interpretative strategies, and account for their responses in terms of the poetry and its rhetoric, teachers engage students in what is indeed a "gymnast's struggle."

Linguistic Features of "Song of Myself"

C. Carroll Hollis

At the end of *Leaves of Grass*, in the poem "So Long!" there is a famous metonymic figure: "Camerado, this is no book, / Who touches this touches a man." Whatever "willing suspension of disbelief" we employ in accepting Walt's final farewell, we have no trouble understanding his intention: he has put so much of himself into *Leaves of Grass* that the book is more truly Whitman than is (or was) the sick old man who died almost a century ago.[1]

But how did he get himself into the book in the first place? He did so in "Song of Myself," the first poem of the first edition, which he revised in later editions. A passage near the end of the poem reads:

> Listener up there! What have you to confide to me?
> Look in my face while I snuff the sidle of evening,
> (Talk honestly, no one else hears you, and I stay only a minute
> longer.) (*LG* 88; sec. 51, lines 1321–23)

The "Listener" is *you*, the reader of the poem and *you* who are now reading this sentence. Whitman writes as though he were talking to you. That is why he calls you "Listener" rather than "Reader." Indeed, the best way to read Whitman is to consider his lines the written record of an oral expression. Here, then, is one of the key linguistic features that distinguishes this poem from the conventional poetry before and after Whitman. The immediacy and intensity of this interchange, and others like it, turned off many contemporary readers (and later ones too), and even led to misreadings. Some couldn't believe a *poet* could be talking-writing to them in this manner— but the speaker was obviously talking to someone—so this must be a nervy manner of addressing God! Now he, admittedly, may be "up there" in heaven, but certainly not subject to a poet's demands, particularly this one.

You the reader, then, are the Listener, but what is the inference of *up* and *there* and why the exclamation mark? *Up* means where you are in reference to the poet-speaker, who is speaking from the book you are holding. *There*, another deictic word, suggests that the poet-speaker is pointing to you. *Deixis*, the language function that relates what is talked about to the position of the speaker, has key significance to Whitman teachers because of the many deictic words and phrases he uses and their textual importance. (See Austin; Bakhtin; Brown and Yule.) I explain the term in the next few paragraphs, but in this passage it is enough to say that you as listener-reader are *up there* not *down here* in the book (in your hand or on the desk in front of you) from which the poet is speaking.

So, in this situation, he is calling "up" to you to get your attention. The exclamation mark parallels what would have been the force and perhaps the intensity of his voice to cut through possible distractions. Once students understand and accept the speaking situation of this poem and many others, the deictic words and phrases fall into place, giving the text an immediacy and everyday reality rarely found in the elevated, formal, refined, and distanced poetry of Whitman's contemporaries.

In "what have you to confide to me?" he asks for your responses, now that you have listened to his explanations, challenges, catalogs, boasts, and judgments for the previous 1,320 lines. But I am here not concerned with his themes so much as with his manner of making poetry out of his utterance. All poetry is language, to be sure, but no other poetry is so importantly *oral* language in its motivation and style. So here what is notable is that he asks you, meaning that you are to be an active (i.e., responsive) participant in this exchange.

But it is the question itself that is important, and we help the poet and the poem by making sure students grasp that they too are being questioned. The fact that we are asked makes us inwardly verbalize an answer, whether we actually utter it or not. And that inner answer is what Whitman wants to originate in us. When he says "look in my face" (i.e., at the pages in this book) and "talk honestly," it is the private response to one's own self that is called for.

Notice too that "talk honestly" is a request, an imperative, and thus a speech act, which we will discuss later. But are there many imperatives in poetry? There are a few, as in Keats's "Ode on Melancholy," where he begins "No, no, go not to Lethe. . . ." But note that here we are eavesdropping on the poet's advice to one of the lovelorn, whereas Whitman's imperative is a direct request to you, his reader. And why does he say, "no one else hears you"? Because reading is a private affair. Your mental response is expected, and he is there as long as you are holding the book and looking at his lines. So why does he say, "I stay only a minute longer"? Because, like you, he is twenty-three lines from the end of this long (1,346 lines ×15 words a line = 20,000 words) communication! He has been doing the talking, to be sure, but you are responding even though you may seem to be talking to yourself. Finally, why is this line in parentheses? Through the first three editions of *Leaves* it was not, but in later revisions he put in many parentheses to indicate asides. Whether the poem is improved by these later emendations is an arguable point and need not deter us here.

The relation between *I* and *you* in language use is the fundamental distinguishing element in communication. In fact the first key language function that we manifest our human nature in mastering is the *I* and *you* reversibility. There is only one *I*, and the glorious mystery of language opens up when we recognize that the speaker is always the *I*, and *you* (singular or plural) are the listener(s) or reader(s). Everything in language communication develops from this basic understanding, from baby language to term paper to sonnet sequence to impassioned oration.

In "Song of Myself," the *I*, as speaker, organizes the communication in relation to his presence. So, at line 8, when he says "I, now thirty-seven years old . . . begin," he means that he was that old when the poem-utterance was printed—and he remains thirty-seven while we are reading the poem. At this point I remind students that this poem is like a play. It is taking place as we hear or read it. In Whitman's self-dramatization he dies at the end of this poem (and revives to die again in "So Long!") but along the way speaks to us as our contemporary.

Now let us look at lines 29–37, a representative question-and-answer segment. Note that the first three questions are framed to lead to the fourth (32) on the meaning of poems. And all four, no matter how you answer them, lead to 33, a personal request (or invitation) to discover your own self in relation to nature and society through the poet's guidance. As a request it is another of those speech acts that will be explained further on. But first let us note how these lines appear on the page. Is this poetry?

We have long acknowledged that poetry does not need rhyme and meter. For this last century poets have been less concerned with the mechanics of poetry than with the appropriateness of form to thought. Notice here that Whitman does not alter the natural order of words in the four questions, nor in the five lines that respond to them, and he does not use the run-on line. He certainly does delight, however, in parading the parallelism that unites lines of comparable meaning. The orator's practice of beginning or ending phrases or clauses with identical words or phrases is not in itself either better or worse than the use of rhyme and meter, but it is more natural and suited to Whitman's thought.

Note here the repetition of the "Have you" questions leading up to the transition about the "meaning of poems," where he has his first chance to give you advice. Check also the skillful organization of the "you shall" clauses, beginning with two positives followed by five negatives leading to a final positive at 37. When we analyze this way, does the sequence seem contrived? Yes, most certainly, but only in the artistic sense in which all poetry, all art, is contrived.

The point we should make for students is that Whitman rejects the contrivances of rhyme and meter but replaces them with other devices drawn from oratorical rhetoric. His lines are not prose paragraphs cut up into segments of uneven length but, rather, fervent expressions of a would-be Jacksonian prophet speaking with "prophessional"—to coin a word—skill and energy. Repetition of words, phrases, and syntactical groupings is still another linguistic and artistic feature in which Whitman follows an oratorical tradition going back to classical and biblical periods.

But not all uses of "you" are to the listener or reader. In the middle sections, the "you" may refer to some other subject. To provoke a good argument in class, ask what each of the seventeen "you"s in section 40 refers to. But in the famous sexual-mystical passage in section 5 (82–90) the "you" refers to the soul in the body-soul union often considered Whitman's explanation of his poetic birth. Lines 91–98, on his response to the new insight now available to him, prepares for section 6 with its first use of *grass* as the central symbol of this poem and of the book.

The child's question about the grass (99) really asks, "What is life?" Starting with the symbol of the grass, the poet goes on to answer with an amazing parade of life's manifestations. Note at 123–24 how he reshapes the child's question to us and answers with a succession of photographically conceived details from the beginning of section 7 through the longest sentence so far in the poem, section 15 (66 lines). Both sections 15 and 33 (161 lines) are famous (or infamous to some) as catalogs and are often mentioned by Whitman critics. Referred to as "inventory" by Emerson and as "thousand of brick" by Thoreau, the catalogs are a language feature comparable to the lists in oral literature of former ages, as Homer's catalog of the ships.

A major linguistic factor, speech act, is appropriately named, for "Song of Myself" is more speech than conventional poem. The term refers to an utterance that carries out what it is saying as it is being said. When the judge says, "I sentence you to five years," and the minister, "I now pronounce you husband and wife," they are both *performing* their legal functions by and with their statements. I have italicized *performing*, for that is the key to speech acts. Indeed, they are often referred to as *performatives* to distinguish them from constative or declarative statements. In "Song of Myself" the first and last lines are both speech acts, as are hundreds in between. If you are ever in doubt, insert a "hereby" between the "I" and the verb: if the expression still makes sense, it is a speech act. A speech act proposes and imposes on the listener some action or reaction. Early in "Song of Myself" the speech acts are fairly mild, as in line 33. When Whitman asks questions, in 123–24, his answer in the following lines is meant for you as well as for himself. But he is not assertive here, perhaps because he is not sure whether you know enough about him to accept his prophetic answers. But the opening questions in section 20 set up the now stronger speech act: "All I mark as my own you shall offset it with your own, / Else it were time lost listening to me" (392–93). These speech acts continue and grow in strength and intensity. Indeed after section 42, where he announces "My own voice, orotund sweeping and final" (1055), the rest of this longest of his poems is almost a series of speech acts.

Section 42 is a turning point, for by now he has most of his audience with him; those who were not sympathetic would have gone long ago. It is amusing to see how those not amenable to his sort of persuasion are treated. Those within the sound of his voice (whether literal or literary) are *you*. When he knows or assumes you are in agreement with him, *you* can become *we*. Those who were not "sympatico" are *they* or *them*, usually treated with scorn or amused tolerance. In section 42, as he is preparing for his windup, which is altogether to *you*, he frees himself from those outsiders, "The little plentiful manikins skipping around in collars and tail'd coats" (1078). He realizes too that this may seem a superior attitude, but he laughs away the implied criticism in another speech act:

I know perfectly well my own egotism,
Know my omnivorous lines and must not write any less,
And would fetch you whoever you are flush with myself.   (1083–85)

Speech acts were originally meant for speeches, so in 1855, 1856, and 1860, line 1084 above was "Know my omnivorous *words* and cannot *say* any less." If anyone wishes to put "Song of Myself" on tape, the first edition would be the one to use.

Section 44 begins with a speech act: "It is time to explain myself—let us stand up." The line has continued in all editions, for presumably the listeners in the public hall and the readers in the library both need to stretch after these 1,100 lines. The last part of the poem, from section 44 to the end, is full of speech acts of the Jacksonian prophet urging his listeners and readers to live the open, chancy, independent, generous lives available to Americans who know and glory in their heritage. The final eight lines of the poem complete this long presentation in the most sensitive *ave atque vale* in our poetry.

Another language feature in "Song of Myself" is the skillful and rhetorically effective use of negation. Surprisingly, Whitman uses many more negatives than any other American or English poet although he is accepted as the most optimistic writer of them all. Many negatives are in clusters, as in 40–43, 355–58, 406–12, 497–504, 684–91, 1124–33, 1204–06—too many to analyze here. But note again 40–43, an oratorical passage that has the same delight in the balance of thought and expression as does the most artful poem. The necessary negatives, two *never*'s and two *nor*'s, control meaning, with all four lines united with and by the repeated ending, *now*. He seems to have delighted in variations of this rhetorical device, as at the opening of section 17 (355–58), or the startling conclusion of 43 (1124–33), with its denial of denial. A memorable passage is that about the animals, 686–91, but it is really about the "civilized" people whose limitations are thus brilliantly excoriated. So, too, 1202–09 tells us what he is by telling us in the middle of the passage, 1204–06, what he is not. The negatives amplify and support its optimism.

There are also more questions in "Song of Myself" than in any comparable poem on record. Like the negatives, the questions support and emphasize the positive response Whitman hopes for. We have noted the four questions at 30–32, all directed to the listener-reader. But some questions are inserted in a narrative sketch and thus are addressed only indirectly to us. In the account of the would-be twenty-ninth swimmer, section 11, the poet asks "which of the young men does she like the best?" (204), to follow with the answer. Then "Where are you off to, lady?" (206), and answers for her in the rest of the stanza. This carefully structured narrative insert, with simple questions and nonjudgmental answers, typifies the care and delicacy with which the poet handles human relations.

But most of the questions are to you, the audience, to encourage your participatory response. Thus the question and answer at 382–83 are followed by four more questions with a partial answer at 384–88. Then, in the self-assertive section 20 (389–91), there are five more questions to shake us up a little. In sections 24 to 30, he breaks the conventional rules for propriety in an amazing presentation of sensual and sexual awareness. There are few questions here, but they are central. In section 24 he speaks of the never heretofore expressed voices that he vows to express. In a startling maneuver he personifies speech so it can challenge him: "*Walt you contain enough, why don't you let it out then?*" (568). He refuses at first, preferring to listen. But even that listening, particularly to "the train'd soprano (what work with hers is this?)" (603), forces him "to feel the puzzle of puzzles, / And that we call Being" (609–10). So, he asks in section 27, "To be in any form, what is that?" (611) and acknowledges that "To touch my person to some one else's is about as much as I can stand" (618). When in section 28 he questions what sense comes closest to the mystery of recognizing one's being, he asks, "Is this then a touch?" (619). His answer, in an extraordinary dramatization of masturbation, includes three further questions as he personifies touch (639, 642, 652).

The poem continues its celebration of life for a few hundred lines without any necessity for questions. Indeed, questions in the famous catalog of section 33 would break the spell of the amazing enumeration. Nor would there be much occasion for questions in the narrative episodes: the shipwreck, the mashed fireman, the Goliad massacre, the John Paul Jones victory. Sections 37 and 38 work out the implications of the poet's full empathy with "all presences outlaw'd or suffering," which he concludes by turning to his followers: "Eleves, I salute you! come forward! / Continue your annotations, continue your questionings" (974–75). The French pupils apparently didn't have any questions, so the imperturbable poet supplies them himself—nine in the next four lines in section 39, a glorified characterization of the American bard he hoped to embody. There are no questions in the famous last stanza, but in the preceding section there are seven. They, as well as eighty percent of the other questions, are directed to you, the "Listener up there!" in one of the most evocative communications in the history of poetry.

The intention of "Song of Myself" is the self-dramatization of the poet. He is speaking about himself and presenting himself in numerous episodes, but his professed purpose is to get us (as listeners and readers) to understand and accept life as he does. He cannot come into our world, nor can we truly join his. But through his bold and skillful use of deixis, speech acts, negatives, and questions, he has created a middle world (that imaginary world we inhabit while reading his poem) in which we can meet and interact.

Because of the length and scope of "Song of Myself," its unusual poetic accomplishment cannot be duplicated in any other work. But Whitman uses certain of these techniques with striking success in other early poems. If your class has time, try "Starting from Paumanok," "Song of the Open Road," "Crossing Brooklyn Ferry," "A Song for Occupations," "A Song of the Rolling Earth," and "So Long!" Even shorter poems are possible if put in the context of "Song of Myself"; "To Think of Time" might be thought of as a stanza taken out of the master poem. By contrast, "The Sleepers" or "Out of the Cradle Endlessly Rocking" is clearly not in this category, and your class can work out why. This difference also applies to "When Lilacs Last in the Dooryard Bloom'd," "Passage to India," and other poems after 1860. Why Whitman gave up the earlier mode we will never know for sure, but his reasons are fascinating to speculate about, and your class may come up with new answers. And if you are looking for a smaller but true challenge, have them try to place "As I Ebb'd with the Ocean of Life"—and when they think they have it nailed, ask them to identify the "you" in the final two lines.

NOTE

[1]There has always been the danger of confusing the persona, the Walt Whitman of the poem, with the author of the poem, the historical person, 1819–1892. The author encourages this confusion by giving his name to the persona twice in the poem (at 497 and 568). As a device, the persona was enormously successful—but it was still a device. It would be silly to keep on making this distinction every time the occasion arises, so let this statement do for all.

"Song of Myself" and the Politics of the Body Erotic

Betsy Erkkila

In teaching "Song of Myself" I begin with a passage from the 1855 preface to *Leaves of Grass* in which Whitman imagines the ideal poet balanced between the values of pride and sympathy:

> The soul has that measureless pride which consists in never acknowledging any lessons but its own. But it has sympathy as measureless as its pride and the one balances the other and neither can stretch too far while it stretches in company with the other. The inmost secrets of art sleep with the twain. The greatest poet has lain close betwixt both and they are vital in his style and thoughts. (*LG* 718)

This vision of a poet stretching within a universe bounded by pride and sympathy had as its political analogue the paradox of an American republic poised between self-interest and public virtue, liberty and union, the interests of the many and the good of the one. The secret not only of Whitman's art but of the American Union, the paradox of many in one, would eventually become the opening inscription and balancing frame of *Leaves of Grass*:

> One's-Self I sing, a simple separate person,
> Yet utter the word Democratic, the word En-Masse.

Balanced between the separate person and the people en masse, the politics of *Leaves of Grass* is neither liberal nor bourgeois in the classical sense of either term; rather, the poems inscribe the republican ideals of early nineteenth-century artisan radicalism, emphasizing the interlinked values of independence and community, of personal wealth and commonwealth.

Whitman's concern with the problem of individual power, balance, and social union was in part a response to the political turmoil of the 1840s and 1850s—a time when traditional republican values were being eroded as America was transformed from an agrarian to an industrial economy and the political Union was itself dissolving under the pressure of the contradiction of slavery in the American republic. In this essay, I discuss ways to read and teach "Song of Myself" as a poem that grows out of, and responds to, revolutionary ideology and the specific political struggles of America on the eve of the Civil War.

Just as the American Revolution had led to a relocation of authority inside rather than outside the individual, so Whitman's myth of origins focused not on the exploits of a historic or mythic figure of the past but on the heroism of a self who was, like the nation, in the process of creation. Whitman mythologizes what he called the "entire faith and acceptance" (*Prose Works* 2: 729) of the American republic in a poetic person who is at once a model of democratic character and a figure of democratic union. Speaking of the analogy between the individual and the body politic, he said: "What is any Nation—after all—and what is a human being—but a struggle between conflicting, paradoxical, opposing elements—and they themselves and their most violent contests, important parts of that One Identity, and of its development?" (*Whitman's Memoranda* 65).

The drama of identity in "Song of Myself" is rooted in the political drama of a nation in crisis—a nation, as Lincoln observed at the time, living in the midst of alarms and anxiety in which "we expect some new disaster with each newspaper we read" (Sandburg vii). Through the invention of an organic self who is like the Union, many in one, Whitman seeks to balance and reconcile major conflicts in the American body politic: the conflicts between "separate person" and "en masse," individualism and equality, liberty and union, the South and the North, the farm and the city, labor and capital, black and white, female and male, and religion and science. In teaching "Song of Myself," one might discuss the ways these conflicts are played out in individual sections. I usually stress the development toward two particularly intense moments of crisis: one in section 28 and the other in section 38. I ask students to discuss the specific nature of the crisis in each section. Both situations involve a momentary loss of balance.

"Swing Open the Doors!" Whitman had declared in one of his *Brooklyn Daily Eagle* editorials in 1846. "We must be constantly pressing onward— every year throwing the doors wider and wider—and carrying our experiment of democratic freedom to the very verge of the limit" (*Gathering* 1: 10). Like the American republic, "Song of Myself" is an experiment in self-governance that both tests and illustrates the capacity of a muscular and self-possessed individual for regulation from within. The poem might be read as a democratic performance in which the poet approaches the limit of sexual appetite and hellish despair but is continually restored to an inward economy of equity and balance. In his famous act of self-naming in section 24, Whitman stresses his sexually turbulent nature:

> Walt Whitman, a kosmos, of Manhattan the son,
> Turbulent, fleshy, sensual, eating, drinking and breeding,
> No sentimentalist, no stander above men and women or apart
>   from them,
> No more modest than immodest.
>
> Unscrew the locks from the doors!
> Unscrew the doors themselves from their jambs!   (*LG* 52)

Here as throughout the poem Whitman celebrates and indeed flaunts his representative status as a poet who absorbs into the "kosmos" of his body and his poem what he called in his journalism the "turbulence and destructiveness" and "freaks and excesses" of the democratic spirit (*Gathering* 1: 3–4).

It is on the sexual plane, through a release of libidinous energies, that Whitman's democratic poet undergoes his first major trial of self-mastery. The main challenge comes with the onslaught of touch in section 28. The passage records a crisis in which Whitman's hitherto balanced persona, stimulated by a masturbatory fantasy, is taken over by the sense of touch:

> Is this then a touch? quivering me to a new identity,
> Flames and ether making a rush for my veins,
> Treacherous tip of me reaching and crowding to help them,
> My flesh and blood playing out lightning to strike what is
>   hardly different from myself,
> On all sides prurient provokers stiffening my limbs,
> Straining the udder of my heart for its withheld drip.   (*LG* 57)

Stimulated and stiffened by the "treacherous" fingertips of himself, the poet not only loses bodily balance. Carried away by a solitary act of onanism, he also loses the balance between self and other and between body and soul that is part of the democratic design of poet and poem. Here one might ask students why a masturbation fantasy occurs at the very center of a poem about democracy. Why is the main battle in this epic of democracy fought not on the battlefield but within the self, on the level of the body and the senses? And why is the masturbatory fit represented in the language of political insurrection? These questions lead readers to reflect on the relation between the fear of democracy and the fear of an unruly body in mid-nineteenth-century America.

Presented in the language of a violent mass insurrection in which touch, as the "red marauder," usurps the governance of the body, the entire episode has a fairly marked political nuance:

> No consideration, no regard for my draining strength or my anger,
> Fetching the rest of the herd around to enjoy them a while,
> Then all uniting to stand on a headland and worry me.
>
> The sentries desert every other part of me,
> They have left me helpless to a red marauder,
> They all come to the headland to witness and assist against me.
>
> I am given up by traitors,
> I talk wildly, I have lost my wits, I and nobody else am the
>   greatest traitor,
> I went myself first to the headland, my own hands carried me
>   there.   (*LG* 57–58; sec. 28)

The poet's "worry" in this passage is at once personal and political. The vision of insurrection and violence within the democratic body of the poet relates not only to the impending crisis of the Civil War but also to the very theory of America itself. If the individual is not capable of self-mastery, if balance is not the natural law of the universe, if the storms of (homo)sexual passion can usurp the constitution of body and body politic, then the theory of America would be cankered at its source. Just as the insurrection within the body of the poet comes from his own hand, so in the political sphere, the main threat to democracy appeared to come from within the body of the republic. The entire sequence links the danger of democracy with the danger of a sexually unruly body. And it is on the level of sex and the body that the poem tests the democratic theory of America.

Whitman resolves the bodily crisis of his protagonist symbolically by linking the onslaught of touch—as a sign of unruliness in body and body politic—with the regenerative energies of the universe:

> You villain touch! what are you doing? my breath is tight in its throat,
> Unclench your floodgates, you are too much for me.
>
> Blind loving wrestling touch, sheath'd hooded sharp-tooth'd touch!
> Did it make you ache so, leaving me?
>
> Parting track'd by arriving, perpetual payment of perpetual loan,
> Rich showering rain, and recompense richer afterward.
>
> Sprouts take and accumulate, stand by the curb prolific and vital,
> Landscapes projected masculine, full-sized and golden. (*LG* 58;
>   secs. 28, 29)

The moment of sexual release is followed by a restoration of balance as the ejaculatory flow merges with, and is naturalized as, the regenerative flow of the universe. The parallel lines formally mark the restoration of balance at the same time they inscribe the process of parting and arriving, efflux and influx that is the generative rhythm of the universe and the main pattern of the poem as the poet advances and retreats, absorbs and bestows.

Read closely, the sequence provides a useful corrective to the popular image of Whitman as the poet of sexual excess. Whitman does not celebrate masturbation in "Song of Myself." On the contrary, his attitude is closer to the antimasturbation tracts published by Fowler and Wells, the distributors of the first edition of *Leaves of Grass*. He presents masturbation as an instance of bodily disturbance—a muted sign perhaps of the unruliness of his own homosexual passion—and a trope for disorder in the political sphere. As a figure of democratic unruliness in body and body politic, masturbation becomes the sexual ground on which Whitman tests the democratic theory of America. By demonstrating the restoration of bodily balance after taking democracy to the very limit in the masturbatory fit, Whitman both tests and enacts poetically the principle of self-regulation in individual and in cosmos that is at the base of his democratic faith.

"Is this then a touch? quivering me to a new identity," the poet asks at the beginning of the touch sequence. Within the gloriously regenerative economy of "Song of Myself," (homo)erotic touching is safe and natural, quivering the poet not to a new and marginal identity as homosexual in heterosexual America but toward the experience of cosmic unity evoked in the lengthy catalog of section 33. But while Whitman successfully manages the onslaught of touch within the symbolic order of the poem, the unruly body—both his own and the bodies of others—would remain a source of anxiety and perturbance in his dream of democracy.

If section 28 involves a loss of bodily balance, section 38 involves a loss of self in empathetic identification with others. In discussing the crisis in section 38, ask students what Whitman means by the lines "I discover myself on the verge of a usual mistake." This inquiry will usually lead back to the end of section 33, where the poet begins identifying with scenes of suffering, carnage, and death: "I am the man, I suffer'd, I was there," he says (*LG* 66). Some of these scenes are linked with the nation's history: the "condemn'd" witch and "hounded slave" in section 33, the Texas war in section 34, and the American Revolution in section 35. While the poet's descent into the American past is presumably intended as a heroic record of personal and national creation, the weight of human suffering and tragedy in the battles he describes registers anxiety about the impending dissolution of the Union and the blood "falling" not only over the past but over the future of America.

The structures of human misery that entrap the human life threaten to overwhelm the poet in sections 37 and 38. As he assumes the identities of a prisoner, a mutineer, and a criminal, he becomes static, impotent, caged:

> Askers embody themselves in me and I am embodied in them,
> I project my hat, sit shame-faced, and beg. (*LG* 72; sec. 37)

No longer "afoot" with his vision, the poet has fallen from the state of democratic grace. His shamefaced beggar is the very antithesis of the proud, self-confident person who straddled continents and cocked his hat as he pleased indoors or out at the outset of the poem.

Having lost his democratic balance between self and other, pride and sympathy, the one and the many, the poet undergoes his second crisis of self-mastery in section 38:

Enough! enough! enough!
Somehow I have been stunn'd. Stand back!
Give me a little time beyond my cuff'd head, slumbers, dreams,
gaping,
I discover myself on the verge of a usual mistake. (*LG* 72)

The poet appears to be on the verge of losing faith in the divine potency of the individual and the regenerative pattern of the whole. He resolves the crisis by remembering the divinity of Christ—the "overstaid fraction"—as a living power that exists within rather than outside of every individual.

Whitman's concern throughout "Song of Myself" with the problem of self-mastery is related to his anxiety about the increasing centralization of institutional authority, whether in the areas of finance, capital, and trade or in response to the issues of slavery, territorial expansion, and the state of the Union. "You cannot legislate men into morality," he had declared as early as 1842 in an article on popular sovereignty (*Whitman of the New York 'Aurora'* 100); and later, in an *Eagle* editorial on government he said: "Men must be 'masters unto themselves,' and not look to Presidents and legislative bodies for aid" (*Gathering* 1: 52). He elaborated his position in *Democratic Vistas*:

> That which really balances and conserves the social and political world is not so much legislation, policies, treaties, and dread of punishment, as the latent eternal intuitional sense, in humanity, of fairness, manliness, decorum., &c. Indeed, this perennial regulation, control, and oversight, by self-suppliance, is *sine qua non* to democracy; and a highest widest aim of democratic literature may well be to bring forth, cultivate, brace, and strengthen this sense, in individuals and society. (*Prose Works* 2: 421)

By imaginatively embodying the individual's capacity for balance—between self and other, body and soul, material and spiritual—and by launching the reader into a process of self-creation, Whitman sought in his poems to cultivate and strengthen the "perennial regulation, control, and oversight, by self-suppliance" as the "*sine qua non* to democracy."

This concept of balance not only as a principle of self-regulation in humanity but as a principle of unity in the cosmos is the culminating lesson of "Song of Myself." In section 50 the poet finds the "word unsaid" of the universe in the generative order of creation:

> Do you see O my brothers and sisters?
> It is not chaos or death—it is form, union, plan—it is eternal life
> —it is Happiness. (*LG* 88)

Like the self-evident truths of "life, liberty, and the pursuit of happiness" enunciated in the Declaration of Independence, Whitman's declaration of faith is rooted in an Enlightenment vision of "form and union and plan" as the natural law of the universe.

Having communicated his lesson of equity and balance, Whitman takes leave of his readers. Moving toward dusk, death, and the future he acts out his message of faith by joyously dissolving into the elements of earth, air, fire, and water:

> I depart as air, I shake my white locks at the runaway sun,
> I effuse my flesh in eddies, and drift it in lacy jags.

> I bequeath myself to the dirt to grow from the grass I love,
> If you want me again look for me under your boot-soles.   (LG 89)

The death of the poet and the completion of the poem correspond, like the fifty-two weeks of the year and the fifty-two sections of the poem, with the completion of the regenerative cycle of the earth. The poet's departure enacts the promise of eternal life not through personal immortality or spiritual transcendence but by merging with the processes of universal creation. Existing under, rather than above, the "soles" of his readers, the poet becomes the uniform hieroglyphic and sign of democracy he began by contemplating as he loafed in the grass.

While the poem, like the final edition of *Leaves of Grass*, inscribes an arc of development from life to death, body to spirit, summer to autumn, dawn to dusk, self to other, and poet to reader, it has no beginning, middle, or end in the traditional sense. The poem moves not by narrative line but by association and recurrence, in the form of a circle. The concluding lines of "Song of Myself" return cyclically to the beginning, with this difference: as the poet had predicted, the reader has now assumed the active and creative role of the poet contemplating the meaning of the grass:

> You will hardly know who I am or what I mean,
> But I shall be good health to you nevertheless,
> And filter and fibre your blood.

> Failing to fetch me at first keep encouraged,
> Missing me one place search another,
> I stop somewhere waiting for you.   (LG 89)

Through the use of present tense and present participles in the final lines, the poet becomes, like the grass, perennially present, waiting in perpetuity not in the past but somewhere down the road in the future where the reader may encounter him. The image of an open-ended process is further underscored by the lack of a period in the 1855 version, an omission that Whitman as scrupulous printer and editor of his own poems surely intended.

"A great poem is no finish to a man or woman but rather a beginning," Whitman said in the 1855 preface to *Leaves of Grass*. "Has any one fancied he could sit at last under some due authority and rest satisfied with explanations and realize and be content and full? To no such terminus does the greatest poet bring . . . he brings neither cessation or sheltered fatness and ease. The touch of him tells in action" (*LG* 729; Whitman's ellipses). In the final lines of "Song of Myself," Whitman refuses the traditional authority and closure of art. His democratic poetics is an activist poetics that incites the reader to the final act of creation—of self and poem, nation and world.

Some Contexts for "Song of Myself"

Roger Asselineau

When I introduce Walt Whitman to students, in France or in the United States, I ask them first to read "Song of Myself"—all of it or as much as they can bear, for one must keep in mind Poe's warning that the common reader cannot read more than one hundred lines of poetry at a sitting.

The reason I choose this poem is that I want to jolt students by exposing them to poetry for which they probably have not been prepared, "pure" poetry, poetry laid bare, divested of its traditional trappings, stripped of all adornments, equally contemptuous of storytelling and moral didacticism, indifferent to prosodical conventions, in short, singing the self without recourse to extraneous matters, as in these lines near the beginning of section 2:

> The atmosphere is not a perfume, it has no taste of the
>   distillation, it is odorless,
> It is for my mouth forever, I am in love with it,
> I will go to the bank by the wood and become undisguised
>   and naked,
> I am mad for it to be in contact with me.
>
> The smoke of my own breath,
> Echoes, ripples, buzz'd whispers, love-root, silk-thread,
>   crotch and vine,
> My respiration and inspiration, the beating of my heart, the
>   passing of blood and air through my lungs,
> The sniff of green leaves and dry leaves, and of the shore and
>   dark-color'd sea-rocks, and of hay in the barn,
> The sound of the belch'd words of my voice loos'd to the
>   eddies of the wind,
> A few light kisses, a few embraces, a reaching around of
>   arms,
> The play of shine and shade on the trees as the supple
>   boughs wag,
> The delight alone or in the rush of the streets, or along the
>   fields and hill-sides,
> The feeling of health, the full-noon trill, the song of me
>   rising from bed and meeting the sun.   (*LG* 29–30)

or in these lines in section 41:

> I heard what was said of the universe,
> Heard it and heard it of several thousand years;
> It is middling well as far as it goes—but is that all?

Magnifying and applying come I,
Outbidding at the start the old cautious hucksters,
Taking myself the exact dimensions of Jehovah,
Lithographing Kronos, Zeus his son, and Hercules his
    grandson,
Buying drafts of Osiris, Isis, Belus, Brahma, Buddha,
In my portfolio placing Manito loose, Allah on a leaf, the
    crucifix engraved,
With Odin and the hideous-faced Mexitli and every idol and
    image,
Taking them all for what they are worth and not a cent more,
Admitting they were alive and did the work of their days,
(They bore mites as for unfledg'd birds who have now to rise
    and fly and sing for themselves,)
Accepting the rough deific sketches to fill out better in myself,
    bestowing them freely on each man and woman I see,
Discovering as much or more in a framer framing a house,
Putting higher claims for him there with his roll'd-up sleeves
    driving the mallet and chisel,
Not objecting to special revelations, considering a curl of smoke
    or a hair on the back of my hand just as curious as any
    revelation. . . .   (*LG* 75)

The Italian essayist Giovanni Papini defined this essential quality of "Song of Myself" very aptly when he wrote:

> I must confess that I, a Tuscan, an Italian, a Latin, have not felt what
> poetry really means through Vergil or Dante—and still less through
> Petrarch and Tasso, luxury poets and consequently men of letters rather
> than poets—but, on the contrary, through the childish enumerations
> and impassioned evocations of the kindly harvester of *Leaves of
> Grass*. (199; my trans.)

After letting my students follow the apparently erratic course of Whitman's self shooting across the sky like a comet, I show them the underlying structure of the poem, its hidden logical pattern. Then I try to bring out its "paraphrasable content," to take up Kenneth Burke's phrase, its implicit metaphysics, that is, Whitman's transcendentalism, pantheism, optimistic faith in the fact that the world "is not chaos or death" but "form, union, plan . . . eternal life . . . happiness" (sec. 50). But it is important not to reduce the poem to a mere paraphrase. I therefore underscore the poet's sense of the infinity of space and "amplitude of time" and refer my students to "A Noiseless Patient Spider," which describes the poet lost in the middle of "measureless oceans of space" but nevertheless trying to anchor the web of his poems by launching forth "filament, filament, filament" out of himself.

Then we come back to earth. So far we have studied only the universal features of the poet, and while Whitman, as André Gide noted, could have written *Leaves of Grass* anywhere (723), or at least what is essential in it, he was also an American and must be studied as such with the help of a good biography (Gay W. Allen's, Justin Kaplan's, or mine) and reattached to the literature of his time with the help of books like F. O. Matthiessen's *American Renaissance*, Newton Arvin's *Whitman*, or Allen's *New Walt Whitman Handbook*. Then poems besides "Song of Myself"—*Drum-Taps*, "Memories of President Lincoln," "Passage to India," "Prayer of Columbus," and so on—become accessible to students in ever-widening circles.

Another approach I sometimes use, though it is of value mainly with advanced students, involves drawing upon Gaston Bachelard's books about the part played in poetry by the four elements—earth, air, fire, and water. In such works as *The Psychoanalysis of Fire, The Poetics of Space, The Poetics of Reverie*, and *The Right to Dream*, Bachelard explores the creative forces of the poetic imagination as the route to revelation, the entrance to reality.[1] He is particularly fascinated by the activity of daydreaming or reverie, which he promotes, believing that it liberates the mind and enables it to associate with the four basic elements. This process, in turn, releases the power of the imagination to generate poetic images, and the creation of new images, according to Bachelard, is the essence of poetry.

When making use of Bachelard's writing, I do not study Whitman's metaphysical and political ideas but instead lay emphasis on his imagery, its secret life in the poet's subconscious and its growth in the poems. This method helps students to understand the creative process and to feel the sensuous and instinctual quality of "Song of Myself" and of many other poems in the *Leaves*.

I thus always use several approaches and absolutely refuse to let myself be guided (i.e., enslaved) by one method to the exclusion of others.

NOTE

[1]A useful selection from Bachelard's writings may be found in *On Poetic Imagination and Reverie*, translated and edited by Colette Gaudin. To those students who can read French I recommend four works that have yet to be translated: *L'eau et les rêves: Essai sur l'imagination de la matière* (1942), *L'air et les songes: Essai sur l'imagination du mouvement* (1943), *La terre et les rêveries de la volonté* (1948), and *La terre et les rêveries du repos* (1958).

TEACHING OTHER MAJOR WORKS

Reconciling Varied Approaches to "Out of the Cradle Endlessly Rocking"

Dennis K. Renner

Whitman scholars have been curious about the sad mood of new poems included in the third edition of *Leaves of Grass*, especially the one eventually retitled "Out of the Cradle Endlessly Rocking." Some attribute this poem's desolation to rekindled emotional conflicts from Whitman's infancy, others to more recent traumas—the loss of a male or female lover or Whitman's foreboding that the nation on which he had staked his civic identity could be dismembered by civil war. Still others believe that a more universal problem—coping with the reality of death—is the appropriate backdrop for the poem. A stellar selection in course anthologies, "Out of the Cradle Endlessly Rocking" is a provocative assignment after the ebullient "Song of Myself." Like the critics whose explications they sometimes consult, students recognize Whitman's emotional transformation but cannot agree about the reasons for it. Helping students understand the diverse possibilities for explication is worthwhile because the poem is pivotal in the Whitman canon and presents many interpretative options new readers will encounter in his other poems.

The situation in the poem is clear enough. Its speaker recalls that just as the mockingbird he watched in boyhood seemed to sing for its lost mate, the speaker has "caroled" poems in a futile effort to regain something lost. But what is equivalent in the speaker's life to the bird's lost mate? Why do "the memories of the bird" still bring tears and why does the speaker claim in the poem's opening lines that he, "of all men," knows "the meanings" of the bird's calls? The poem concludes by embracing the word *death* as a consolation for whatever has been lost; at this point students probe the relation between the word the sea is "hissing" and what the mockingbird and the speaker hold in common. Since the text does not speak directly on the matter, I usually survey the options with my students, acknowledging the ambiguity. Then we settle for our own consolation: we admire the poem's aesthetic achievements. A better closure for class discussion of "Out of the Cradle Endlessly Rocking" would reconcile critical approaches to the poem, which I propose to do in this essay.

The dominant approach in published criticism is biographical, stressing the poet's personal relationships. Although this perspective appeals to those familiar with Whitman's life, the evidence is sparse and inconclusive. Critics who approach the poem this way acknowledge that "solid facts" are lacking "upon which to make a specifically biographical interpretation," yet they often suggest that "some bereavement . . . may have taken place in or just before 1859" (Chase, *Walt Whitman* 121). The loss might have been "some lover [who] had died" (Holloway 162), perhaps a "beloved companion and mistress" (Stovall, "Main Drifts" 9); or Whitman may have experienced "some sort of unhappy love relation with a man, one that brought him a brief glimpse of happiness and then plunged him into bitter suffering" (Whicher 12–13). "So far as known," however, "Whitman had not experienced such a loss" (Allen, *Solitary Singer* 235). It is known, though, that Whitman experienced conflicts in his relationship with his father, the basis for readings that discern primal oedipal strivings in "Out of the Cradle Endlessly Rocking" (E. H. Miller, *Whitman's Poetry* 48–49, 174; Black 74–76). According to this interpretation the poem's conflicts are at least partially resolved when the speaker turns from the shore, personified as a father, to the sea, the "old mother" who provides the consoling word. And finally, critics have suggested that while the origin of the desolate mood in the 1860 edition of *Leaves of Grass* was oedipal, it was also related to Whitman's disappointment that his parents, especially his father, did not support his poetic vocation. In maturity, Whitman is thought to have been troubled by his father's denial of "comradeship and confirmation" (Cavitch 145). Not only "Out of the Cradle" but also "As I Ebb'd with the Ocean of Life," a poem of desolation from the same period, has been discussed from this perspective (Zweig 309). Plausible textual patterns in the poems support this biographical approach, which emphasizes personal, as opposed to public, relationships.

A second biographical approach, which places the text against the backdrop of the poet's public life rather than his domestic relationships, has been applied to many poems but rarely to "Out of the Cradle Endlessly Rocking." This approach considers Whitman's life as citizen and journalist, the two roles that preceded and shaped his conception of poetry. Because it displays political themes from Whitman's involvement in electoral politics and from his long career as a newspaper writer and editor, the third edition of *Leaves of Grass*, assembled in Boston before the outbreak of civil war, lends itself to this perspective (Hoople 181). Kenneth Burke has observed that "the entire scheme" of Whitman's poetry "was based upon an ideal of all-pervasive and almost promiscuous Union," and thus "the motives of secession that culminated in the Civil War necessarily filled him with anguish" ("Policy" 97). Critics who approach the poetry from this perspective believe that the political stridency and expressions of despair in poems composed during the crisis years are more than coincidental. Manuscript studies suggest a correlation between ominous signs of disunion in the popular press and Whitman's renewed composition of poems for the 1860 edition (Bowers; Renner 204–07, 249–52). The prospect of civil war is not mentioned in "Out of the Cradle Endlessly Rocking," and the text offers none of the political stridency found in the many 1860 poems that do allude to the secession crisis, but figurative patterns and allusions to the South suggest that the threat of secession may be more pertinent to this poem than has been recognized.

An alternative to these biographical approaches—a more strictly generic approach—appeals to students who come to Whitman poems with strong backgrounds in literary study. This approach focuses on "aesthetic form," "conventions of certain kinds of poems," and "the way poems in general work" (Allen and Davis vii; P. Fussell 28). There is less interest here in the poet's life apart from his decision to try to write one or another kind of poem. Critics observe that Whitman's poem reminds them of "basic motifs" from "the great parallel poems of world literature" (Spitzer 218), and they note the presence of allegory (Allen, *Solitary Singer* 235), similarities to the "standard Romantic lyric of reminiscence" (Fussell 30), and elements of Italian opera (Faner, *Walt Whitman* 173–77). What matters is not the resemblance to "episodes" of Whitman's "actual experience" but "the significant shapes of a world of universal forms. . . . the only valuable experience the poem offers us is a wholly artistic one" (Fussell 29–30). Some students are satisfied by the resulting generalizations that "Out of the Cradle" is a "kind of subjective drama" in which the poet creates "a symbolical language for the life of his own mind" (Whicher 25), that its "theme is the origin in boyhood of the lyric impulse and its precarious maintenance into a cooler world of manhood" and that it uses "the shore-surf relationship," like other American shore odes, to provide "a natural 'uniform hieroglyphic' of a Romantic reconciliation of dualisms" (Fussell 32); or that it is a narrative about "a boy's triple discovery—of love, of death, and of poetry, a new kind of life" (Waskow 119).

To pinpoint differences in these approaches to "Out of the Cradle Endlessly Rocking," let's return to the basic interpretative problem of the poem. The speaker, like the bird, seeks his "mate," but since the exact equivalence to the bird's mate is not stated, the nature of the speaker's loss is ambiguous. Generic critics say the least about this problem. Since they are more interested in conventions, formal aspects, and other more purely aesthetic matters, what provoked the composition of this elegiac poem is not crucial to them. In fact, they would probably remind us that the situation may be wholly imagined rather than substantially biographical.

For example, Gay Wilson Allen and Charles T. Davis, who pointedly read Whitman's poems "for their intellectual content and aesthetic form" (vii), conclude that "Out of the Cradle" faces what "sooner or later in life everyone has to face"—"the stern fact of death in the natural order of things"—and does so admirably. "Whether fact or fiction, the death of the female mockingbird is a good symbol of this fact in nature," they observe, and they like the way the poem ends "on the note of implied hope and faith to be found in every great cultural myth and world religion" (165–67). When Richard Chase concludes, however, that "Out of the Cradle," one of "Whitman's best" poems, is nonetheless of "second rank," he does so because the speaker's emotion is "all too easily come by" and the poem's conflicts are unresolved. To sustain his complaint that the emotion is unearned, Chase has to address the problem of what the poet has lost. His interpretation is psychoanalytic: the poem is a "work of personal confession"; the loss is of a father's love. In Whitman's "world bereft of the father-principle, the mother is all-encompassing, like the sea," which seems so consoling. There is comfort in the rocking and whispering of the figuratively spiritual and maternal sea, yes, but Chase also discerns "anxiety and ambivalence toward the mother"—evidence of "neurotic regression which generates powerful and sinister impulses that threaten the destruction of personality." In Chase's view, such unresolved conflicts bespeak "sentimental nihilism" and melodrama rather than literary insight (" 'Out of the Cradle' " 53, 69–71).

These two approaches lead to different assessments. Allen and Davis, who do not address the problem of what has been lost, can admire the poem unreservedly; Chase, who presumes that Whitman's disrupted relationship with his father is the crucial psychological motive for the poem, must qualify his admiration by acknowledging its flaws.

Because psychoanalytic theory is complex, the nuances and elaborations that Chase and other Freudian critics develop are beyond the scope of the present essay. Similarly, a psychoanalytic approach to "Out of the Cradle" is not as practical for undergraduate students as a biographical approach emphasizing the poet's public roles as citizen, journalist, and poet. Because most students are familiar with the events in antebellum American history that troubled Whitman, they regard the political context of the 1860 edition as an outgrowth of his earlier roles. They are also comfortable looking through the entire volume for help in explicating a subordinate passage such as the poem in question. I propose to reconcile the varied approaches to "Out of the Cradle" accordingly, examining the poem against the backdrop of the crisis decade and accepting interpretative promptings from "Protoleaf," the prefatory poem in the third edition of *Leaves of Grass*.

The mockingbirds in "Out of the Cradle" have a direct counterpart in "Protoleaf," which introduces themes and figurative patterns for poems in the third edition. (Verse numbers in parenthesis for quotations from the poems, are from Pearce's facsimile edition.) For their first appearance in this edition, the birds are not on Long Island, as in "Out of the Cradle"; instead they are both *from* Alabama and *in* Alabama, and they are happily together there. It is notable that before the lines about them appear at the center of "Protoleaf," the poet-speaker has declared his New World hopes for "victory, union," and "indissoluble compacts" (2). Also he has presented his prospectus for poems that refer directly to the secession crisis—"a song for These States, that no one State may under any circumstances be subjected to another State," which alludes to disputes over the Fugitive Slave Laws; "a song that there shall be comity by day and by night between all The States," which alludes to threats of violent sectionalism; and "a song of the organic bargains of These States," which refers to the compacts of the Union originating in the American Revolution. Finally, as if the political context were not clear enough, the poet promises "a shrill song of curses on him who would dissever the Union" (20). The antagonistic forces that threaten what the New World promises—the affirmations of "Protoleaf" and sub- sequent poems—are all rooted in the political intrigues of the crisis decade leading to the Civil War.

It is instructive to compare lines about the mockingbirds from "Protoleaf" and "Out of the Cradle" against this political backdrop from the larger poetic unit. The poet's first encounter with the birds in "Protoleaf" is wholly positive and joyful, unlike the sadness of the second passage. The origin of the poet's muse is not just in the desolation of "Out of the Cradle," which critics often stress, but also in the first, joyous encounter with the "birds together," which does not involve a loss. What the he-bird "really sang for was not there only, / Nor for his mate nor himself only," lines from "Protoleaf" read, "But subtle, clandestine, away beyond, / A charge trans- mitted, and gift occult, for those being born" (40). While the poet-speaker pauses to hear the bird, "near at hand, inflating his throat, and joyfully singing," he resolves to do the same:

Democracy!
Near at hand to you a throat is now inflating itself and joyfully
    singing,
Ma femme!
For the brood beyond us and of us,
For those who belong here, and those to come,

> I, exultant, to be ready for them, will now shake out carols
> stronger and haughtier than have ever yet been heard upon the
> earth.   (41, 42)

Even here, in lines of affirmation and hope, "the true poem" is said to transcend death. Indeed, the entire movement from encountering the birds, to recognizing their precedent for "caroling" poems, to declaring that death is not final appears in both "Protoleaf" and "Out of the Cradle." The difference between the passages is that the bird's mate disappears in the second poem.

This difference helps us address our original questions about the analogous situations of the poet-speaker and the despairing bird in "Out of the Cradle." Answers to these questions are suggested by subtle references to the South in the poem. In lines from the bird's joyous song before its mate is lost, the refreshing winds blow both "South" and "North"—capitalizations seem more than incidental here—and the birds, though presently in the North, are "guests from Alabama" (1–3). (Whitman had used Alabama as a metonym for the South as early as 1850 in "The House of Friends," a poem attacking northern Democrats who seemed to be conceding too much to the South in the Compromise of 1850: "Why do you strain your lungs off Southward? / Why be going to Alabama?" [Brasher 36]). These reminders of sectionalism, plus directions from the prefatory lines about the mockingbirds, prompt the recognition that the equivalence in the speaker's life to the bird's lost mate is the future of "Democracy! . . . the brood beyond and of us" toward which the poet has directed his own love songs. In the face of the South's impending secession, because the Union seemed crucial to Whitman's hopes, democracy has become a lost cause. Thus the poet, whose songs for democracy have seemed futile, "of all men" knows the meaning of the bird's calls for its own lost love, and the speaker embraces death, the word whispered by the sea, expressing his faith in immortality. The acceptance of intolerable defeat in this instance is as grudging as our personal resignations sometimes are. The sea that comforts the speaker is characterized, paradoxically, as a "savage old mother"—"incessantly" moaning and crying (28). The word *death* may be "delicious" in its spiritual import, as the poet declares, but it is nonetheless hissed (33). Whitman's is not a facile acquiescence.

To reconcile varied approaches to "Out of the Cradle Endlessly Rocking" I have considered interpretative precedents in the preface of the 1860 edition of *Leaves of Grass*. I have combined generic and biographical approaches stressing Whitman's public roles. As for private biography, Whitman's domestic life undoubtedly found expression in subtexts that add richness and complexity to the poem through latent motives from his unconscious. Moreover, reader-response theory suggests that a community of readers, perhaps so inclined by their own latent motives, will always tend to emphasize the Freudian subtext of "Out of the Cradle," particularly when the poem is read apart from its original context in *Leaves of Grass*. As for the traditional formalist approach, interpretations from this perspective are easily accommodated. There is much that is lyrical, allegorical, and romantic in "Out of the Cradle." At its highest and more nearly universal level of meaning and for a community of readers unfamiliar with its setting in nineteenth-century American life, this American ode—lofty, solemn, ceremonially public—will always be a poem about human aspiration, death, and the origin of the poetic muse.

The Disseminal Whitman:
A Deconstructive Approach
to *Enfans d'Adam* and *Calamus*

Robert K. Martin

The young man that wakes, deep at night, the hot hand seeking to
repress what would master him—the strange half-welcome
pangs, visions, sweats,
The pulse pounding through palms and trembling encircling
fingers—the young man all colored, red, ashamed, angry. . . .

Enfans d'Adam

The poet as masturbator? What are we to make of this passage or of many
like it throughout *Leaves of Grass*? Is this an element of confession? a political
act? a statement of aesthetics? Will we simply pass over such passages,
embarrassed for ourselves or our students? Or will we address them? But
in what terms?

Recent criticism has made Whitman's sexuality an inescapable concern of
any biographical approaches. No one is likely to introduce Whitman these
days without at least briefly suggesting his place in the history of American
homosexual identity. But is his sexuality merely a headnote to the poems?
Will it suffice to identify such lines as "symptoms" of an "equivocal" sexuality?[1] Or should we consider masturbation one of the central acts and
central tropes of Whitman's poetry and explore its consequences?

The interdiction of masturbation was a major strategy of power in mid-
nineteenth-century America. It was undertaken as a crusade, couched in
moral terms, and designed to preserve the power of an elite against a newly
mobile male working class, whose spokesman Whitman was (or posed as).
Masturbation was to controlled, harnessed sexuality what the newly urban-
ized young men were to their village fathers: a rebellious, headstrong force
that seemed to threaten the body politic.[2] Whitman's words locate his young
man at a point of personal and cultural rupture. Although he seeks to "repress
what would master him," he can accomplish that only through the use of
his own "hot hand," agent of both masturbation and writing. His responses
are the product of cultural repression (he is "red" and "ashamed"), but they
have also reached the point of rebellion (he is "angry," and the "pangs" and
"visions" [wonderfully double] are "half-welcome"). Whitman's masturbatory
poems are thus both the revelation of a repressed self and a cultural act of
some magnitude; they apply to the body the political impulses of the revolution, fulfilling the parricide by a new reign of brothers.

While his age sought the control of sperm, Whitman called for its dispersion. Held within, it could only cause a "vexed corrosion," like a "pent-
up river" that seeks its release (*Enfans d'Adam* 5.28, 4.33).[3] In opposition
to the economic theory of sexuality that held sperm to be a precious and

finite commodity, Whitman proposed the dam-burst theory, based on an organic metaphor expressing repression in physical terms, much as Freud would do three generations later. Unlike Freud, however, Whitman bases his theory of art not on sublimation, or release in a substitute form, but on an undirected expense of seminal energy. Whitman's "love-spendings," his denial of the spermatic economy (Barker-Benfield; Killingsworth, "Whitman's Love-Spendings"), become "gushing showers" that revive the earth (*Enfans* 4.38,40). For Whitman the recovery of sexuality is not only a personal project for release from self-hatred and guilt (the "vexed corrosion") but a cultural project for the reappropriation of a chthonic energy, a spirit of renewal located in the individual, not in any transcendent god.

As sexual energy is at once evoked and dispersed, so too verbal energy. Whitman's place as the first great American modernist is due largely to his destruction of the tyranny of order, to his discovery of the apparently casual and natural, founded in an appreciation of an undirected seminality: "this bunch plucked at random from myself, / It has done its work—I toss it carelessly to fall where it may" (*Enfans* 5.44). Whitman's own verbal structures, their extraordinary power of inclusiveness and accretion, represent a revolt against hierarchy at the level of language. To the student who wonders at Whitman's garrulous inability to get to the point, one must reply that a certain pointlessness is indeed "the point." Whitman begins his greatest poem, after all, by announcing that he will "lean and loafe at [his] ease," and his first mystical sexual experience is introduced by a call to the soul (or reader or friend) to "Loafe with me on the grass" ("Song of Myself" 1.5, 5.75),[4] in an experience that will lead to the annihilation of the "imperial self" (Anderson). The dispersion of seminal energy is thus for Whitman a recurring figure for the destruction of all hierarchies, a way through the renewal of the body (of the text as well as of the person) to the renewal of the earth.

Whitman's language strikingly anticipates what the French critic Roland Barthes would call a poetics of bliss, or *jouissance* (*Pleasure of the Text*; Barthes uses *jouissance*, meaning "joy" and "orgasm," in opposition to the more controlled *plaisir* 'pleasure'). Why, a student is likely to ask, must we have "Yahonk!," the cry of the wild gander ("Song of Myself" 14.239)? And why the specificity of reference, the painstaking construction of lists of place names or of trees and fruits ("twigs of maple, and a bunch of wild orange, and chestnut, / And stems of currants, and plum-bows, and the aromatic cedar" [*Calamus* 4.22–23])? Whitman takes joy in making us trip over words, in discovering the power of sounds when words are freed from their function as transparent signifiers and released into sensual being. Their strangeness preserves their freshness, their resistance to reading as mere extraction of meaning. Whitman's constant touching and playing, his responses to the physicality of language, restore words to their function as things. The objects of the physical world are introduced precisely to prevent the poem from becoming a mere vehicle of meaning. They are presented in an apparently random order that reflects a democratic poetics (love is not more poetic than grass), a denial of dualism (soul is not superior to body), and a reclamation of the (undifferentiated) body (the genitals or the armpits are as important to the body as any other part,[5] and the currant is as important as the cedar). Students with lingering New Critical notions of the text's autonomy are challenged by reading Whitman. There is no text apart from the self of the poet: he and the poem are one. Whitman's poems question assumptions about aesthetics; they ask us to rethink notions of the important and the beautiful. Whitman does not lend himself to easy anthologizing, because there are no gems to extract. To read Whitman students must plunge into the chaos. If time is available, they may be asked to work their way through an edition of Whitman, preferably the 1855 or 1860 edition, both now available in paperback. Only then can they grasp Whitman's organic poetics, see that Whitman has redefined poetry in a way that allows for its dispersion rather than its concentration into the rare, commoditized, and valuable. They must experience the slow meander of the text. They can make use of this experience to question assumptions they have made about other poems and about the process of canonization that has placed the short lyric ahead of other verse forms.

Even when Whitman is working within the conventions of a short poem, his is a poetry of process, not of product. One should address this issue in relation to American social history, seeing Whitman's open forms as a response to an increasingly industrial and commercial society. One may also want to look at the relation between textual practice in Whitman and painterly practice, by examining the capacity of photography to capture the momentary and the emphasis of impressionist painting on plein air and a deliberate lack of finish. The spontaneity and process in Whitman's verbal structures can be seen in his use of present participles in a poem such as "We two boys together clinging" (*Calamus* 26). Each line of this ten-line poem, except the last, ends with a participle in the present tense, suggestive of activity and change: clinging, leaving, making, clutching, loving, threatening, dancing, leafing, chasing. Out of a total of only eighty-one words there are twenty-nine present participles, creating an exceptional sense of movement. This verbal energy is one with the poem's content, its exuberant proclamation of boyishness. The opening image of the two boys "never leaving" each other both affirms fraternal love and indicates the threat posed by the young male couple to structures of power. Lines 5 and 6 offer an instructive opposition: the very capacity of the boys for "loving" offers a spirit that is "threatening" to any "law." Students might compare the spirit and language of this poem with the spirit and language of Mark Twain's *Huckleberry Finn*, where the same antisocial energies of boys' friendships are explored but ultimately contained. The boys of Whitman's poem complete themselves by "mocking" the "statutes," not by finding a convenient escape from them. Recapturing their own "natural" forms ("branching and leafing"), they free themselves from convention. The verbal structures, with their own lack of conclusion, thus become an integral part of the dispersion, a sense of constant post-ponement that amounts to a continuation of play. As the boys prolong their youth and its freedoms, so the participial clauses work against closure until the end of the poem.

From contemporary deconstructive theory we have learned to question the notion of the fixed and circumscribed. The self is seen, in this view, as something that is always contingent. Whitman's self is constantly decon-structed and remade in new forms. There is no single Whitman in the poems but rather a myriad of voices and experiences that are constantly re-created in the process of reading as writing. Although Whitman's meliorism seems sometimes to go against such a view of contingency, he is aware, as he affirms himself and his identity, that these are merely provisional. His famous elu-siveness can be seen not so much as a fault of character as an acknowledge-ment of the multiplicity of the self. He is "dying—always dying!" at the same time that he "stride[s] ahead, material, visible, imperious as ever" (*Calamus* 27.2,4). The self dies, not to create a single new self, but to create a constantly changing self that asserts its power even in its contingency. The self is what it hears, what it feels, what it experiences. It does not exist outside its creation of itself. It offers no victory over time except its power of permutation; it sloughs its skin like a snake, buries the past, and continues its way. To accept that state of constant flux is to reverse the pattern of the poem's opening, to transform "dying—always dying!" into "living! always living!" To resist change, to assert permanence, is to die, while to embrace change, to deny permanence, is to live.

Death is omnipresent in the *Calamus* poems, but it is no longer feared, since this life is given no privileged position over any other. As Whitman asks in "Song of Myself," "To be in any form—what is that?" (27.611). In *Calamus* 17, the speaker dreams that his lover is dead and looks for the burial place. He finds death everywhere and this particular tomb nowhere. From his experience he learns to celebrate the dead everywhere, in the midst of life. He accepts death as a dispersion of the self. The body is now merely the corpse, the relic of an earlier self, and its destruction is also its propagation, as in the paradox originally established by the sperm that is spent for "recompense richer" after the "rich showering rain" ("Song of Myself" 29.644). The corpse of the lover or the poet's own corpse may be "rendered to powder," but by this act of physical destruction it is merely transformed and thus becomes a liquid to be "poured in the sea" or "dis-tributed to the winds" (*Calamus* 17.12–13). The pouring out, distribution, or dispersion of the self requires its destruction. Whitman's "death" poems, although they may be read at one level as comments on burial practices and a Victorian obsession with the dead, also concern the nature of the self. They enable us to confront the assumption of the priority of a rational this-world over an imaginary no-world. For the acceptance of death is also the acceptance of the loss of ego, a challenge in deconstructive terms to the power of Logos.

Although Whitman's figure for dispersion is always dissemination, the role of this process in a critique of Western logocentrism (see Derrida, *Dissemination*, and introduction by Johnson) may provide a way of working Whitman's strategies into a feminist project that might, at first glance, seem to be left out of such a male-centered world. One must begin by suggesting that students distinguish between the penis as male organ and the phallus as site of power. Whitman's insistence on the inclusion of the male genitals is a way of restoring the genital to a world from which it had been banished. But at the same time his strategies for extending its energies, his national and cosmic seminality replace the phallus as particular site and directed energy with a figure of oceanic wholeness. His *jouissance* is not concentrated in a single organ but moves from the organ to the body as a whole and to the body of the continent.[6] In this way he responds to the American (and Western) tradition summed up best by the metaphor "the lay of the land" (Kolodny). Whitman's repeated insistence on the implication of the entire body challenges the idea that mind is superior to body as man is to woman. The feminist reader can make use of Whitman to explore the role of language in maintaining structures of power.

Students who want less challenging models for the placing of the unitary authority in question (including the authority of the author) might be directed to *Calamus* 21, in which the poet does not speak but hears, acting as a receiver and filter of voices that lie outside him (much as he elsewhere declares "I think I will do nothing for a long time but listen, / To accrue what I hear into myself—to let sounds contribute toward me" ["Song of Myself" 26.584–85]). He recognizes, in the characteristic pattern of recognition used in the *Calamus* poems, that when he was "untaught" he "did not hear," while "now" he can hear. What he hears is the chorus, with each of the parts assigned a separate textual line and a separate vocal line, and then in the "triumphant tutti" (Whitman's Italian once again serving not as a sign of knowledge but as an intrusive sound) the instruments come together with the chorus. The joining of sounds, in a union that does not involve a loss of identity, is a figure for the poet's ability to record the multiplicity of experience, to evoke the simultaneous difference and unity, much as Beethoven does in his Ninth Symphony. Whitman's language, similarly inclusive, attempts to join without destroying, and his divisions of the poem give voice to different ages as to different emotions or loves.

Whitman's frank avowals of homosexual desire in *Calamus* are thus deliberately balanced by the "heterosexual" sequence of *Enfans d'Adam*, even if Whitman had to change some of the pronouns to achieve this balance (the famous case of *Enfans* 9, originally written about a man). Readers who are troubled by Whitman's frankness should be shown the exceptional courage that Whitman displayed. It may be necessary to explain the consequences of announcing homosexual desire and identity in 1860 and to examine possible models available for Whitman. It should be emphasized that in large part Whitman was inventing a sexuality through his poetry. While it would be cowardly or dishonest to avoid discussions of the coming-out experience recorded in *Calamus*, one should perhaps stress the title's allusion to the reed as a symbol of writing. More than almost any other artist, Whitman insists on the personal and sexual origins of art, on his own origins in the "margins" (*Calamus* 1.2). He insists that his body is the book. A deconstructive reading can be faithful to the historical position of Whitman in the emergence of a gay identity in the nineteenth century while at the same time insisting on the nature of process. Whitman does not view himself or his book as concluded except by death (and death concludes only the bodily self, since the book remains alive in every reading of it).

Looking at the poems in the 1860 edition reminds us that Whitman's structure substitutes process for teleology, circularity for linearity (see *Enfans* 10). From the recognition of the body and spiritual rebirth in *Enfans d'Adam* we leave the garden behind and enter the world in "Poem of the Road" (later "Song of the Open Road"), a poem structured around the repetition of the revolutionary imperative "Allons" ("Let's go"), suggesting movement and change. Accepting the "adhesiveness" of "Road" (see R. K. Martin 33–47; M. Lynch), the reader can now move on, holding Whitman's hand, to the confessions of *Calamus*. Here the "lovers, continual lovers" remind us of perpetual change accepted in and of the body and, by their denial of exclusivity and permanence, allow us to accept the poet's death in *Calamus* 45. In anticipation of "Crossing Brooklyn Ferry" on the facing page, we enter into a timeless world in which factual time ("I forty years old the Eighty-third Year of The States") is meaningless. Tenses shift with dizzying speed, as the poet offers his poems (his sperm, his blood) to "you, yet unborn" and then, in the second stanza, imagines a reversal (or chiasmus) in which the poet seeking a reader is replaced by the reader seeking the poet.

The act of reading thus becomes for Whitman, as it is for Barthes, an act of writing. The poems are "realiz[ed]" in the mind, or voice, or hands, of their reader, for whom Whitman may still be present, not as author, but as lover (as in *Calamus* 10). The printed poems are but potential poems, still to be made and enacted for the reader, whose love will simultaneously restore the poet to his physical being. Whitman affirms life not as the opposite of death, but as something ongoing, changing, uncertain. The renewal of which he speaks is not an event but a process to be undergone as many times as there are readers, just as love may be re-created in the minds and bodies of the lovers who crowd these pages.

The self waits, "willing and naked," stripped of its defenses and its social roles, devoid of any claim to eternity or even permanence, asking for "the souse upon me of my lover the sea" (*Enfans* 5.34), for passage from the proclaiming self to the passive receiver, the body immersed in a sea of sperm, in an oceanic loss of the personal. Whitman's sexual poems, in their awareness of sexual ambiguity and contingency, in their willingness to, as it were, turn over (see the paradigmatic mystical-sexual experience of "Song of Myself" 5.79), offer a model for the denial of certainty that is at the heart of much modern thought. They present a parade of shifting identities ("shifting forms of life" [*Calamus* 2.34]), a carnival of masked figures offering themselves for "one brief hour of madness and joy" (*Enfans* 6.29). They affirm the paradox of life-in-death against the illusion of a centered, controlled life: as Whitman writes at the end of the 1860 edition, "I am as one disembodied, triumphant, dead" ("So long!"), a wonderful phrase that in its apparent contradictions is the perfect expression of a life and a poetry that is protean, elusive, and multiple:

> Failing to fetch me at first keep encouraged,
> Missing me one place search another,
> I stop somewhere waiting for you   ("Song of Myself" 52.1334–36)

NOTES

[1]Whitman has, according to David Cavitch, a "divided personality" that was "never fully integrated" (41) or, according to Edwin H. Miller, an "unstable ego" (*Whitman's Poetry* 150). Sandra M. Gilbert calls Whitman's sexuality "equivocal" (127).

[2]See Carroll Smith-Rosenberg 81 for the new generation of young men and 105 for the relation of masturbation to social change. For a more general background to the problem, see Norman O. Brown, especially chapter 6, "Language and Eros."

[3]Quotations from *Enfans d'Adam* and *Calamus* are cited from *Leaves of Grass*, 1860 edition, edited by Roy Harvey Pearce. Numerals refer to poem number and line numbers as they appear in that edition.

[4]Quotations from "Song of Myself" (title used only later) are cited from *Leaves of Grass*, 1855 edition, edited by Malcolm Cowley. Numerals refer to section number (as used in later editions) and line numbers (from first edition).

[5]See "Song of Myself" 24.538, and notice how the celebration of the male genitals concludes in the horticultural metaphors of equality and difference: "Trickling sap of maple! Fibre of manly wheat!"

[6]Students may want to consider how this term, first used by Barthes, has become a crucial element of French feminism in writers such as Hélène Cixous and Julia Kristeva (Marks and de Courtivron).

A Jungian Approach to the Self
in Major Whitman Poems

Lorelei Cederstrom

The central yet most confusing concept in Whitman's *Leaves of Grass* is the self that Whitman posits as the organizational principle of his work. Critics have called this self aboriginal (D. H. Lawrence, Karl Shapiro), cosmic (Richard Bucke, Bernice Slote), imperial (Quentin Anderson), and mystical (V. K. Chari, James E. Miller, Jr.). The teacher can bring together this diverse catalog of selves by presenting Whitman's self as an archetypal (Jungian) self, for Jung's concept not only subsumes the others but provides a structural model for the growth pattern in *Leaves of Grass*. Comparative study reveals that Whitman was exploring the archetypal psyche in terms that Jung would validate in his clinical writings fifty years later; therefore, Whitman's *Leaves* and Jung's psychological paradigms illuminate each other when juxtaposed. The instructor can begin by noting the correspondence in their definitions of the self. For both, the archetypal self is a completed personality, the culmination of a process of development in the psyche. Whitman and Jung emphasize the same pattern of psychological growth: through painful confrontation with the unconscious the personality develops from a time-bound consciousness centered in the ego into a unifying self that mediates between the conscious and unconscious. This individuated self, to use Jung's term, becomes the "ordering and unifying center of the total psyche just as the ego is the center of the conscious personality" (Edinger 3). The self is cosmic because it sees the eternal archetypal patterns that unite all persons in all times and places.

The problem of teaching *Leaves of Grass* as a whole is simplified when one approaches the work as an example of the growth of the individuated self. From a Jungian perspective, *Leaves of Grass* traces the process of growth in the psyche as it moves from youth to age and expands through confrontation with, and assimilation of, inner conflicts made conscious. The development of the self begins with the assertions in "Song of Myself" of a healthy, youthful ego, which has intuitively identified with the transpersonal dimension of the self. Next, the psyche encounters the realities of the "other" (male and female) in *Children of Adam* and *Calamus*. Through this confrontation, the psyche grows to include the world as other in "Salut au Monde" and "Song of the Open Road," developing the idea germinated in *Calamus* of a universal comradeship. The vision of brotherhood darkens to include war in *Drum-Taps*, but, eventually, the poet achieves a union with all humankind, good and evil, in "Crossing Brooklyn Ferry." In "The Sleepers" the poet explores the unconscious, and the expansion of the psyche through the union of the personal consciousness with the archetypal unconscious is completed. Once individuation has been achieved, the psyche changes its focus. *Autumn Rivulets* describes the movement at middle age away from youthful expansion toward contemplation and the assimilation of earlier encounters. Finally, the psyche confronts the physical changes and "whispers" of "heavenly death" at old age, which reveal that the end of life is the completion of a cycle rather than a termination. Although this pattern is quite straightforward, Whitman describes a painful struggle at each stage of development; growth is based on a confrontation between the oppositions in human nature.

The concept of growth through a confrontation with oppositions is crucial, for this pattern separates Whitman from the mystical consciousness with which he has so often been associated and aligns him instead with Jung. Whitman goes beyond the mystical or cosmic idea of the self for he does not preach the doctrine of a self that lies beyond oppositions. Instead, he maintains the strength of the individual personality at the heart of the opposites; the self holds polarities in balance and unites them within. Whitman shares with Jung this emphasis on polarities as the basis for psychological growth. Whitman's style also affirms the centrality of polarities and oppositions to his view of the self. Students are troubled by the many paradoxes in Whitman's work, but these are a necessary means of expressing the oppositions that are united in the self. A paradox is the perfect medium for the expression of polarities held in balance, since in a paradox, oppositions are in a state of suspension, separate but united in a moment of intuition. Jung describes the development of the self through individuation in terms that help to explain Whitman's reliance on paradoxical expression. He notes that individuation requires the realization of a balance between opposites occurring not through logical argument but through "symbols which make the irrational union of opposites possible" (316). Thus, teaching *Leaves* from a Jungian perspective amplifies not only the nature and development of the Whitman self but the overall structure of the work and the organizational principles behind the random catalog and uneasy paradoxes gathered together through the intuition of Whitman's "fluid and swallowing" self ("Song of Myself," line 800).[1]

With these basic concepts out of the way, the instructor can turn to the details of self-development in *Leaves of Grass*. Although the first poem, "Song of Myself," describes the outlines of the Whitmanian self and hints at the oppositions that self will confront, the concepts here are best approached as the expansion of a youthful (or aboriginal) self, modified and brought to completion in the later poems. The assured voice in Whitman's first song is more that of the ego than that of the self and is in a state of inflation. Through the power of its intuition, the ego has glimpsed and identified itself with the transpersonal dimension of the self. The condition of the ego at this youthful stage can be compared with that of Adam in Paradise, resting securely upon an identification with the good that precedes self-realization. The progress and growth of the psyche require the bitter fall into experience.

With *Children of Adam* and *Calamus* the poet moves into the world of the "fall" characterized by oppositions. Jung has emphasized that, in its early stages, individuation forces a confrontation with society and its values. Critics have noted consistently that in these poems Whitman is dealing with all the ambivalences regarding human sexuality; he not only affirms the value of sexuality for procreation but confirms, as well, the "pent-up aching rivers" of physical desire. In this connection, Whitman also deals with the old man-woman, body-soul polarities. The body is seen not only as necessary to spiritual fulfillment but as central and perfect in itself. Whitman's emphasis on the sexual equality of women is immediately relevant in a contemporary classroom. Students readily appreciate that Whitman does not accept the superiority of male sexuality; he rejects the Platonic view permeating so much of Western literature in which a man's love for a woman is a means of moving from physical to spiritual love. Women are equal and important and female sexuality is as valuable as the male's. He writes, "Be not ashamed women, you are the gates of the body, and you are the gates of the soul" (*Children of Adam*, "I Sing the Body Electric" 67). Thus, it is crucial to emphasize that physical love and spiritual love are not separable; the dark yearnings of the physical are, for Whitman, the strivings of the spirit. Whitman affirms the unity of the physical and spiritual in words heard nowhere else in the nineteenth century: "sex contains all, bodies, souls" (*Children of Adam*, "A Woman Waits for Me" 3).

Physical sexuality, women's sexuality, and bodily yearnings are not the only shadows of love Whitman confronts and absorbs. *Calamus* can be taught from the perspective of the growth of the self through confrontation with the dark, unconscious aspects of sex and love. In this poem, he comes to terms with homoerotic stirrings as well as with the psychological unity between love and death. He recognizes that love and death as polar opposites cannot exist without understanding each other. "What indeed," he asks, "is finally beautiful except death and love" ("Scented Herbage of My Breast" 11). Death, for the poet, lurks in the processes of life and completes them. Whitman shares Jung's view that "everything requires for its existence its own opposite or else it fades into nothingness" (185–86).

After confrontation with love's shadow in *Children of Adam* and *Calamus*, the poet's consciousness again undergoes an expansion. Conflict with society's sexual mores and confrontation with the sexual face of the shadow have enabled the self to achieve an important intuition about the nature of being. Whitman's next few poems, which describe the sense of completion arising from the successful assimilation of the shadow, can be taught as the achievement of a new level of awareness. Describing the effect of the kind of confrontation the poet has undergone, Jung writes, "Everyone who becomes conscious of his unconscious gets outside his own time and social stratum into a kind of solitude" (224). Whitman in "Song of the Open Road" ordains himself "loos'd of limits and imaginary lines" (53). He asserts that he is his "own master total and absolute"—divested of "all the holds" that would keep him (52–55). The student can note here that although this flight is similar to the one described in "Song of Myself," the ego is now firmly grounded in the realities of its shadow. The self is not simply identified with its transcendent aspect but has become aware of both its positive and negative, physical as well as spiritual, elements. The Jungian psychologist Erich Neumann has noted that "inclusion of the unconscious always entails inclusion of the bodily at the same time" (118). The Whitman self is moving forward in its drive to unite conscious and unconscious, body and spirit. From his new perspective, Whitman describes the self as a mixture of "reality and immortality" ("Song of the Open Road" 81). He sees life as a journey both temporal and eternal in which each ending gives rise to new beginning. Again, Whitman asserts what he learned about the growth of the self through polarities. Each forward movement on the open road is made firmly in spite of the inner shadow that would hold one back. He describes this shadow as "another self, a duplicate of every one, skulking and hiding it goes . . . death under the breastbones" (198, 202). The conclusion of the poem establishes the movement along the open road as a symbol of the growth of the psyche through conflicts: "it is provided in the essence of things / that from any fruition of success, no matter what, shall / come forth something to make a greater struggle necessary" (209–10).

"Crossing Brooklyn Ferry" is central in the Jungian pattern of psychological growth because the union between the ego and the self is completed. The time-bound world of the ego and the eternity of the self are no longer opposites but are linked in the poet's understanding of the psyche. Some of Whitman's central paradoxes are presented here. Difficult though they are, they yield when taught from the Jungian perspective. Whitman resolves the crucial opposition of time and eternity through the realization that although the individual is bound to time, the individuated self shares in eternal patterns. Jung writes, "The fact that all men share the same psychological processes gives rise to an intuition of the 'eternal' continuity of the living" (325). Whitman notes that one can be "disintegrated" yet "part of the scheme" (7). The body, which is temporal, is the means by which the eternal spirit is given life. Whitman describes this with the paradox of being "struck from the float forever held in solution" (62). Whitman also establishes again the importance of the body, for identity requires a body: "That I was I knew was of my body, and what I should be I knew I should be of my body" (64). Above all, the shadow, darkness and evil, are recognized as part of the self. Whitman affirms, "I am he who knew what it was to be evil" (70).

These realizations are continued in "Song of the Answerer," Whitman's poem on the function of the poet. The self is a conjoiner of oppositions, and Whitman emphasizes that the role of the poet is to express the unities of the self. "One part does not counteract the other part, he is the joiner, he sees how they join" (32–33). The poet and his vocation can thus be taught as a model of the self and its functions. For Whitman, the true poet reveals the universal through the particular. He shows that the patterns of the individual psyche are part of the general human condition: "the words of the maker of poems are the general light and dark" (57). Finally, Whitman returns to the idea he expressed in "Open Road" of endings leading to new beginnings. The answerer sees death itself as a new beginning in a "sweep through the ceaseless rings" (83).

The eternal cycles that all share contribute to the bond of comradeship, a central theme in the poems of Whitman's middle years. The poet's joy in the idea of America, "the clew of the union of them" ("Our Old Feuillage" 80), the "Song of Joys" of the "vast elemental sympathy" (23) among all people, the paradox of the "unseen soul" that exists in "objects gross," all rest upon the pivotal idea of the self, which joins all persons and things through all time. *Birds of Passage* can be taught as a work that brings together the insights of these years. The poem opens with a reminder of the realization of polarities as necessary to the growth of the individual. In the "mystic evolution" (20) of the spirit, Whitman notes that it is "not the right only justified," but "what we call evil also justified" (21). Whitman realizes that the problem of evil, the Jungian shadow, is bound up with the transformation of the personality throughout life. Erich Neumann stresses this crucial re-alization as well:

> The shadow is not a transitional stage or "nothing but" the instinctual side considered simply as the soil in which the roots of life are bedded. It is the paradoxical secret of transformation itself, since it is in fact in and through the shadow that the lead is transformed to gold. It is only when a man learns to experience himself as the creature of a creator who made light and darkness, good and evil, that he becomes aware of his own Self as a paradoxical totality in which the opposites are linked together as they are in the Godhead.   (145)

Whitman writes similarly of the Godhead as a "Belief of plan in Thee enclosed in Time and Space" ("Song of the Universal" 60). As one who has taken responsibility for good and evil upon himself, Whitman speaks as an indi-viduated self of the universality of human experience: "where I am or you are this present day, there is the centre of all days, all races, / And there is meaning to us of all that has ever come of races and days, or ever will come" ("With Antecedents" 39–40).

The psyche is never static and the dynamics of its growth, stasis, and regrowth continue to shape the movement of *Leaves of Grass*. After expan-sion through identification with the eternal patterns of the self, the psyche again regresses. The poet expresses doubts and a loss of faith in the very principles of which he was recently so sure. The student will note the change in "As I Ebb'd with the Ocean of Life," in *Sea-Drift*, which describes this reversal: "I perceive I have not really understood anything, not a single object and that no man ever can" (32). Darker still than self-doubt is the realization of the dark side of comradeship. While the brotherhood of man seemed possible to a self linked to eternal processes, the realities of a war between brothers in the states forces a new confrontation with the shadow. In *Drum-Taps* Whitman asks, "Must I indeed learn to chant the cold dirges of the baffled? / and sullen hymns of defeat?" ("Year That Trembled and Reel'd beneath Me" 5–6). In spite of the note of despair here, the Jungian approach reveals that the poet's confrontation with the evils of war leads to an ever greater reliance upon the strength of the individuated self. For although wars represent a collective evil, Whitman sees that the solution to wars can come from the individual. Erich Neumann, in his attempt to deal with the psychological basis of the atrocities of the Second World War, emphasizes the role of the self. He writes:

> The individual who is brought up against the overwhelming problem of evil and is shaken by it . . . naturally defends himself against destruction. In order to survive at all he needs . . . the aid of the forces of the deep unconscious; in them and in himself he may be able to find new ways, new forms of life, new values, new guiding symbols. (29)

Whitman, recoiling from the war, reassesses the meaning of America in "By Blue Ontario's Shore." He concludes that greatness does not lie in "civilizations, governments, theories" (253) but with individuals. The self, for Whitman, includes everything: "I see flashing that this America is only you and me" (273). He takes responsibility for all evil as part of himself: "The war, (that war so bloody and grim, the war I will henceforth forget), was you and me" (278). Whitman refuses to "shirk any part" (282) of himself. He takes all the "rude forms" (312) and wickedness of the world as his own. The poet must be prepared to sing not only with patriotic fervor but with responsibility for the evils toward which such fervor can lead. Like Neumann, Whitman realizes that the individual is "the retort in which the poisons and antidotes of the collective are distilled" (30).

By now, the instructor and student will be aware of a consistent pattern. Whitman repeatedly merges himself with the dark oppositions that confront him and emerges anew. He understands that the recognition and acceptance of darkness is the basis for understanding life. He emphasizes that one cannot identify only with the good but must see that it is conjoined with evil in the self. This is stated explicitly in "Song of Prudence" in *Autumn Rivulets*:

> What is prudence is indivisible,
> Declines to separate one part of life from every part,

Divides not the righteous from the unrighteous or the living from
    the dead,
Matches every thought or act by its correlative. . . .   (46–49)

This idea of a "correlative" provides a new term in the classroom analysis
of oppositions in Whitman's work. In "Passage to India," Whitman matches
the efforts of modern science with the correlative of the dark past out of
which the New World has grown. He reminds the enlightened world, which
can link continents with its wonders, of its basis in darkness, "the teeming
gulf—the sleepers and the shadows" (11). The separations between East and
West, between today and the past, cannot be brought together by science,
but only, Whitman stresses, through the efforts of a seer-poet whose spirit
moves between the world of "primal thought" (165) wherein all things are
unified, and the modern world. Whitman sees the archaic correlative of the
modern world and understands that one cannot reject either old or new
ideas; both are necessary. Again, this can be related to individuation through
assimilation of opposites. Jung notes:

> Whoever protects himself against what is new and strange and regresses
> to the past falls into the same neurotic condition as the man who
> identifies himself with the new and runs away from the past. . . . In
> principle both are doing the same thing: they are reinforcing their
> narrow range of consciousness instead of shattering it in the tension
> of opposites and building up a state of wider and higher conscious-
> ness.   (283)

By accepting both modern science and the past, the poet achieves such a
state of "wider and higher consciousness." At the conclusion of the poem,
he writes of a self that has mastered the orbs, mated Time and filled "the
vastnesses of Space" (209–10). It must be emphasized here that this expansion of consciousness is firmly rooted in "correlatives"—the matching of
every thought by its opposite in the "indivisible" self.

The poem that summarizes most clearly Whitman's view of the unconscious is "The Sleepers." Here Whitman presents a thorough examination
and affirmation of the value of the unconscious and its patterns to the total
psyche. The poet merges himself with the sleepers, becomes one with the
good and evil conjoined in their realm, and returns, renewed, to the world
of waking consciousness. This poem can be taught as a paradigm of the
function of the unconscious in Jungian psychology. Jung's description of the
dream world applies directly to "The Sleepers":

> The dream is a little hidden door in the innermost and most secret
> recesses of the soul, opening into that cosmic night which was psyche

long before there was any ego-consciousness, and which will remain psyche no matter how far our ego-consciousness extends. . . . All consciousness separates; but in dreams we put on the likeness of that more universal, truer, more eternal man dwelling in the darkness of primordial night. There he is still the whole, and the whole is in him, indistinguishable from nature and bare of all egohood.   (53)

In sleep, the poet, too, moves in the world of the primordial psyche preceding ego consciousness. In this world he is one with all the other sleepers whose waking identities have been negated as well. It is important to point out Whitman's emphasis on the positive aspects of the unconscious. For Whitman, good and evil are "averaged" (142) in this state, and through emergence in the primordial element all the sleepers are "likened" and "restored" (143). The poet is at peace with all mankind in the "matrix" in which he "lay so long" before birth and to which he will one day return. He looks toward the unconscious, without fear, as a place of renewal and beauty.

Whitman views death in terms similar to those describing the unconscious. Death, too, is greeted without fear; it is seen not as a terminus but a gateway to another cycle. Living, for Whitman, consists of many deaths, an idea expressed incontrovertibly in "O Living Always, Always Dying." He emphasizes here that each day brings death to what we were yesterday. Again Whitman and Jung agree, for Jung writes, "any going beyond oneself means death" (324). Each of Whitman's poems at old age expresses this view of death. Once again, however, the professor and the student must be prepared for paradox as Whitman reflects upon the implications of death for the idea of the self. He returns once more to the paradox of a timeless self confronting its end in a world of time and death. "To Think of Time" affirms that life has a "systematic pattern" (76) nonetheless. The laws of past and present, of good and evil are purposeful, leading the poet toward his central insight, which is couched in paradoxical terms: "the purpose and essence of the known life, the transient, / Is to form and decide identity for the unknown life, the permanent" (101–02). The professor must make clear here that for Whitman the development of the self, which mediates between the world of time and the timeless realm of the archetypal unconscious, creates an entity that will not terminate when one part of its cycle is complete. Since the unknown life of the self is permanent, known life, which is transient, becomes merely a state in endless cycles of transformation. Death and life are the final polarities that are absorbed in the growth of the self. In "Pensive and Faltering" Whitman writes that "living are the Dead, / (Haply the only living, only real, / And I the apparition, I the spectre.)" (3–5). To the end, Whitman affirms the self as "the final substance—that out of all is sure" ("Quicksand Years" 4).

Teaching Whitman's *Leaves of Grass* with respect to the structure and dynamics of the Jungian self provides significant insights into the organization of the poem as a whole as well as the meaning of its individual parts. Whitman's poem describes, above all, a dynamic self growing through oppositions into a unified and unifying being. Because it has come to terms with its shadow and incorporated both sides of the basic polarities of existence, Whitman's self is able to move beyond the limitations of the temporal and personal into the realm of the eternal and collective. Whitman has accepted the "creative relationship of light and shadow" (Neumann 147) as the basis of selfhood. In an uncollected manuscript fragment, Whitman affirms this idea: "I have all lives, all effects, all hidden invisibly in myself . . . they proceed from me" (Bradley and Blodgett 707). Through his creation of the dynamic self at the center of *Leaves of Grass*, Whitman has achieved the stature of the true poet, who, in his words, stands "as blender, uniter, tightly holding hands" with both body and soul.

NOTE

[1]Quotations of Whitman's poetry are from the *Norton Critical Edition*, edited by Bradley and Blodgett.

Listening to Whitman:
An Introduction to His Prosody

Martin Bidney

Whitman's meanings and motions of spirit are conveyed through his innovative music. Study of his verse rhythms can make the poet's voice come alive: to achieve this goal is the Whitman teacher's main challenge (students may have heard little about prosody but usually like it when they catch on). The teaching of Whitman's metrical music should be both inclusive, covering the fullest range of musical effects, and richly comparative, offering insights into the relations of his distinctive but universally appealing musical achievements to those of kindred spirits in other times and places.

To free the ear from the dominion of the eye, I change the typographical format of some Whitman lines. To help students hear the rhythm of section 1 in "Song of the Broad-Axe," I readjust Whitman's first (six-line) stanza by dividing lines 3 and 4 in half and then dividing the resulting eight-line poem into two stanzas—all this for easier grasp of the meter. Also, to defamiliarize the poem in an amusing way, I repunctuate Whitman's phrases in the manner of another mid-nineteenth-century American poet. The student then reads:

> /   /   /   /
> Weapon shapely, naked, wan—
> /   /   /   /
> Head from the mother's bowels drawn—
> /   /   /   /
> Wooded flesh—and metal bone—
> /   /   /   /
> Limb only one—and lip only one—
>
> /   /   /   /
> Gray-blue leaf—by red-heat grown—
> /   /   /   /
> Helve produced from a little seed sown—
> /   /   /   /
> Resting the grass amid and upon—
> / /   /   /
> To be lean'd—and to lean on.[1]

This compact Whitman lyric, with its four heavy beats per line, is a riddle poem of precisely the type that Dolores Dyer Lucas finds recurring in Emily Dickinson's works. Dickinson's terse stanzas and meters are comparable too. In the following untitled riddle poem by Dickinson that I use for comparison, most lines have three stresses (the optional fourth stress appearing only in lines 1 and 7). The first two of this poem's stanzas will make the similarity clear enough:

One Síster have Í in óur hóuse,

And óne, a hédge awáy.

There's ónly óne recórded,

But bóth belóng to me.

Óne came the róad that Í came—

And wóre my lást year's gówn—

The óther, as a bírd her nést,

Búilded our héarts amóng.   (1: 17; poem no. 14)

The answer is sister-in-law (Lucas 28). The comparative presentation becomes livelier if you teach some Dickinson riddle poems first and then
introduce the Whitman axe riddle, possibly without identifying its author.
Bringing in a few Anglo-Saxon riddle poems generates further discussion of
meters and mentalities. Whitman liked to speak of "the riddle and the
untying of the riddle" ("Song of Myself," sec. 17); I like to teach the "Song
of the Broad-Axe" as the progressive untying of an initial riddle. Part of
Whitman's persona is surely that of a riddler: in "Whoever You Are Holding
Me Now in Hand" (a *Calamus* poem) he assures us that "these leaves . . .
will elude you at first and still more afterward . . ." (28–29).

Each aspect of prosodic study, then, will simultaneously disclose a facet
of Whitman's persona or self and a relation to other poetic personae embodied
in comparable forms of rhythmical music. Take as another example Whitman's use of the spondee. In section 33 of "Song of Myself" he is afoot with
his vision

Where the chéese-clóth hangs in the kitchen, and ándírons straddle

the héarth-sláb, and cóbwébs fall in festoons from the rafters . . .

—and a litany of spondees takes over the stanza:

Where the péar-sháped balloon is floating aloft . . .

Where the lífe-cár is drawn on the slípnóose . . .

Where the shé-whále swims with her calves . . .

Where the stéamshíp trails híndwáys its lóng pénnant of smoke,

Where the ground-shark's fin cuts like a black chip out of the water,

Where the half-burned brig is riding on unknown currents,

Where shells grow to her slimy deck. . . .   (740–46)

Harvey Gross (159–61) notes the prominence of spondees in Ezra Pound's rhythms in the *Cantos*. I read "A Pact" (which Pound addresses to Whitman) as a display of spondees and an acknowledgment of metrical indebtedness:

I come to you as a grown child

Who has had a pig-headed father; . . .

It was you that broke the new wood, . . .

We have one sap and one root—. . . .   (3–4, 6, 8)

Before Whitman was afoot with his metrical innovations, no one seems to have noticed how the spondee pervades our American conversation or how musical its effects can be. A poetic voice that delights in spondees is one that favors robust, natural talk, forthrightness, and a bit of swagger. Whitman's rhythms reveal his poetic personality, and they disclose unexpected kinships with other personae in the tradition he helped to found.

Two or three times I've offered an undergraduate course in Blake and Whitman: here too, musical study plays a large role. Consider the correlation between expansive vision and expanded poetic line in "Song of Myself" and *The Four Zoas*. First Whitman (sec. 31):

In vain the plutonic rocks send their old heat against my

approach,

In vain the mastodon retreats beneath its own powdered bones,

In vain objects stand leagues off and assume manifold shapes. . . .

Next Blake (110.6–8):

So Man looks out in tree & herb & fish & bird & beast

Collecting up the scattered portions of his immortal body

Into the Elemental forms of every thing that grows. . . .

Whitman's self or Blake's Albion is gathering up the dispersed, the orphically dismembered Cosmic Body, whose reconstitution has required a musical awakening. Each Whitman or Blake line tends to have at least six or seven beats, sometimes eight or nine; pentameter will not do for these huge orchestras (see Bidney 39).

In teaching the scansion of Whitman's verse, I use the traditional accent marking as shown above. (I don't distinguish between accent and stress according to the Andrei Biely system, which Nabokov has made familiar to readers of English, because this system is useful only with poets who use regular meters.) Ivan Marki thinks that Bradley's 1939 essay on Whitman's meter is still the best, but when I tried scanning some stanzas using Bradley's theory of the floating or hovering accent, colleagues and students quite rightly told me that the supposed hoverings were impossible to locate or describe with any precision. So experience suggests that the "hovering" theory will not work. Whitman's frequent use of spondees may help explain much of that spreading out of the stress over more than one syllable that Bradley heard.

When the famous catalog problem comes up, I suggest that complaints about Whitman's long-drawn-out lists usually refer to the less musical listings. When rhythms get flat, interest flags: "The coon-seekers go now through the regions of the Red river, or through those drained by the Tennessee, or through those of the Arkansas" ("Song of Myself," sec. 15). But enumerations can be lovely when their rhythms are at once powerful and varied, vigorous and supple, as in this list of adornments for the burial house of Lincoln:

$$\overset{/}{\text{Pic}}\text{tures }\overset{x}{\text{of}}\overset{x}{}\text{ grow}\overset{/}{\text{ing}}\overset{x}{}\text{ spring }\overset{/}{\text{and}}\overset{x}{}\text{ farms }\overset{/}{\text{and}}\overset{x}{}\text{ homes,}\overset{/}{}$$

$$\overset{x}{\text{With}}\text{ the }\overset{x}{}\overset{/}{\text{Fourth}}\text{-month }\overset{/}{\text{eve}}\text{ at }\overset{/}{\text{sun}}\overset{x}{\text{down,}}\overset{/}{}\text{ and the }\overset{\|x}{\text{gray}}\overset{x}{}\text{ smoke }\overset{/}{\text{lu}}\overset{/}{}\overset{/}{\text{cid}}\overset{x}{}$$

$$\overset{x}{\text{and}}\overset{/}{\text{ bright,}}$$

$$\overset{x}{\text{With}}\overset{/}{\text{ floods}}\overset{x}{\text{ of}}\overset{x}{}\overset{/}{\text{ the}}\overset{x}{}\overset{/}{\text{ yel}}\text{low }\overset{x}{\text{gold}}\overset{x}{}\overset{/}{\text{ of}}\text{ the }\overset{x}{\text{gor}}\overset{/}{\text{geous,}}\overset{xx}{\text{ in}}\text{dolent, }\overset{/}{\text{sink}}\overset{x}{\text{ing}}$$

$$\overset{/}{\text{sun,}}\overset{/}{\text{ burn}}\overset{x}{\text{ing,}}\overset{x}{}\overset{/}{\text{ ex}}\text{pand}\overset{x}{\text{ing}}\overset{/}{\text{ the}}\text{ air. . . .}$$

("When Lilacs Last in the Dooryard Bloom'd," sec. 11)

The flowing iambic pentameter of the first line has an initial trochee to bring it alive. The second has spondaic ("Fourth-month"; "sundown"; "gray smoke") interspersed with anapestic rhythms ("With the Fourth-"; "and the gray"; "-cid and bright") plus an elegant symmetric structure created by the caesura. The third is a gorgeous mix of fluent anapests and iambs.

No one will complain about listings like these. Catalogs are inevitable in an ecstatic poet who believes that we are here to sing praises; Thomas Traherne, like Whitman, shows how successful enumerations can be when the poet sings a new song:

/   / x /
Limbs rarely poised
     x   /   x   / x
  And made for Heaven:
/ x x /
Arteries filled
       x   x / x   / x
    With celestial Spirits:
/   x x   /   / x
Veins, wherein Blood floweth,
      x / x   /   x /
    Refreshing all my flesh,
       x   / x
      Like Rivers.

("Thanksgivings for the Body" 48–54)

Whitman and Traherne illuminate each other's musical achievements by together showing students that catalogs constitute a subgenre of the poetry of ecstatic praise: when metrically diversified, lists expand on the principle of plenitude, begetting a manifold world.

x /   / x / x   / ||/ x   x /   x   x
I sound my barbaric yawp over the roofs of the
  /
world   ("Song of Myself," sec. 52)

—rarely has a yawp been less barbaric. A hexameter, the line is related to Homer's and Vergil's traditions; even the caesura is rightly placed. Perhaps no single speech unit in Whitman's writing shows us so clearly the need to hear the music while we take in the meaning: here the meter conveys the poet's ironic wink at the civilization he claims to have fled.

Anthony Burgess notes that Whitman's basic line is "often hexametric": the link with the classical tradition points to a larger connection, in Whitman as in the classics, between poetry and oratory as expressions of an ideal of majesty or grandness (Bradley and Blodgett 972). Whitman also loved the poetry of Ossian (in Macpherson's alleged translations) and compared his rhythmic style with that of the Bible (Waskow 53–55); here too we see the link between written poetry and prophetic or bardlike or oratorical declamation. (Allen in 1933 showed biblical analogues for Whitman's prosody ["Biblical Analogies"].) Christopher Smart, another admirer and adapter of biblical style, said that loud public prayer was "good for weak lungs and for a vitiated throat" (*Jubilate Agno*, frag. B1, line 225); this wonderful phrase aptly describes Whitman's verse and Smart's as well. When I teach Whitman, I invariably distribute copies of passages from Smart, Macpherson, and the Bible to help situate the American bard in a venerable, high-energy tradition of long-lined, free-rhythmed, large-lunged verse.

Talk of hexameters easily leads us to dactyls—in

```
 /  x   x  /  x /   x   x  /  x
"Out of the Cradle Endlessly Rocking,"
```

Whitman's luxuriant musical triumph, the title sets up and repeats the effective rhythm pattern unique to this poem: a dactyl followed by a trochee. It is the poem's musical leitmotif—a word peculiarly appropriate to this Wagner-like love-death aria. In the last dozen lines the dactyl-trochee motif builds to a swelling climax:

```
 /  x x /   x
steadily up to
 /  x x   / x
softly all over
 /  x  x    /  x
demon and brother
 /  x    x  / x
thousand responsive
 /  x    x/  x
strong and delicious
 /  x   x  /  x
rocking the cradle
 /    x   x  /   x
swathed in sweet garments
```

By a curious coincidence, a similar pattern of alternating threes and twos pervades the erotic orchestral climax of *Tristan und Isolde*. The last time I taught "Out of the Cradle," I simply sang the first couple of lines to a tune of my own composition. Next time I intend in addition to play a recorded selection from Wagner's opera.

Whitman's well-known love for opera (see Faner, *Walt Whitman*) is expressed in some of his most evocative musical writing: metrical study of this material dramatizes for the student opera's central importance for the poet himself. Such an examination also helps call attention to a wider tradition of music lovers among America's poets. The attractive and protean mixture of double- and triple-foot structures in the description of the orchestra's effects is typical of Whitman:

```
x  /  x      x  /  x  /   /           x  x   /      x
It sails me . . . . I dab with bare feet . . . . they are licked by
  x /  x x    /
the indolent waves,
/ x   x   /       /  x / x  x    / x    /
I am exposed . . . . cut by bitter and poisoned hail,
 /    x x  / x    /   x      x  /  /
Steeped amid honeyed morphine . . . . my windpipe
    x    x   x /  x  /
squeezed in the fakes of death. . . .
```

("Song of Myself," sec. 26; Whitman's ellipses)

Compare the double-triple mixture (dactyls or anapests interspersed with trochees or iambs) from Edgar Lee Masters's unjustly neglected and profound lyric "Beethoven's Ninth Symphony and the King Cobra":

/ x x / x / x /
So by magnetic waves of fire

x / x x / x x / x x
Does Beethoven enter the cage of the

/ x
cobra,

x / x / x x | |x x / x
And start to torture it with colossal

/ x x
mystery,

x x / x / x /
Which the cobra cannot strike.   (sec. 4)

(Sidney Lanier's *Symphony* fits into this tradition too; see C. S. Brown 52, 128–36.) For Whitman, as for Schopenhauer, music is metaphysics, the expression and mirror of cosmic power.

Whitman has sometimes been patronized for his attempts at linguistic cosmopolitanism—his cameradoes and élèves and révolutionnaires—but the rhythmic experiments he carried out, in particular his long poetic line, which has become the most influential musical legacy of nineteenth-century poetry to our age, have engendered precisely that international poetic sharing he had hoped for. He inspires Horace Traubel, D. H. Lawrence, Theodore Roethke, Allen Ginsberg, but beyond that, without Whitman it is nearly impossible to imagine the startling new rhythmic effects we hear in, say, the *Cinq grandes odes* of Paul Claudel. Whitman's self is unbounded, and nowhere is this clearer than in his sea music:

Sail forth—steer for the deep waters only,
Reckless O soul, exploring, I with thee, and thou with me,
For we are bound where mariner has not yet dared to go,
And we will risk the ship, ourselves and all.
                    ("Passage to India," sec. 9)

Compare Claudel:

Ah, je n'en ai pas assez! Je regarde la mer! Tout cela me remplit
    qui a fin.
Mais ici et où que je tourne le visage et de cet autre côté
Il y en a plus et encore et là aussi et toujours et de même et
    davantage! Toujours, cher coeur!
Pas à craindre que mes yeux l'épuisent! Ah, j'en ai assez de vos
    eaux buvables.   ("Deuxième ode" 37–40)

Ah, I don't have enough of it! I look at the sea! I'm tired of things
that have limits.
But here and everywhere I turn and on that other side too
There's more of it and still more and there also and always and the
same and more! Always, dear heart!
No fear that my eyes will exhaust it! Oh, I've had enough of your
drinkable waters.   (my trans.)

In every poetry course I teach, I read at least a couple of lyrics to the
students in some language other than English. Whitman's universalism encourages this "one world" approach.

Students are interested to learn that Whitman's musical explorations relate
to some of the most important poetic developments now under way in both
the United States and Russia (Latin America, too, as we learn from Doris
Sommer's essay in this volume). American poets like David Antin and Jerome
Rothenberg build on oral tradition in ways Whitman would have found
intriguing. And the declamatory recitations of Soviet poets Yevgeny Yev-
tushenko and Andrey Voznesensky stem from the tradition of futurism established by Vladimir Mayakovsky and Velimir Khlebnikov, both clearly
akin to Whitman. The title of Mayakovsky's poem "To His Beloved Self the
Author Dedicates These Lines" has a familiar ring, but of the two futurist
pioneers Khlebnikov is the truer Whitmanist. Charlotte Douglas has called
his "first major poem"—"O Garden of Animals!" ("Zverínets")—a "homage
to Walt Whitman"; she is surely correct in claiming that "Whitman's long,
variable line was a model for the young Khlebnikov" (Khlebnikov 14, 17).
In the lyric's closing lines I hear echoes of "The Sleepers" and even more
of section 32 of "Song of Myself" ("I think I could turn and live awhile with
the animals . . . They bring me tokens of myself"):

Where the beasts have learned to sleep while we gawk.
Where the bat hangs sleeping, and its capsized body resembles a
Russian's heart.
Where a sable displays two tiny ears, like a pair of nights in
springtime.
Where I search for new rhythms, whose beats are animals and men.
Where the animals in their cages glow, as meaning glows in language.
O Garden of Animals!

We can see Khlebnikov as Whitman encouraged us to see himself in the
last poem in *Children of Adam*—"As Adam early in the morning, / Walking
forth from the bower refresh'd with sleep," ready to name in new rhythms
every aspect of the unbounded Self.

A nondogmatic approach is best in teaching metrics. I'm aware that not
all the scansions I've proposed above will be favored by everyone—there's

plenty of room for discussion and debate. Refinements may be added: it's often useful to insert a vertical line to separate two rhythm units. A leftward-leaning slash can be used to indicate a secondary accent. When a developing rhythm pattern within a line seems to call for stress on a syllable not ordinarily accented in conversational English, the resulting tension can be signaled by putting an accent mark in parentheses. I usually ask students to devote at least one page of a ten-page Whitman paper to analysis of the poet's music. (Students who have trouble with scansion may be mistaking pitch for accent: discussion helps clear up this problem.) Sometimes the "music page" proves the best part of the student's essay.

NOTE

[1]Quotations of Whitman's poems are from the *Norton Critical Edition*, edited by Bradley and Blodgett, except for those from "Song of Myself," which are from *The First (1855) Edition*, edited by Cowley.

Leaves of Grass as a Sexual Manifesto: A Reader-Response Approach

William H. Shurr

Literary criticism is rightly concerned with the question of where the author places himself or herself in the text. How does the author choose to relate to the reader, with the text as surrogate? Theoretically it is impossible to read a text without coming to some implicit decision about this relationship. With Whitman, the college student will find no doubt.

Whitman clarifies his intended relationship to us at many points in his poetry, telling exactly how we should read him. His approach is consciously and blatantly seductive. He presents his book as his physical person and his purpose as a sexual relationship with the reader. As students notice this, they become personally involved with the poet. For many the relationship is disquieting, as Whitman predicted it would be.

One of the *Calamus* poems of 1860 is addressed to "Whoever you are holding me now in hand" (*LG* 115). The nonresisting reader experiences a moment of shock in realizing that he or she is now holding this book as if it were a human being held in the lap. The poem immediately charges any reader who cannot yield physically to Whitman the seductive writer to "let go your hand from my shoulders" (*LG* 116). The reader who does give in to Whitman's solicitation is invited to accept the reward of kissing the book with an erotic kiss, not some reverential kiss such as one might give to the Bible. It is "the comrade's long-dwelling kiss or the new husband's kiss." The sympathetic reader is then charged, now that the book has been accepted as a real person and an erotic partner, with "thrusting me beneath your clothing, / Where I may feel the throbs of your heart . . ." (*LG* 116).

Whitman perfected the technique of reader seduction long before Roland Barthes wrote the theoretical text on it (*Pleasure*). Whitman did not invent erotic literature, but he did invent the text that is itself erotic and self-consciously seductive. The last line of the last *Calamus* poem reads "Be it as if I were with you. (Be not too certain but I am now with you)"—reminding the reader who has gone this far that he has agreed to take the book along as a permanent erotic partner.

This seduction of the reader is no small or partial aspect of the poems, no momentary mood. It appears throughout his work. The famous "Crossing Brooklyn Ferry" is another important poem in Whitman's campaign to seduce his reader. Students who have been given these hints on reading Whitman are usually eager to read through the poem carefully to identify the seductive passages. In this poem, Whitman once more presents his book as a physical body before the reader: "Closer yet I approach you," he announces as the poem begins to mount to its climax, "Who knows but I am enjoying this? / Who knows, for all the distance, but I am as good as looking at you now, for all you cannot see me?" Whitman as author lurks in the shadows of his text, yearning for the moment of sexual contact. This authorial presence, at once physical and invisible, urges upon the reader a relationship that is undeniably sexual union: he insists at the climax of "Crossing Brooklyn Ferry" that it is a relation "which fuses me into you now, and pours my meaning into you" (LG 163–64).

Once they understand the technique of reader seduction, students will see that it served Whitman well in later collections, such as Drum-Taps, where Whitman imagines himself and his reader as individuated drops from the great ocean of life, momentarily separated but destined again to merge into indissoluble unity. These poems are written, he tells the reader, "for your dear sake my love" (LG 107). The living writer presents himself disguised as the book the future reader is holding: "(As I glance upward out of this page studying you, dear friend, whoever you are)" (LG 322).

Whitman is explicitly aware that many regard the sexual activity he proposes to the reader as evil: depending on the context it is either unconventional, immoral, or illegal. The most dangerous of all of his poems begins "As I lay with my head in your lap camerado." In this seductive situation he warns:

> The confession I made I resume, what I said to you and the open air
>   I resume,
> . . . .
> I know my words are weapons full of danger, full of death,
> For I confront peace, security, and all the settled laws, to unsettle
>   them,
> . . . .
> And the threat of what is call'd hell is little or nothing to me,
> And the lure of what is call'd heaven is little or nothing to
>   me. . . .   (LG 322)

Whitman is a disturbing and demanding presence in his literature. He confronts the student with all the dangers of illicit sexual encounter and all the potential ecstasy as well. Students who grasp what kind of sexual activity Whitman is proposing may debate whether it is necessarily homosexual. Constant reference to the texts is the only method of finding evidence here. Following reader-relationship clues through whatever group of texts is chosen will always involve the students more personally in studying Whitman.

Whitman's sexual relationship with his reader received special emphasis in the middle editions of Leaves of Grass. Advanced students might be interested in studying one of the six editions (selected almost at random) to track the specific addresses to the reader (Whitman's seductive suggestions vary interestingly from edition to edition). The following poignant six lines were placed in a dramatic position, at the end of both the 1860 and 1867 editions:

Now lift me close to your face while I whisper,
What you are holding is in reality no book, nor part of a book;
It is a man, flush'd and full-blooded—It is I— *So Long!*
—We must separate awhile—Here! take from my lips this kiss;
Whoever you are, I give it especially to you;
So long!—And I hope we shall meet again.   (*LG* 604)

This is reluctant parting of lovers, at the conclusion of what must surely be America's most personal book.

The sentiment of this poem must have met with Whitman's approval, with his sense of how the collection should end, since he incorporated a powerful version of the same seduction at the very end of all later editions of *Leaves of Grass*, in the poem called "So Long!" Here the poet finally drops his book disguise:

Camerado, this is no book,
Who touches this touches a man,
(Is it night? are we here together alone?)
It is I you hold and who holds you,
I spring from the pages into your arms—   (*LG* 505)

In this poem Whitman seems to depend on the reader to guide him through the complete sexual act. The author now becomes the passive partner and the reader is expected to take the active part in their lovemaking. He continues:

O how your fingers drowse me,
Your breath falls around me like dew, your pulse lulls the tympans
    of my ears,
I feel immerged from head to foot,
Delicious, enough.

Then, as a passive, manipulated lover who rises toward climax and satiation, he continues:

Enough O deed impromptu and secret,
Enough O gliding present—enough O summ'd-up past.

The parting must then finally come; but it is the parting, Whitman insists, of lovers who have shared a sexual experience:

Dear friend whoever you are take this kiss,
I give it especially to you, do not forget me. . . .   (*LG* 505–06)

Quite likely, no college student has had to cope with this kind of authorial demand before, with so intense an involvement with a writer. Some readers have even seen the famous catalogs as seductive, as if Whitman were casting the widest net possible to catch every reader in one or other of his categories. He will let no one escape his seductive lure.

Whitman's seduction of the reader is no minor adjunct to his poetic work. It is thoroughly appropriate and even essential in view of his major theme. In the first poem of the earliest edition of *Leaves of Grass*, he solicited the attention of the serious reader, whom he addressed as the one who is "so proud to get at the meaning of poems." In fact, he proclaimed that he would reveal to this careful reader something of the greatest value: "Stop this day and night with me and you shall possess the origin of all poems." Whitman went on to specify what he thought this origin might be: "Urge and urge and urge, / Always the procreant urge of the world." Whitman grew clearer and bolder the next year. In his second edition of *Leaves of Grass*, he repeated himself: "Always the procreant urge of the world" and then added the phrase "always sex" (*LG* 30–31).

The proclamation—that the sexual urge is the origin of poetry—stands like a great arch at the beginning of *Leaves of Grass*, orienting us toward a proper understanding of its content. This is the gateway through which can be seen the main thematic materials of the whole collection, its profound and pervasive sexuality. Students can explore the possibilities latent in this suggestion that the sexual drive is the same as the drive to create artistic works. The picture is complicated by Freudian suggestions concerning the narcissistic temperament that seem relevant to Whitman's first great artistic and ecstatic experience in section 5 of "Song of Myself." This intense inaugural vision of the poet may be homosexual, heterosexual, or a narcissistic fantasy of sexual self-fulfillment. (Freud's thoughts, recorded mainly in his essay "On Narcissism," seem relevant to Whitman's personality.)

This proclamation of both the sexual origin of his poetry and its sexual subject matter stands unchanged through all the many printings of "Song of Myself." Students can easily enumerate the number and variety of sexual experiences Whitman goes on to describe, even in his first edition. Whitman, in fact, fills his first edition of *Leaves of Grass* with descriptions of many sexual experiences never before described in public writings.

The poem that would become "Song of Myself" begins with the famous scene of vaguely symbolized oral sex and rises to a first crisis that sounds like something similar to gang rape, when a group of frolicking young men suddenly become mean and dangerous as they turn all of their sexual play on one of their group. This is also the poem in which Whitman acts out a role as the female voyeur, watching the twenty-eight bathers and then imagining herself, unseen, swimming and playing intimately with them (sec. 11). Still later in the first edition of the poem, contact even with the earth is an extreme sexual experience: "Prodigal! you have given me love! . . . . therefore I to you give love! / O unspeakable passionate love!" (Cowley 45). Then some lines later: "Something I cannot see puts upward libidinous prongs, / Seas of bright juice suffuse heaven" (Cowley 50). Even the experience of listening to a soprano is intensely erotic. "She convulses me like the climax of my love-gripe" (Cowley 52).

The next poem in *Leaves of Grass*—one that would come to be called "The Sleepers"—describes not only the sexual manipulation of sleeping persons but solitary masturbation and an assignation with a lover on the beach as well.

The first-edition poem that would later be called "I Sing the Body Electric" and that would become the most important poem in the *Children of Adam* collection deliberately eroticizes the human body, featuring the sexually arousing details first of the male and then the female body. This is no merely aesthetic exercise; the description ends with "loveflesh swelling and deliciously aching, / Limitless limpid jets of love hot and enormous. . . . quivering jelly of love . . . white blow and delirious juice, / Bridegroom-night of love working surely and softly into the prostrate dawn . . ." (Cowley 119). In this poem Whitman imagines himself sharing the mother's breast with her infant, as he continues to explore a broad range of sexual experiences. Watching a parade of firemen he focuses on what he calls "the play of the masculine muscle through the cleansetting trowsers and waistbands" (Cowley 117).

Even his own sexual origins are described and celebrated in the poem that would become "There Was a Child Went Forth": he records his father, "he that had propelled the fatherstuff at night, and fathered him . . . and she that conceived him in her womb and birthed him . . ." (Cowley 138–39; Whitman's ellipses).

For Whitman the newly discovered area of sexual experience is both the cause of his new poetry and the subject that is described and celebrated in this first edition. He can be forgiven the enthusiastic reports of an explorer and discoverer.

Most of Whitman's critics and biographers have been extraordinarily shy about the revolutionary sexuality explored in his work. There is something overly sanitized and genteel in the academic handling of Whitman, which has left this central force of his writing untouched. Critics and biographers have preferred to write about Whitman's debts to opera or phrenology and his supposed illegitimate children; they have discussed Whitman and Emerson or other figures, his style, his politics, or his catalogs—thus missing the central point he labored a lifetime to express. Academic critics have bent Whitman's poetry away from his intent, have finally trivialized a great writer by refusing to read the main message of his manifesto. They do not begin to describe the powerful energies set up in his poetry.

Students can discover and appreciate one of Whitman's main accomplishments through close reading and discussion of his poetry. They can readily perceive striking and wonderful new images for experiences that had rarely been approached before, at least in literary America. The poem "From Pent-up Aching Rivers," for example, yields fresh images, new fantasies, and emotive words for experiences that had not yet been described. Students can discuss to what extent Whitman's work is a sexual manifesto paralleling the *Communist Manifesto* of Marx and Engels in the previous decade. Sexual experience is the armature on which Whitman wound the long strings of his words. The poet who sang the body electric would approve of the electrical figure.

This class presentation and discussion of Whitman, then, stresses three points: Whitman declared the origin of poetry to be the sexual drive; his subject matter is primarily the exploration and definition of a variety of sexual experiences; and finally, his method of relating to the reader throughout the canon of his literature is chiefly by sexual seduction, achieved by placing himself within the text as an erotic partner for the reader. His work comes to us as a manifesto (in an age of manifestos) of sexual description and exploration. Whitman can overwhelm the student with a richly complex but unified and forceful experience.

Teaching Whitman's Old-Age Poems

Donald Barlow Stauffer

Not every instructor has the opportunity or the inclination to teach much of the poetry that Whitman wrote after, say, "Passage to India." Yet these poems of Whitman's old age should not be dismissed too lightly: in addition to what they reveal about his life, they have an interesting relation to the structure and themes of *Leaves of Grass* as a whole. They can be read profitably in an undergraduate course in Whitman (or Whitman and Dickinson) and in a graduate course or seminar.

When students read the poems Whitman wrote in the last nineteen years of his life, they are struck by the contradictions they find. On the one hand he seems to be trying to preserve as much of his health and vigor as possible, projecting for his reading public the image of the exuberant and affirmative self he had carefully created over the course of his career. On the other hand he gives ample evidence of his physical deterioration and failing creative powers. When students think about how he reconciled this conflict, they note two solutions. One, on which Whitman came to rely heavily, was to view his life's work as a whole and to emphasize its autobiographical quality. The other was to ignore as much as he could the less pleasant aspects of aging; this he did quite deliberately in a number of poems that sustain the idealized views of old age he had presented in his earlier work.

In January 1888, for example, Whitman published in the New York *Herald* a highly romanticized and even sentimentalized poem about old age that he called "Halcyon Days":

Not from successful love alone,
Nor wealth, nor honor'd middle age, nor victories of politics or war;
But as life wanes, and all the turbulent passions calm,
As gorgeous, vapory, silent hues cover the evening sky,
As softness, fulness, rest, suffuse the frame, like fresher, balmier air,
As the days take on a mellower light, and the apple at last hangs
    really finish'd and indolent-ripe on the tree,
Then for the teeming quietest, happiest days of all!
The brooding and blissful halcyon days! (*LG* 513)

It would seem, in the light of the strokes and other illnesses Whitman suffered during the fifteen years preceding this poem's composition, that his picture of a serene and untroubled old age, facing the sunset years with equanimity, is not based upon his own experience but is merely a literary or artistic conception, written in the affirmative tone of his early poems. This posture is possibly not so much deception or self-deception as it is a way of continuing and sustaining the themes and attitudes of his life's work. As he often said, he was determined to keep as much as possible of his own sickness and pain out of his poems; at the same time, however, he wanted

to be honest and to put as much of his own personal experiences into them
as he could. These contradictory aims account for the conflicting attitudes
toward his own aging that we find in his later poems. And in the context of
other poems they have read, students can see these old-age poems as part
of Whitman's philosophy of contraries: he could assert that his loss of energy,
weakening mental powers, and even his fears of senility were not to be
resisted but were to be viewed as part of the life cycle and as part of a
greater spiritual totality.

Only two days after the three strokes that came close to killing him in
June 1888, Whitman had a remarkable conversation with Horace Traubel,
his Boswellian companion and biographer, in which he examined his present
condition in the context of his life, his beliefs, and what he had recently
described in "A Backward Glance o'er Travel'd Roads" as his program to
"exploit [my own] Personality, identified with place and date, in a far more
candid and comprehensive sense than any hitherto poem or book" (LG 563):

> I often ask myself, is this expression of the life of an old man consonant
> with the fresher, earlier, delving, faiths, hopes, stated in the original
> Leaves? I have my doubts—minor doubts—but somehow I decide the
> case finally on my own side. It belongs to the scheme of the book. As
> long as I live the Leaves must go on. Am I, as some think, losing
> grip?—taking in my horse? No—no—no: I am sure that could not be.
> I still wish to be, am the radical of my stronger days—to be the same
> uncompromising oracle of democracy—to maintain undimmed the light
> of my deepest faith. I am sure I have not gone back on that—sure,
> sure. The Sands have to be taken as the utterances of an old man—a
> very old man. I desire that they may be interpreted as confirmations,
> not denials, of the work that has preceded . . . I am not to be known
> as a piece of something but as a totality.   (Traubel 1: 271–72)

"The Sands" he refers to is the Sands at Seventy collection, first published
in 1888 in the November Boughs volume. Whitman had not come by this
title easily; he had considered such possibilities as "Halcyon Days," "Sands
on the Shores," and "Carols Closing Sixty-Nine" (LG 507n). These late poems
are clearly not the work of a poet in fullest command of his powers, but we
find occasional flashes that recall his younger self. The dominant themes of
the collection are old age and death, but since Whitman's interest in what
was happening in the world was still strong he touched upon many other
subjects as well. There are occasional poems on Election Day 1884, the
death of General Grant, the burial of a famous Iroquois chief, the Washington
Monument, the death of an operatic tenor, and Whittier's eightieth birthday.
The poems are all relatively short, perhaps indicating that he was no longer
able to sustain the energy that went into producing the long poems of his

prime (although he remarked in "A Backward Glance" that he had learned from Poe about the virtues of the short poem).

Talking to Traubel about the subject matter of these poems, Whitman said, "Of my personal ailments, of sickness as an element, I never spoke a word until the first of the poems I call Sands at Seventy were written, and then some expression of invalidism seemed to be called for" (2: 234). He realized that if he were to be true to his own stated goal of reflecting the life of an old man in his poems he had to include references to his sickness and invalidism, since they had become so much a part of his life. Yet he was concerned that these poems of old age might strike too querulous a note, as he said in "As I Sit Writing Here":

> As I sit writing here, sick and grown old,
> Not my least burden is that dulness of the years, querilities,
> Ungracious glooms, aches, lethargy, constipation, whimpering *ennui*
> May filter in my daily songs.   (*LG* 509–10)

I like to assign this poem, which Whitman placed in the same collection as the extremely positive "Halcyon Days," in order to show students that old age did not make him less likely to contradict himself. They can see that the latter poem is the result of very carefully filtering *out* what old age actually was becoming for him and treating it in more transcendent terms as an idealized part of an idealized life cycle. They may also realize that some of the same painful self-awareness that formerly centered on sexual questions in the *Calamus* poems and elsewhere was in later life directed toward the experience of growing old. This questioning mood is contained in "Queries to My Seventieth Year," published about a month before Whitman's seventieth birthday:

> Approaching, nearing, curious,
> Thou dim, uncertain spectre—bringest thou life or death?
> Strength, weakness, blindness, more paralysis and heavier?
> Or placid skies and sun? Wilt stir the waters yet?
> Or haply cut me short for good? Or leave me here as now,
> Dull, parrot-like and old, with crack'd voice harping, screeching?
>   (*LG* 510)

In connection with this poem I like to look at "Prayer of Columbus," written many years earlier in 1874, in which Whitman indirectly refers to his own condition. It had become clear to him by that time that he would never achieve the national fame and recognition he had hoped for, and after his first stroke he necessarily became more aware of his illness, his oncoming old age, and his mortality. The passages in which he describes the aging

Columbus, the "batter'd, wreck'd old man" who ended his life despised and defeated, quite clearly refer to himself as well:

> My terminus near,
> The clouds already closing in upon me,
> The voyage balk'd, the course disputed, lost,
> I yield my ships to Thee,
>
> My hands, my limbs grow nerveless,
> My brain feels rack'd, bewilder'd,
> Let the old timbers part, I will not part,
> I will cling fast to Thee, O God, though the waves buffet me,
> Thee, Thee at least I know.   (*LG* 423)

Three poems in the *Sands at Seventy* collection are similarly indirect in their treatment of old age. In "The Dismantled Ship," he describes an "old, dismasted, gray and batter'd ship, disabled, done." "After free voyages to all the seas of earth," Whitman writes, the ship is "haul'd up at last and hawser'd tight, / Lies rusting, mouldering" (*LG* 534). "Twilight" (1887) shows that Whitman was thinking more and more about death—not death in an abstract philosophical way, but his own death, including the death of consciousness:

> The soft voluptuous opiate shades,
> The sun just gone, the eager light dispell'd—(I too will
>   soon be gone, dispell'd)
> A haze—nirwana—rest and night—oblivion.   (*LG* 532)

I like to call students' attention to the untypical word *oblivion*, which seems, as it did to many of Whitman's readers who objected to it, inconsistent with his own philosophy. But it was just the word he wanted, he told Traubel, "both as furnishing sense and rhythm to the idea I had in mind" (1: 141). Another interesting word is *nirwana*, which reinforces the idea of a Buddhist release from self or the Hindu reunion with Brahma through the suppression of individual existence.

This contradiction between his own feelings and the posture he wanted to maintain as a poet often gave Whitman trouble. In the fall of 1888, when the immobility resulting from a severe and almost fatal stroke forced him to sell his horse and carriage, he remarked to Traubel, "It marks a new epoch in my life: another stage on the down-hill road." Traubel replied, "I shouldn't think with your idea of death that you would speak of it as a *down* road." And Whitman answered, "Sure enough—the word was false: *up* road: up —up: another stage on the up-hill road: that certainly seems more like me and I want to be like myself" (2: 273).

Even less direct in its use of imagery suggestive of old age is "You Lingering Sparse Leaves of Me." In this poem Whitman compares himself to a tree in autumn, whose "leaves" are "tokens diminute and lorn—(not now the flush of May, or July clover-bloom—no grain of August now;)." Still the lingering sparse leaves are, he says, "my soul-dearest leaves confirming all the rest,/ The faithfulest—hardiest—last" (*LG* 532). Once again we hear a note of insistence—he protests too much in his claims that these last leaves are his best—but the word *confirming* is interesting, since it reflects his attitude, often stated, that the group of poems in *Sands at Seventy* adds up to a totality.

One poem that Whitman considered especially important was only later included in *Sands at Seventy*, but it was, he told Traubel, "an essential poem—it needed to be made" (2: 289). "Old Age's Lambent Peaks" characterizes old age as a time to look at the world and at life "in falling twilight." Old age casts its soft, flickering light (the word *lambent* seems carefully chosen) in a way that reveals new points of view and new knowledge:

> So much i' the atmosphere, the points of view, the situations
>   whence we scan,
> Bro't out by them alone—so much (perhaps the best) unreck'd
>   before;
> The lights indeed from them—old age's lambent peaks.   (*LG* 535)

The phrase "perhaps the best" again seems an effort to justify this stage of life, and it is stated in Whitman's characteristic affirmative tone. It contradicts much of what he said as a young man with his emphasis on manly vigor, but it is a direct continuation of the attitude in "Song of Myself" that whatever he is experiencing at the moment is for the best.

Whitman was aware, however, that his powers were failing, so much so that he considered ending his writing career with another, final "annex" to *Leaves of Grass*. This mood is clearly stated in a letter he wrote to William Sloane Kennedy in June 1890, shortly after his seventy-first birthday:

> Did I tell you my last piece (poem) was rejected by the *Century* (R. W. Gilder)—I have now been shut off by *all* the magazines here & the *Nineteenth Century* in England—& feel like closing house as poem writer—(you know a fellow doesn't make brooms or shoes if nobody will have 'em)—I shall put in order a last little 6 or 8 page annex (the second) of my *Leaves of Grass*—& that will probably be the finish—   (*Correspondence* 5: 54)

The "last little annex" became the thirty-one poems and the miscellaneous magazine pieces Whitman first collected in *Good-Bye My Fancy* (1891). He later gathered the poems into a "Second Annex" to the 1891–92 *Leaves of*

Grass. This is a mixed bag: occasional poems on such subjects as the Paris Exposition, the burial of General Sheridan, and the Johnstown flood; miscellaneous poems on various Whitman themes, the bulk of them on old age and death.

Two of the best poems in this section are "To the Sun-Set Breeze" and "Unseen Buds." In the first of these, the breeze is a messenger and comforter to the speaker, "old, alone, sick, weak-down, melted-worn with sweat" (*LG* 546). It brings him reminders of the sky, prairies, oceans, and forests: the entire world, the universe, and God. The poet moves very quickly from the particular to the universal, as he moves from his own physical and mental weariness to call up once again his cosmic vision of the universal One. This vision is a capsule version of his great early poems; he treats these subjects with his typical expansive sweep. In this unpretentious and even understated poem we find again the sure touch of the master, whose confidence and assurance about the truth of what he believes keep him from faltering or striking a false note in a poem that, as Ezra Pound once noted, contains much "deliberate artistry" (Bergman 60).

The other fine poem in the *Good-Bye My Fancy* collection is "Unseen Buds." Here Whitman uses a strange and unusual image: buds hidden under snow and ice with a latent potential to flower, mysteriously suggesting the idea of the universe as an eternal process of becoming:

> Billions of billions, and trillions of trillions of them
>   waiting,
> (On earth and in the sea—the universe—the stars there in
>   the heavens,)
> Urging slowly, surely forward, forming endless,
> And waiting ever more, forever more behind.   (*LG* 557)

In the context of these late-in-life poems, "Unseen Buds" assumes a special significance, as Whitman moves away from an individual confrontation with death and places it on a truly cosmic scale. He becomes merely one of the many trillions of germinal presences that eternally and infinitely expand, grow, and die to make room for their successors—a view of death he had frequently expressed in his younger years.

Students encouraged to give an attentive and sympathetic reading to the poems collected in *Good-Bye My Fancy* most likely will not dismiss all of them as the last scribblings of a weakened and failing poet. "Unseen Buds" and "To the Sun-Set Breeze" have intrinsic merit and recall the themes and artistry of Whitman when he was in full command of his powers. They may discover that other poems dealing more specifically with his aging, sickness, and confrontation with death reveal interesting qualities about the man himself: his intellectual lucidity, his honesty, and his unwillingness to soften his increasingly harsh reality or to deny the unavoidable.

Two other poems in *Good-Bye My Fancy* are of especial interest. One is "Supplement Hours," a poem about extreme old age—about the tranquility that comes after the striving and activity of a full life. The "supplement hours" are the bonus given at the end of life to be used for contemplation and enjoyment of life and nature. There is something much less facile about this poem than the earlier "Halcyon Days," which describes a state of mind and feeling the poet thought was somehow appropriate to old age but which does not ring true. This poem, with its Wordsworthian movement away from books to nature, seems to come from his genuine feelings as an old person rather than from cultural stereotypes about aging. Whitman apparently attached considerable importance to it, since many manuscript versions exist, as well as several different titles, such as "Notes as the wild Bee hums," "A September Supplement," and "Latter-Time Hours of a Half-paralytic" (*LG* 578–79n).

The last poem Whitman ever wrote he began in November 1891 and handed to Traubel ten days before his death in March 1892. "A Thought of Columbus" is a tribute to the great discoverer with some ideas harking back to "Passage to India" and "A Prayer for Columbus." Here Columbus is viewed not as the "batter'd wreck'd old man" suffering from defeat and despair but as a much more abstract figure—the agent of a divine plan bringing about the fulfillment of an age-long process of completion. He is "A phantom of the moment, mystic, stalking, sudden," which gives rise to the development of the "Western World," the "long-deferr'd éclaircissement of human life and hopes" (*LG* 582). This is a vision Whitman still sees in his dying days as the central fact of the universe: the connection between the growth of democracy in the Western Hemisphere and the unfolding of our cosmic destiny.

Like many of his other later poems, "A Thought of Columbus" cannot be ignored or dismissed as the product of feebleness or senility. It demonstrates that Whitman was still afoot with his vision, to which he remained faithful to the end. The structure and the confident tone of serenity and assurance permeating the poem make it in these respects similar to many works he wrote twenty years earlier. Clearly, he continued to live a rich intellectual and spiritual life even in these later years of paralysis, loneliness, and neglect, when his physical world was shrunken almost entirely to the four walls of his Mickle Street "den." The exuberance, the confidence, the assurance, and the strong rhythms may still be heard in this eloquent apostrophe to the discoverer of America and moving farewell from its solitary singer.

The Poetic Uses of Whitman's Prose

Susan Day Dean

Whitman's prose is indispensable to the study of his verse for many reasons. In this essay I argue that because the prose is more rooted and less fluid than the poetry, it offers a medium in which students may engage and wrestle with the ways Whitman uses language to construct and carry meanings.

I refer to seven prose works, well-known and easily available:

> 1855: preface to the 1855 edition of *Leaves of Grass*
> 1856: preface to the 1856 edition of *Leaves of Grass*
> 1871: *Democratic Vistas*
> 1872: preface to "As a Strong Bird on Pinions Free"
> 1876: preface to *Leaves of Grass* and "Two Rivulets"
> 1882: *Specimen Days*
> 1888: "A Backward Glance o'er Travel'd Roads," preface to *November Boughs*; appended as afterword to 1890–91 *Leaves of Grass*

For convenience I use the word *prefaces* to speak of all five essays that Whitman published in various editions of *Leaves*, even though "A Backward Glance" was attached as an afterword, not a foreword. For these five prefaces I use the 1973 *Norton Critical Edition* (ed. Bradley and Blodgett), the only one-volume edition that reproduces the scholarly text and line numbers of the many-volumed New York University Press edition. For *Democratic Vistas* and *Specimen Days*, I use the New York University Press edition, *Prose Works 1892*. All are cited by date of publication.

I use these seven texts to suggest ways of approaching certain features in Whitman's writing that may be estranging to our students—unlikely, as vehicles, to move those younger versions of ourselves. I sketch out a few techniques of locating and using "estrangement" and explain what seems to me their direction and value.

The best way for students to know the twists of Whitman's language is to work with it closely, and there are several useful exercises that bring about this contact. One is to read difficult passages aloud—for instance, the three long and sustained ones in the 1855 preface, on Liberty (lines 375–472), on Truth (461–78), and on Prudence (479–580). Each of these is an assertion that depends for its meaning on a final double negative that is easy to miss on a casual first reading. Each assertion has been built on certain assumptions drawn from the Western liberal tradition that Whitman (along with many readers who share that tradition with him) takes for granted as applying to human psychology universally. Once the double negatives are located, students can question their underlying assumptions as though they were unfamiliar propositions.

Another exercise, old-fashioned but helpful, is sentence diagramming.

When Whitman's characteristically long sentences are put into simple diagram form, with grammatically parallel entities (phrases or clauses, subjects or verbs or objects) lined up vertically, students can visualize what usually comes through only to the inner ear: Whitman's habit of setting element in counterpoise with element, so that his apparent "mélange" of words has a pattern of balance within its motion.

Exercises like these give students a sense for the way Whitman's formulations carry his meanings. Once they have this sense they will be in a position to scrutinize places where the meaning is not clear. They should begin with Whitman's pronouns, halting and questioning any pronoun whose referent is unspecified. In line 440 of the 1855 preface, for instance, who or what is "they"? the varieties of tongues, subjects, and styles? the poets of the kosmos? the large proprietor and legal owner? Some of these answers make more sense than others, and discussion of them is useful. In line 134n of the 1876 preface, what is "they"? the *Leaves*? morals? Here, both possibilities fit, and Whitman's imprecision is likely to be intentionally aggregative. And in "A Backward Glance," line 199, what is referred to in "them"? our lands? the concrete realities and theories of the universe? both? Again, the available interpretations do not cancel each other out or even conflict; one makes the other true, and they are congruent with one another inside the pronoun that "fetches" them. By questioning Whitman's referents and getting the context to deliver all available answers, we get a firsthand sense of Whitman's tendency to preserve common denominators and suspend unnecessary distinctions. We are alerted to look for plurality of reference in the pronouns of poems such as "Crossing Brooklyn Ferry" and "As I Ebb'd" and to see in them also this characteristic and meaningful inclusiveness and nonspecification.

This questioning attitude should be brought to the ideas asserted in Whitman's prose, especially when they appear and reappear in the same work. The 1855 preface, for example, features a list of the free-spirited qualities of the common people of America and gives as the last item on its list "the President's taking off his hat to them not they to him" (41), a reference to a fine old Quaker gesture of insubordination that Whitman would have known from his ancestors. Whitman's wording suggests that this Quakerly attitude can be attributed to the generality of American people in 1855—a suggestion that might make us envious in our twentieth-century, when such republicanism has been in short supply. But later in the same preface, in a passage of directions on what to "do" (what to trust in, rather than putting trust in superficial supports), we find Whitman commanding his American reader: "take off your hat to nothing known or unknown or to any man or number of men" (204–05). In the first instance Whitman refers to the virtue as if it is already achieved; in the second, as though it is not yet and ought to be. A small contradiction like this can force students to think themselves into Whitman's position as writer: if the second usage is closer to actual needs in 1855, why does Whitman put forth the "ideal" claim first and the more modest, reasonable, persuasive one later? Coming up with possible motives requires empathy with the writer and respect for his intelligence, and so the student who makes an effort to respond to this challenge has already moved closer to Whitman. After such a contradiction has been worked through once, it can be recognized as a rhetorical device in other texts. For instance, in the 1888 "Backward Glance," lines 235–77, we meet again the puzzle of the covered versus uncovered head in two apparently conflicting claims: first, that the young Whitman encountered the great poems of the past with "uncovered head"; and second, that he read them outdoors where they and he were equally subordinated before the great presence of nonhuman nature. Once more we must look for an explanation beneath the apparent inconsistency. (Best explanation: "His head must have been uncovered not to anyone's great poems but to the open air.") Each occasion for questioning takes us to a deeper understanding of Whitman's textual intentions.

In general I recommend a policy of giving full weight to the measured claims of the later essays and a different policy of taking figuratively and rhetorically the sweeping terms of the early essays. Lines 120–61 of the 1855 preface ("Of all mankind the great poet is . . ." through the whole of "The presence of the greatest poet . . ." to the end of the paragraph) provide a good working example. There the "great poet" is ascribed such superlative and redemptive powers that readers who have not built up a prior sympathy for Whitman's enterprise may well react with instinctive disapproval and distaste for his claims, thinking them proof of the writer's personal conceit or of his naïveté about how society works, or both. I ask students to specify what verbal changes would be necessary to make the claims in the passage acceptable to them. At first the suggestions are comic: "Just add *it is not true that* throughout"; or simply, "Add *not* to all his statements about that 'great poet.' " But after such disbelief and resistance are voiced, students can take a closer look at the various actions on Whitman's list of claims. Each action can be perceived as the result of an adjustment in vision, such as is released in us in certain moods by our imaginations and in society when its artists and prophets are inspired to speak and we to listen. The class is then in a position to add a more consciously cooperative addition to the text: perhaps, "The *kind of* great poet *I want to be* does such and such" or "a great poet *such as I envision* does this and not that."

I find that this kind of intrusive reading is justified when it brings about an increase in thinking *with* Whitman and in sympathy for his rhetorical position. But even should reactions in class discussion stay at the first level of skepticism and amusement, I believe it is valuable for readers to engage with Whitman's claims and to articulate the points of their skepticism, rather than to censor their reactions and to close the book silently on problematic aspects of Whitman's vision. But, of course, to superscribe over Whitman's universal manifesto claims a qualifying phrase that would make them hold

conditionally is an act of interventionist hermeneutics and, like any inter-
vention, should be employed not routinely but critically and self-critically.
Does it illuminate this statement and a class of statements? Is there some
rationale by which we can justify our use of the limiting phrase, and can we
offer a theory as to why it might have been an implicit part of Whitman's
meaning rather than an explicit one? The test of an interpretive procedure
is in its ability to clarify our questions and help us with our problems,
scholarly and pedagogical.

I believe this interpretive strategy can help two groups of readers. One
is the younger undergraduate who comes to the introductory-level class
without a developed sense of literary history but with a sensitive awareness
of his or her personal history and the need to establish an adult identity and
to define it in some relation to the known past. If such readers, quick to
detect and distance themselves from conceit and naïveté in a writer, can be
shown a way to look at Whitman's overlarge claims as situational and tactical,
then these problematic passages may work with, rather than against, the
self-consciousness these young adults carry into their reading. The American
Declaration of Independence is a good analogy to bring in to class discussion,
for all readers will share with Whitman some knowledge of that precedent-
shattering, precedent-setting document, and that knowledge has shaped all
our subsequent declarations, whatever our nationality, politics, or chronological age. When that text claims "these [far from evident] truths to be self-
evident" and appeals beyond the dominative authorities immediately concerned to Universal Reason, to Nature, and to "the opinions of mankind,"
young and old can identify with the reaching out for equal justice, can
sympathize with the need to gain a hearing and "decent respect," and can
admire the rhetorical bravado. From there we can extend a similar sympathetic identification with the manifestos of the young Whitman, when he
holds that what is "in fact" still latent, unformed, and true only in some
hoped-for, future-conditional sense, is "really" self-evident, manifestly and
unconditionally true.

Furthermore, this strategy should be useful to the advanced student who
brings to Whitman's prose a historical knowledge of literature that is likely
to be at variance with many of Whitman's generalizations about American
art. Throughout his prose Whitman attempts to describe the New World
art that America needs. Some of these descriptions turn into prescriptions
for "universal" works eschewing any kind of particularity that could be con-
strued as partisan and divisive. These prescriptions turn into prophecies
most students of literary history will know are too narrow; literature over
the last century has given us works that Whitman could not have imagined
and that have achieved "universality" through motives and in forms he did
not describe. If, over these universal predictions and pronouncements, we
superscribe "In my theory and programme," such generalizations need no
longer conflict with "objective" facts of literary history outside of Whitman's

own practice. As self-descriptions, they can be turned inward, like beams of light, to elucidate Whitman's "subjective" intentions for his work and to illuminate his views on "subjective point of view."

Perhaps the most estranging feature in the prose is to be found in the honorific nouns Whitman uses throughout these seven works. Usually capitalized, they seem to carry more status and significance than do the uncapitalized words next to them on the page. I include a brief list here, grouped to show that there are two traditions, religious and secular, in Whitman's honorific diction.

Religion	Democracy
Soul	Science
Transcendence	Personality
the Poet	Individualism
Immortality	Independence
Being	Culture
	Sex
	Nature

Whitman uses these words prominently, to name qualities in human life that "co-operate" with democracy and to argue that democracy, better than any other social arrangement, can bring together the individual and the mass and preserve the rights of both. Behind these words lie enormous and complex issues that no one can claim have been satisfactorily resolved in history. So, when Whitman attempts to address them in a vocabulary that without explanation or apology mixes the religious with the secular, his language itself has to come under suspicious scrutiny: does he believe in some unacknowledged divinity, some deus ex machina that will miraculously solve democracy's contradictions and make it work? For many readers of Whitman the only way to get past this problem of credibility is to suspend one's disbelief—rather as one does with other poets who write out of belief systems one does not share. But this is a belief system we still care about; why suspend the problem of credibility? I like to show students that Whitman's prose becomes believable if its religion is viewed as entirely "modern": that is, not set *against* modern science but coming *out* of it. I ask them to take quite seriously Whitman's assertions of naturalism, beginning with these unambiguous assertions in 1855:

. . . the whole theory of the special and the supernatural departs as a dream.   (344–45)

What has happened . . . what happens and whatever may or shall happen . . . the vital laws enclose all . . . They are sufficient for any case and for all cases . . .   (345–46; Whitman's ellipses)

. . . any [exceptional] miracle of affairs or persons [is] inadmissible in the vast clear scheme where every motion and every spear of grass and the frames and spirits of men and women and all that concerns them are unspeakably perfect miracles referring to all and each distinct and in its place.   (348–52)

They can be found throughout the prefaces, through to this reaffirmation in 1888 of

the concrete realities and theories of the Universe furnish'd by science, and henceforth the only irrefragable basis for anything, verse included.   (196–97)

By establishing everything, "verse included," on this "irrefragable basis," Whitman puts us on notice to look for "modern" principles of naturalism and empiricism in everything he says and does. Thus we are told to read the words on our list naturalistically: those that bear connotations of super-naturalism are to be translated into terms that fit the ordinary powers and experience of ordinary human beings. (For example, in the third passage quoted above, *miracles* would be translated as "ordinary wonders, part of the miracle of life and death.") When the words are so translated (as they can be, one by one), the whole of Whitman's prose becomes more accessible to readers of today—more tenable, more interesting, more radical.

After such an exercise, when we come across the many instances where Whitman attempts to describe the great balancing acts of democracy (as we do in the prose of 1871, 1872, 1876, 1882, 1888), we will find that one of our interpretive problems has been removed. We will not jump to the suspicion that Whitman is showing himself, in slips of the tongue, to be depending on the supernatural to deliver on his hopes; that suspicion is too complicated, not as simple and radical as the principle we have chosen to read by. Furthermore, Whitman's many reformulations of what democracy can and must do, which might strike us as insistently reiterative, can now be viewed empirically, as experimental, exploratory in purpose—sketches toward what democracy should attempt, rather than declarations of what it already does.

What evidence is there to support this scientific, empirical picture of Whitman, so different from the salesman that he seems to be at a first meeting? Here I send students to read *Democratic Vistas* and *Specimen Days*. In these works, where Whitman has more space than the prefaces allow, he views his subjects, democracy and nature, from a wide variety of angles and perspectives. These works may be called "perspectival registers," since their variety of views acts as an implicit recognition of the relative and finite nature (and at the same time, of the necessity and worth) of every subjective point of view.

For further evidence that Whitman's explanations and formulations are put forth as propositions and that his "great words" too are meant less as achieved facts and more as conscious propositions, I have students look in the prose for statements like these:

> We have frequently printed the word Democracy. Yet I cannot too often repeat that it is a word the real gist of which still sleeps, quite unawaken'd. . . . It is a great word, whose history has yet to be enacted. It is, in some sort, younger brother of another great and often-used word, Nature, whose history also waits unwritten. (1871, 937–43)

> Behind all else that can be said, I consider "Leaves of Grass" and its theory experimental—as, in the deepest sense, I consider our American Republic to be, with its theory. (I think I have at least enough philosophy not to be too absolutely certain of any thing, or any results.) (1888, 39–42)

> But what is life but an experiment? and mortality but an exercise? with respect to results beyond. And so shall my poems be. If incomplete here, and superfluous there, n'importe—the earnest trial and persistent exploration shall at least be mine, and other success failing, shall be success enough. (1872, 13–16)

Such statements by Whitman can of course be taken as defensive, their purpose to cover up the disappointment to his hope that his poetry would be readily embraced by an America "awaken'd" by it to democracy. But they can also be read as evidence of an awareness, abiding alongside his hope, that all our knowledge, all our enterprises are provisional in status, subject to the conditions and test of experience. If we read Whitman in this way, treating his words as testable propositions whose proposer was aware of his own and their finitude and fallibility, we are not taking him "off the hook," removing his thought experiments from range of our criticism. Each of Whitman's propositions about nature and human nature is put forth earnestly and persistently to be answered by "results" and judged by fellow souls; he invites this judgment in each of his prefaces from 1855 to 1888. We will be able to criticize those propositions more attentively, rather than less, when we move beyond the assumption that they are all the result of naive double-thinking. But while the judgment of each soul and each generation of souls is an important part of the "results," it too is not conclusive, not definitive, but subject to ongoing review as long as human perception renews itself. Our criticism is relativized, set on the same "irrefragable basis" as is that which it criticizes.

Here let me summarize the claims of this essay. I have been proposing that Whitman's best-known prose writings—the five prefaces and the two longer works—will yield up, when read actively, much that readers need for understanding his verse. The prose teaches the theory of *Leaves of Grass* (see 1888, 39–40), by which we gather not only what meanings to look for but also the means to find them: questioning referents; assuming problematic terms and assertions have intentions that can be discovered by sympathetic attention and cooperation; expecting Whitman's text to be strong enough to stand up to our challenges and return answers in context to them. We will not be satisfied at every point with the partial answers that emerge, but we will be reading Whitman as he would have us read:

> Books are to be call'd for, and supplied, on the assumption that the process of reading is not a half-sleep, but, in the highest sense, an exercise, a gymnast's struggle; that the reader is to do something for himself, must be on the alert, must himself or herself construct indeed the poem, argument, history, metaphysical essay—the text furnishing the hints, the clue, the start or frame-work. Not the book needs to be the complete thing, but the reader of the book does. That were to make a nation of supple and athletic minds, well-train'd, intuitive, used to depend on themselves, and not on a few coteries of writers.   (1871, 1957–66)

The purpose described here—to call into being a nation of independent minds—summons us to become cocreative, copoetic readers of the prose and verse of *Leaves of Grass*. Whitman's challenge applies to us still, whether we will it or not, and cannot be sidestepped by deflecting charges of naïveté, optimism, overcertitude, or mystification. He and we and all, democracy, and life itself are participants in the same vast experiment.

WHITMAN IN THE LOWER-DIVISION COURSE

Whitman in the Undergraduate Survey
Robin Riley Fast

Whitman is the last writer I teach in the first term of a two-semester American literature survey, a course required for all English and English-education majors and available as an elective to students in other fields ranging from engineering to French and psychology. Because our literature courses have no prerequisites, this survey could as easily be a student's first college-level literature course as it could be the last course in a student's major before graduation.

Despite my students' diversity, I have come to anticipate certain initial responses to Whitman and his poetry. Poetry is daunting for many, even for English majors. Yet these same students often find that they can understand Whitman more easily than they had expected. Their satisfaction is complicated, though, because they aren't sure "Song of Myself," their first assignment, is really poetry—it may seem "too easy" to some. When they find the poetry difficult or unrewarding, they may observe that "he rambles," or that "he could have said it more concisely." This response can become the basis for discussion of Whitman's beliefs about poetry and the purposes possibly underlying his techniques. More important, while a few may express uneasiness about his religious views or direct treatment of sexuality, many are drawn, from the beginning, to his persona of the miraculously ordinary guy and to his invitation to "Come to us on equal terms" (McMichael 1: 1778; 1855 preface). Much as critics might question the notion of universality, most undergraduates, in my experience, don't. For them, a sense of commonality, of experience shared with an author who "speaks to" them, can be extremely important, and the fact that they find this in Whitman disposes them favorably to him. It also may enable some to consider his differences more tolerantly than otherwise they might (e.g., his homosexuality; his apparent alienation from the kinds of ambition many of them are moved by and admire in Benjamin Franklin); and it can become the basis for discussion of the difference between author and character, poet and persona.

My own reading is informed by feminism, by concern for the relations between a work and the writer's life and social-cultural-political surroundings, and by my interest in the structures and techniques of poetry. Feminism prompts me to invite students to think about Whitman's treatment of women in relation to his democratic and egalitarian aspirations and to his contemporaries' depictions of women, and to ask whether his ideal American could as easily be female as male. I sketch the contexts of the poetry in an introductory lecture on Whitman's life and his responses and contributions to the politics and society he knew, drawing on Gay Wilson Allen's and Justin Kaplan's biographies and on Whitman's prose; especially illuminating are the descriptions of New York street and river scenes and of soldiers and wartime hospitals in *Specimen Days* and the criticisms of American culture and politics in *Democratic Vistas*. Whitman challenges my inclination to close reading, but this approach seems essential if students are to recognize his full significance and begin to think of him in relation to the development of American poetry. Thus we read the poetry aloud and discuss its formal qualities and the relations between form and content. This discussion allows students to think of Whitman in the context of transcendentalism and Romantic organicism.

Teaching Whitman in the survey offers an important advantage and a serious dilemma. The advantage is that by the time we reach Whitman at the end of the term, students have been exposed to his literary-cultural background and his contemporaries. I can remind students of works and writers they've recently read and suggest connections or contrasts with Whitman. They can think of his imperialist leanings in relation to the Puritans' sense of mission, his cultural nationalism in relation to Emerson's. When I speak of the influences of Quakerism and of political radicalism, they recall John Woolman and Thomas Paine, a friend of Whitman's father. Whitman's Free Soil politics and his depiction of the runaway slave have special meaning because they've recently read Frederick Douglass and Harriet Jacobs. They are often struck by Whitman's exuberant urbanism, which they can contrast with the disillusionment of Melville's "Bartleby" and with Franklin's optimistic pragmatism when he was a young man on the rise in a young city.

If students' familiarity with the literary background is the great advantage of teaching Whitman in the survey, the great dilemma, also the product of a densely populated syllabus, is how to select assignments. The survey syllabus, I believe, should include relatively many writers and should allow a number of them to be discussed in depth. For Whitman, this means at least three class sessions, and with luck four. I want students to develop a sense of the unity, continuity, and variety of his poetry. Thus besides "Song of Myself," I assign the ten *Drum-Taps* poems in the anthology (most recently volume 1 of McMichael's *Anthology of American Literature*, from which all quotations in this essay are taken). To promote attentive reading and real discussion I assign only parts of "Song of Myself." Colleagues who assign the whole poem in the survey feel that students should experience the full sweep of the poem; I don't disagree, but I do believe that my approach offers advantages. (Of course, I encourage students to read the whole poem, and some invariably do.)

Obviously, one could select excerpts that support a particular thesis, and this may seem a danger to some teachers. I think, however, that the continuity of themes and variations in the poem guards against distortion; varying the selections somewhat from term to term also helps me avoid taking the poem for granted. Carefully chosen selections can promote productive discussion, which in turn enables students to read the whole poem with greater confidence and comprehension; finally, Whitman himself warns readers against assuming that any one interpretation (perhaps supported by the teacher's selections) is obligatory or exclusively correct.

A typical assignment in my survey, then, comprises the following sections of "Song of Myself": 1, 2, 5, 6, 8–10, 15, 17, 19, 27–29, 31, 34–38, 46, 47, 51, and 52. Depending on the students and the calendar, I might give all the passages as one assignment, or I might end the first day's reading at section 19. This selection provides numerous examples of most major motifs and the opportunity to see how Whitman develops or varies them in the poem. The speaker appears as the celebrated average American (1), as a childlike wonderer (6), as an observer of, or participant in, his fellows' lives (8–10, 15), as a natural (31), sexual (5, 27–29), spiritual (5) being; the reader is variously characterized, challenged, and invited to join him (1, 2, 17, 38, 46, 47, 51, 52); poetry itself is explicitly and implicitly defined (2, 6, 15, 17, 51, 52); the poem's religious (5, 19, 46) and democratic (8–10, 15, 17) impulses are evident, as are the importance of nature (2, 31, 47, 49) and Whitman's acknowledgment of the dangers of betrayal and the horrors of violence and oppression (28, 29, 34–38).

In making the assignment, I ask students to consider why his first readers were astonished by Whitman's poetry. *Astonished* seems the best word for this question: stronger than *surprised*, it lacks the negative connotations of *shocked*, and turns out to fit many students' initial responses. It is also consistent with Whitman's own sense of his poem: "Do you take it I would astonish?" (line 384). I ask them, too, to consider how Whitman characterizes himself and them, as readers. This second question, depending upon the students' interest and ability, will at least prepare them to discuss sections 1 and 2 and may carry them through the whole assignment.

Why were Whitman's readers astonished by *Leaves of Grass* in 1855? Students' responses vary, but usually they suggest as possible reasons the overt sexuality, the "bragging" or "self-centered" tone, the "ordinariness" of the people described and of the language ("it's not hard to read, but what he's saying is pretty shocking"), the sheer length (this comes across even in excerpts), and the fact that "it just doesn't seem like poetry." I note down all of their responses and try to weave them into the discussion over the two or three days we have for the poem, asking students to elaborate on them whenever possible—my experience is that these comments are all relevant to the central issues, and it's important for students to see their insights being used in this way. What I focus on for the rest of the first day's discussion is the poem's form and Whitman's characterization of himself and his reader-listener.

Once students have specified what makes the poem seem "unpoetic" (usually this means identifying what's missing), I ask a couple of them to read some passages aloud: the opening lines and any part of section 15 are my choices here, but any passages would do. Listening, they hear the rhythm and go on to point out other aspects of form—for example, lexical and grammatical repetition, the line as the unit of meaning; I identify techniques, like the "envelopes" Allen discusses in *American Prosody*, that they will be able to recognize in rereading. The point here is to acknowledge that Whitman's poetic structure is looser than the conventional norm, yet it is neither coincidental nor spontaneous. If students are either unconvinced or very interested in these questions, Arthur Golden's facsimile edition of the "blue book," which shows revision in progress, can be passed around in a later session.

One can then ask why Whitman might have chosen to write like this. This question can lead to discussion of Whitman's democratic ideals or his ideas about language and poetry; if students' observations and questions seem to warrant further inquiry, we may stay with this topic for a while. Otherwise, and more often, I simply remind them of Emerson's poetics and his own poetry, suggesting that they consider Whitman as in part responding to Emerson's challenge, and then turn toward the other question I posed when first making the assignment: how does he characterize himself in the poem? Some students will do a fairly close reading of sections 1 and 2; others will take a more wide-ranging approach, pointing out, for example, the sexuality in section 5, the priestlike role in section 19, the perhaps contradictory rural and urban identities implied in different sections, the childlike stance of section 6. Passing around copies of the title page and frontispiece from the 1855 edition—reprinted in Malcolm Cowley's facsimile edition—will give students visual evidence for this discussion. Whatever direction students' ideas about the speaker's characterization take, I can easily raise the question of how he characterizes and relates to the audience, integral as this relationship is to his own self-depiction. This question is bound to elicit personal reactions as well as literary analyses (again, sections 1 and 2 are a natural beginning for the more analytical approach); some are enchanted by, some highly skeptical of Whitman's intimacy: "I might not tell everybody, but I will tell you" (line 388). I read from the 1855 preface to reinforce our observations about the relationship between speaker and audience: "He is a seer . . . he is individual . . . he is complete in himself . . . the others are as good as he, only he sees it and they do not"; "the American bards shall be marked for generosity and affection and for encouraging competitors . . . hungry for equals night and day" (1775, 1778; Whitman's ellipses). Such passages also allow me to circle back to the question of Whitman's stylistic choices.

I can now suggest connections between the characterizations of self and reader and the "ordinariness," relative informality, "easiness," and inclusiveness of the poem's form, and I make some observations about Whitman's poetics and his conception of the poet. Indeed, by this point students have probably begun to make such connections themselves. They can now see that Whitman's style is part of his self-characterization as a natural who encompasses and speaks for all people and the whole range of ordinary and extraordinary experience. And they can see that this style reflects his conviction that the poet must acknowledge his consanguinity with "the others" in words that invite and challenge them, at once reflecting the vast sweep of history and geography and growing naturally from the individual lives of the poet and his fellows. On the one hand, Whitman affirms universal, common experience; on the other, he validates diversity and difference. My students have observed that his style contributes to this multiple affirmation, with its apparently endless, all-inclusive series of particularized images: the suicide, the prostitute, the young sister, the fare collector, and so on.

During the first day I also try to discuss the relation between soul and body, which is integral to Whitman's self-characterization and to the whole poem. I concentrate on section 5 because it is rich in related motifs, it is structurally interesting, it expands the inclusiveness of the democratic catalogs (that students will inevitably have mentioned), and in all of these respects it demonstrates the belief in organic unity that Whitman shared with the transcendentalists. Because I want to pull all these points together economically and use them to forecast the second day's discussion, I usually analyze section 5 in a brief lecture. Of course, we may not get to this on the first day.

In the one or two days remaining for "Song of Myself," I discuss section 6, the structure of the whole poem, and section 52. Since the last section and the overall scheme can be covered briefly, largely by lecturing, we usually have time to discuss additional sections or topics chosen by students from the assignment.

There are numerous bridges from the first day's discussion of section 5 to section 6: the theme of organic inclusiveness makes an easy transition; students have also observed that sections 5 and 6 are comparable in tone and address, as Whitman speaks both to his soul and the grass and to us about them. Looking at section 6, we discuss the various "hints" that the grass symbolizes Whitman's poetry, the implications of such symbolism, and whether this seems an appropriate symbol for Whitman's poetry. By this point, students are making numerous connections, generally apt and sometimes wonderful, to other parts of the poem. These comments, in turn, often become bridges to discussion of sections they've chosen or of questions they have raised earlier. In the (unlikely) absence of such choices or questions, I challenge them to reconcile the self-betrayal in section 28 or the massacre in section 34 with the tone and characterization of the rest of the poem. Good readers will point out that Whitman's speaker recovers from his revulsion and despair in sections 29 and 38; the question then becomes how the recoveries or reconciliations come about and whether they're convincing.

Before the last period in which we discuss the poem, I ask students to consider its overall structure. I acknowledge that they are at a disadvantage, having read only parts, but encourage them nonetheless to think about how the poem is unified, if at all, and what metaphors they might use to describe it. The basis for the question, as for a similar one earlier in the term about *Walden*, is Whitman's own assumption of organic unity. The question also offers another opportunity for them to think about sections not previously discussed in class. I first ask students for their ideas; often they'll suggest the journey motif and the speaker himself as unifying devices. I observe that there are numerous ways of seeing the poem and that they often don't contradict but in fact coexist with and even illuminate one another. I then describe several critics' "maps" of the poem: Malcolm Cowley's and James E. Miller's (*Critical Guide*) analyses of it as a visionary or mystical experience, and Robert K. Martin's as a homosexual love poem, indicating some of the key passages for each interpretation. I also mention that Richard Chase characterized the poem as a comic drama of identity but denied the existence of any tight structure (*Walt Whitman*), to remind them that although they may find one or all of the models helpful, they are not obliged to accept an elaborate scheme for the poem.

Finally, we move to section 52 by recalling section 6; I point out some of the ways in which this last section builds both from early parts of the poem and from the sections that immediately precede it. I try to show that if those relationships imply a kind of completion, the journey motif implies continuity. Last, I observe that if the first and last sections are placed side by side, we can see that the emphasis subtly shifts, in 52, to "you," the reader and student, who is once more challenged and invited to set out independently. Although this is the end of class discussion of "Song of Myself," the final Whitman assignment does allow students to continue thinking about the issues the poem has presented.

For the final day on Whitman, I assign all of the *Drum-Taps* poems in the anthology: "Beat, Beat Drums," "Cavalry Crossing a Ford," "Bivouac on a Mountainside," "Vigil Strange I Kept on the Field One Night," "A March in the Ranks Hard-Prest," "A Sight in Camp in the Daybreak Gray and Dim," "The Wound-Dresser," "Long, Too Long America," "Give Me the Splendid Silent Sun," and "Reconciliation." I observe that the war presented an enormous challenge to Whitman's faith and ask students to notice the changing emphases and feelings evident in these poems (which fortunately appear in the same order as in Whitman's book) and to be aware of continuities with, and differences from, "Song of Myself."

My own experience as a student was that I was awed by "Song of Myself" but first admired Whitman as a poet when I read some of the *Drum-Taps* poems. Many of my students seem to respond similarly. I begin the class on *Drum-Taps* by reminding them of the questions I'd asked them to consider and eliciting their ideas in an open-ended way. Two kinds of comments usually predominate. Students are able to trace the outlines of Whitman's progress from enthusiasm for the war, through increasing awareness of its realities and anguish at its cost, to reconciliation. They also single out particular poems that impressed them so much that they reread them and are ready to declare that "he can really write."

Building on their responses, I briefly summarize the structure of *Drum-Taps*, pointing out some aspects that students haven't noted or the anthology omits. I also want to make clear here that anguished as he was and grisly as "The Wound-Dresser" is, Whitman didn't become an antiwar poet but rather searched for redeeming meaning in the war.

For the rest of the session, we concentrate on poems that students have found particularly impressive, reading them aloud and discussing them in some detail. "Cavalry Crossing a Ford," "A Sight in Camp," "Vigil Strange," and "Reconciliation" especially lend themselves to this approach. Students are struck by the visual images, the irony, the understatement, the quietness, and the relative lack of emphasis on the speaking self in some of these poems.

At the end of the period, I summarize our observations and suggest some of the ways in which the *Drum-Taps* poems might be related to "Song of Myself." Reminding the class that a survey gives only an incomplete view, I encourage them to read more of Whitman's work and particularly recommend "When Lilacs Last in the Dooryard Bloom'd" as the culmination of the Civil War poems. I again recall Emerson's agenda for American literature and observe that Whitman, by realizing that agenda and surpassing it, radically changed American poetry. I may mention Dickinson, whom they'll read in American Literature II, as also making radical, but very different, innovations, in part because of Emerson's influence, adding that the second term of the survey, where Dickinson is the first writer on my syllabus, will give them the opportunity both to compare these two great poets' works and to see how they continue to influence twentieth-century poetry.

Whitman's Use and Abuse of Poetic Predecessors

Kenneth M. Price

Many of the rich complexities of Whitman's relation to the literary past are presented in the opening words of the 1855 preface to *Leaves of Grass*:

> America does not repel the past or what it has produced under its forms or amid other politics or the idea of castes or the old religions . . . accepts the lesson with calmness . . . is not so impatient as has been supposed that the slough still sticks to opinions and manners and literature while the life which served its requirements has passed into the new life of the new forms . . . perceives that the corpse is slowly borne from the eating and sleeping rooms of the house . . . perceives that it waits a little while in the door . . . that it was fittest for its days . . . that its action has descended to the stalwart and wellshaped heir who approaches . . . and that he shall be fittest for his days. (*LG* 709; Whitman's ellipses)

Paradoxes abound here. Whitman denies that he repels the past but describes a corpse needing to be carted out and a cultural residue he must "slough" off. Confronted by a European and an American literary past that he regards—or, more accurately, wishes to depict—as essentially foreign, Whitman intends to shed the past and yet be its "wellshaped heir." Later in the preface, Whitman varies this imagery, suggesting that he will interfuse life into death: the ideal poet "drags the dead out of their coffins and stands them again on their feet . . . he says to the past, Rise and walk before me that I may realize you." Having learned "the lesson" he "ascends and finishes all" (*LG* 716; Whitman's ellipses).

Whitman sometimes tried to "finish all" by finishing off his predecessors. In his 1856 open letter to Emerson, he urged Americans to "Strangle the singers who will not sing you loud and strong" (*LG* 732). "Old forms, old poems, majestic and proper in their own lands here in this land are exiles." Such poetic models, he asserted, "are useful to America today to destroy them, and so move disencumbered to great works, great days" (*LG* 734). One might argue that these extreme statements are uncharacteristic: before writing *Leaves of Grass* Whitman spoke favorably—at times reverentially —of other writers, and in his final years he returned to a generous attitude. Yet it is the aggressive Whitman of approximately 1855 to 1871, the period of his best poetry, who is so interesting, and the vigor with which he denies other writers suggests that he had predecessors worth denying.

Our criticism—and my guess is most of our teaching—has gravitated to one of two poles: the presentation of Whitman as a rough, instinctive poet, working with little sense of the literary past, or as a paradoxical outgrowth of transcendentalism ("Emerson with a body" as one recent commentator puts it [Hyde 169]). Certainly there have been exceptions—helpful examinations of Whitman's debt to individual English predecessors and some richly documented examinations of his extraordinarily wide-ranging self-education. But even such studies tend to belittle all of Whitman's American predecessors except Emerson, arguing, for example, that "Whitman avoided a direct confrontation with the traditional New England poets . . . leaving the Frogpond to its quiet effusions" (Soule 39) or, more directly, "no American literary writer except Emerson had any appreciable influence on the . . . poems of the 1855 edition" (Stovall, *Foreground* 282).

I test such claims, these assertions that Whitman responded only to Emerson among American writers, when I teach the survey course covering the first half of American literature. I grant (and try to clarify) the importance of Emerson in Whitman's development, but I move beyond this established connection to explore what remains to be determined: the strength of Whitman's links with other predecessors. I find it helpful to organize, within the survey, a unit of study dedicated to nineteenth-century poetry. Instead of considering individual authors one at a time in discrete classes, I approach the poetry of Longfellow, Poe, and Bryant first on its own terms and then in relation to *Leaves of Grass*. Specifically, I often discuss Longfellow's "Excelsior" in conjunction with Whitman's "Excelsior," Poe's "Raven" with Whitman's "Out of the Cradle Endlessly Rocking," and Bryant's "Thanatopsis" with Whitman's "To Think of Time" and "This Compost." The Bryant-Whitman connection seems to me especially intriguing. Reading Bryant and Whitman together can raise crucial issues relating to tradition, literary history, and what Harold Bloom calls the "anxiety of influence."

During his most assertive years, Whitman argued that he was a poet of such magnitude as to make irrelevant all comparisons with the likes of Poe, Bryant, and Longfellow. He opened one review of his own work by denying with a single salvo the work of his compatriots: "An American bard at last!" Another of his anonymous reviews made explicit the need for work "essentially different from [that of] the old poets, and from the modern successions of jinglers and snivellers and fops." "English versification," he added, "is full of these danglers, and America follows after them. Everybody writes poetry, and yet there is not a single poet" (Traubel et al., *In Re* 13, 28). By most ways of reckoning, American antebellum artists had to measure up to British standards. Yet Whitman reversed matters, disqualifying American artists precisely for being *English* artists.

Bloom has argued that "poetic strength comes only from a triumphant wrestling with the greatest of the dead," an idea that may have encouraged us to think Whitman would not have been concerned with American poets (*Map* 9). But the muscular force of Whitman's assertiveness suggests that he was not wrestling with phantoms but that he keenly felt the double pressure of both a British and an American poetic past. Ever since canon makers of the 1920s relegated Bryant and Longfellow to marginal status, to what Van Wyck Brooks termed "a limbo of the non-elect" ("On Creating"

340), it has required historical imagination to understand Whitman's creative context, to appreciate the circumstances of the aspiring poet. Whitman knew perfectly well that "up to 1845 no [American] poet was read more eagerly than William Cullen Bryant" (Charvat, *Profession* 109). In fact, writing in the *Brooklyn Daily Eagle* on September 1, 1846—only a year, most scholars believe, before he began notebook entries in the manner of *Leaves of Grass*—Whitman greeted Bryant on his return from Europe, describing him as "a poet who . . . stands among the first in the world" (qtd. in Stovall, *Foreground* 121).

Only by becoming more self-conscious of our "truth" about the past can we begin to understand the very different past Whitman knew. If we recall the stature of Bryant and Longfellow in nineteenth-century America (and of Poe in the wake of "The Raven"), we can appreciate the audacity of Whitman's effort to alter his past by shrinking these poets into "little creatures" (*Prose Works* 2: 388–89). One way to rewrite history was to impose his criteria for poetry on them. In one of his 1855 anonymous reviews Whitman asked, "If [*Leaves of Grass*] is poetry, where must its foregoers stand?" (Traubel et al., *In Re* 31). Of course, the answer is nowhere or, at best, in a wholly different sphere. Only by becoming, as he called it, "disencumbered" could Whitman speak as if situated at the dawn of time. This myth was crucial for Whitman's attempt to wrest from Bryant the distinction generally accorded him at midcentury, the role of originator of the American poetic tradition.

The desire to gain historical perspective guides my approach to teaching. One advantage of pairing Whitman and Bryant is that it allows one to demonstrate significant continuities despite revolutionary changes as one moves chronologically from this "schoolroom" or "fireside" poet to Whitman and from Walter Whitman to Walt. Walter Whitman's pre–*Leaves of Grass* poetry, written from 1838 to 1850, draws recurrently on "Thanatopsis," as can be seen in "The End of All," "The Love That Is Hereafter," "Death of a Nature Lover," and "Ambition" (*Early Poems*). I usually present one of these poems when entering into discussion of Whitman's mysterious transformation during the period from 1847 to 1855. Whatever the reason for Whitman's great change, he learned the crucial difference between borrowing that is derivative and use that is transformative.

In discussing Whitman's mature work that responds, at least in part, to "Thanatopsis," I often share with my class Whitman's longest comment on Bryant's poem, an undated fragment probably from the 1870s:

> *July by the Pond.* The same thoughts and themes—unfulfilled aspirations, the enthusiasms of youth, ideal dreams, the mysteries and failures and broken hopes of life, and then death the common fate of all, and the impenetrable uncertainty of the Afterwards—which Wordsworth treats [in] his *Intimations of Immortality* Bryant in his

Thanatopsis and in the *Flood of Years*, and Whittier often in his pieces, W. W. also treats in *Leaves of Grass*. But how different the treatment! Instead of the gloom and hopelessness and spirit of wailing and reproach, or bowed down submission as to some grim destiny, which is the basis and background of those fine poems. Instead of Life and Nature growing stale—instead of Death coming like a blight and end-all. . . . (*Notebooks* 3: 981)

Whether or not Whitman is fair to these poets is largely beside the point: as Bloom argues (*Map* 4), what is important for a poet is not reading fairly but reading creatively. This passage depicts Whitman consciously seeking to oppose Bryant, Whittier, and Wordsworth, poets who, broadly speaking, resembled Whitman in their use of a plain poetic style. Moreover, Whitman implies that Whittier and Bryant, by following their major British predecessor, have absorbed a "stale" outlook, a symptom of an old European civilization burdened by what Whitman typically called "ennui." Whitman adopted an important defense against the English charge that America lacked the cultural achievements, the rich storehouse of associations, necessary for great art. He turned the argument on its head, asserting that the rich English past had led to an impoverished present, to a civilization in decline that was given to reminiscence. Whitman argued that Americans, possessing a vital present and a promising future, should avoid the lassitude and the gloom he saw in English (and anglicized American) poems.

I cannot prove indisputably that "To Think of Time" was written with Bryant in mind because Whitman was largely successful, after much effort, in purging the 1855 *Leaves of Grass* of allusions to other writers. But as Claudio Guillén has argued, there is an important difference between allusion and influence, and there can be profound influence even where there is no direct textual echo (36–37). "To Think of Time" speaks to "Thanatopsis" in many ways and often through similar images so that, if the poems are read together, a dialogue develops (similar to the one Robert Weisbuch has heard between "Song of Myself" and *The Prelude*) that makes the case for influence sufficiently secure (221–32).

At first glance, "Thanatopsis," of all poems, might seem safe from charges that it was inadequately "American." This work confronted the English argument that Americans lacked a worthy heritage of their own by tying American experience to the ancient past. Moreover, the implicit politics of the poem seem shaped by American experience. Death is seen as the great democratizer, the equalizer that places matron and maid and speechless babe with patriarchs and kings in one mighty sepulcher.

There is, however, a particular bias in Bryant's poem that Whitman, more clearly than most critics, highlights. In "To Think of Time" Whitman purposefully calls to mind "Thanatopsis" by echoing its theme, by reproducing the sweep of its geographical and temporal vision, by adopting its description of the coffin as a "house," and by depicting the endless dying of humanity as a train or caravan. Like Bryant, Whitman notes the worthies who go to death: Bryant's matron and maid, patriarch and king become Whitman's "good-doers," "heroes," and "distinguished" people. But Whitman establishes a general likeness in order to stress a more important difference. Bryant's apparently democratic outlook, Whitman believes, is finally select, exclusive, aristocratic: as Whitman says, "there is more account than that." He implicitly chastizes Bryant for failing to achieve a truly inclusive vision. Here, he says in effect, is a sampling of what Bryant does not discuss: the "interminable hordes of the ignorant and wicked," "the barbarians of Africa and Asia," "the common people of Europe," "the American aborigines," "A zambo or a foreheadless Crowfoot or a Camanche," infected immigrants, the murderer, the mean and shallow person, the prostitute, the mocker of religion—all these, Whitman points out, enter the world tomb, and all these are "not nothing."[1]

Whitman meant his poem to be more encompassing and ultimately more affirmative than Bryant's, and Whitman forces the reader to reach the affirmations only after facing death squarely. Bryant's form had distanced the reader through the use of a speaker given to dignified cadences and abstractions. These characteristics are enough to keep in control even the most troubling thoughts. Whitman allows far less distancing partly through his use of the vernacular, asking the reader "Have you dreaded those earth beetles?" and do you believe that bodily decay leads to "ashes of dung?" Whitman's questions, a marker of his early oratorical style, may well build on Bryant's own sermon-based oratorical style, though Whitman, characteristically, presses matters further, addressing sixteen of nineteen questions directly to the reader (Hollis, *Language* 90).

A second Whitman poem, "This Compost" (1856), also responds to "Thanatopsis." Bryant had urged readers, when confronted with the "last bitter hour," to "Go forth under the open sky, and list / To Nature's teachings." In nature's presence, one would hear the "still voice." When Whitman confronts death, however, he finds Bryant's advice misleading. Rather than recommending a turn to Nature as a trusted teacher, "This Compost" opens with a warning: "Something startles me where I thought I was safest, / I withdraw from the still woods I loved." The speaker of "Thanatopsis" found that the lesson of nature is decay, and he fled to a social vision after contemplating horrible violations: the oak that "pierces" the body in the grave, "the rude swain" who plows through and treads upon the dead. Whitman takes issue with Bryant's poem by placing his emphasis not on decay but on nature's baffling ability to produce exquisite beauty out of "distempered corpses." Seeking to understand this transformative power, Whitman himself (not an archaic "rude swain") decides to "run a furrow with my plough, I will press my spade through the sod and turn it up underneath, / I am sure I shall expose some of the foul meat." Unlike Bryant, who turns away from nature to a social vision, Whitman says that nature is enough. Nature is terrifying, not in the fearful way that Bryant implies, but in its awesome powers of transmutation. Whitman's poem of death becomes a meditation on the interdependence of death and life.

It must be stressed that Whitman did not use his predecessors only as negative examples. Whitman's adoption of key images and themes from Bryant indicates how much he saw to admire in a work such as "Thanatopsis." Whitman had to know the best of America's conventional verse if only to understand how he could be innovative. As a poetic rival working with the taint of England in his lines, Bryant was a predecessor that Whitman needed to "slough" off in the molting process. Yet complete as the rejection might appear, there was also common blood and indebtedness that made Whitman the "wellshaped heir." By virtue of having realized more completely than his predecessors the implications of democracy for literature, Whitman made good his claim to be the poet "fittest for his days."

NOTE

[1]Quotations from "To Think of Time" are from Malcolm Cowley, *Walt Whitman's Leaves of Grass: The First (1855) Edition.*

Whitman's Language as the Basis for a Scientific or Technical Report

Sherry Southard

Instructors of required courses in college composition, introductory literature, and beginning technical writing may have students from scientific and
technical areas who are not interested in humanistic subjects. They, like
some teachers in their fields, want class assignments that they view as relevant to their major areas of study—assignments practically and directly
related to what they will be doing after they graduate. Some scholars, however, argue that it is valuable for students in scientific and technical fields
to study humanistic subjects (see Harris; C. Miller; for a summary of the
literature dealing with this controversy, see Rubens).

Assuming that the liberal arts are valuable for these students, instructors
can devise research projects that make humanistic subject matter the basis
of a scientific or technical report. Instructors are not restricted to using this
approach only in technical- or scientific-writing courses. The project described in this article, especially with the suggested supplemental work, is
suitable for any number of English courses that have a writing component,
as long as faculty members and students are flexible.

For this project, students analyze the vocabulary in a section of Walt
Whitman's poetry and then present the results of their research in a technical
or scientific report. By completing this assignment, students employ the
proper procedure for gathering and analyzing data to be presented in a
research paper (the scientific method); become familiar with the format of
scientific and technical reports, including matters such as the major sections
and expected content and the use of headings and graphics; use the *Oxford
English Dictionary* and the *Dictionary of Americanisms* (Mathews); and
investigate Whitman's vocabulary in *Leaves of Grass*.

Thus, students deal with matters of practical value to those in scientific
and technical fields and with matters in the realm of the humanities.

In this essay, I discuss the scientific method, the general format of scientific
and technical reports, and a suitable humanistic research project based on
the vocabulary in *Leaves of Grass*. Each discussion concludes with a section
entitled "Supplemental Work," in which I indicate additional information
and exercises for students.

The Scientific Method

Teachers can begin by explaining the general procedure for gathering and
analyzing data for a research project, particularly the procedure followed
when the results will be presented in a report. Persons in scientific and
technical fields generally use the label *scientific method* when discussing
this procedure while those in the liberal arts refer to it as the process of
writing a research paper; however, the methodology is the same in all cases.

To use the scientific method, researchers first isolate and define the problem they will study and attempt to solve. Then they observe the evidence to form a hypothesis. Next they devise an experiment or project that allows them to collect objective data that verifies, disproves, or modifies their hypothesis. After studying the collected data, they formulate a theory that accounts for the data gathered.

Since instructors have already defined the problem students are to study and solve (determining the characteristics of Whitman's vocabulary), students focus on the second stage of the scientific method, observing evidence to formulate a hypothesis. By collecting and analyzing data about Whitman's vocabulary in *Leaves of Grass*, they can determine the characteristics of his diction in the passages they are studying. Researchers often use the inductive approach as part of their method; students must learn to gather specific data, analyze it, and draw general conclusions.

Supplemental Work

Teachers can have students read and discuss writings from science, engineering, and technology that illustrate the scientific method. For example, Robert Lynch and Thomas Swanzey in *The Example of Science: An Anthology for College Composition* divide the scientific method into five steps and provide readings to illustrate each step.

Instructors can explain the mechanics of gathering data: for example, how to use note cards to record both bibliographical data and other information gathered methodically and accurately.

A General Format for Scientific and Technical Reports

After students understand how to use the scientific method in a research project, instructors can discuss the following general format, which is appropriate for many scientific and technical reports.

Title

I. Introduction
   A. Subject and purpose
   B. Scope
   C. Audience
   D. Overview of results
   E. Plan of development
II. Literature review
III. Background
IV. Materials and equipment
V. Methods and procedures

VI.   Results
VII.   Conclusions
VIII.   Recommendations, if appropriate
IX.   References
X.   Appendices

Supplemental Work

When explaining the section called "Literature Review," teachers can discuss using reference works and secondary sources as well as primary sources, paraphrasing and quoting from other sources, preparing annotated bibliographies, and basing new research on earlier research by others. For this supplemental work, instructors can have students read secondary sources about Whitman's theory of words and language (see Southard).

When describing the types of information researchers put in the "Background" section, instructors can either have students read secondary sources or lecture about such matters as Whitman's life (Allen, *Solitary Singer*) and poetical theory (Allen, *Whitman Handbook*; J. E. Miller, *Critical Guide*).

When discussing the "Results" section, instructors can teach students about support graphics, for example, how to use visuals to supplement prose and to replace prose that is prolix. Instructors can also explain how to prepare correctly visuals suitable for an expert audience (tables and figures) or for a general audience (bar graphs, pie charts, and other simple types of graphics).

When explaining the "References" section, instructors can review some of the different methods of documentation used in various fields in the humanities and sciences. They can also briefly describe style manuals.

Humanistic Research Project

After explaining the scientific method and discussing a format for presenting the results of research, teachers are ready to assign the problem—the study of Whitman's vocabulary. Students can use the outline below to gather data about and analyze the words Whitman uses in selected passages from *Leaves of Grass*.

I.   Subject, purpose, scope
   A.   Gather appropriate data
   B.   Analyze data to determine the characteristics of the vocabulary used by Walt Whitman in a poem or a passage from a poem in *Leaves of Grass*
II.   Materials
   A.   *Leaves of Grass*, Blodgett and Bradley's *Comprehensive Reader's Edition* (1892)

    B. *Oxford English Dictionary (OED)*
    C. *A Dictionary of Americanisms on Historical Principles*, Mitford
        M. Mathews
III. Procedures
    A. Select a passage from *Leaves of Grass*
    B. Choose the vocabulary to be analyzed
        1. Use "content" words
        2. Omit "function" words such as articles, prepositions, and
            conjunctions
    C. Record certain information taken from the *OED*
        1. Language origin
        2. Earliest date of written use
        3. Special information such as status labels and subject labels
    D. Record information given in *Dictionary of Americanisms*

After students tabulate and analyze the data they have collected, they write
a short report presenting their findings and including appropriate headings
and support graphics.

For a paper five hundred to one thousand words long, they use the following abbreviated version of the general format given earlier:

Title

    Introduction: What are you investigating? How have you limited
your research? Who is your audience? Briefly, what are your conclusions? What are the major sections of your report?
    Procedures: What are your sources of data and how did you obtain
your data? Can the reader redo what you did exactly the way you did
it?
    Results: What data did you obtain? What did you find when you
analyzed your data? (Explain, using support graphics as well as details
and examples.)
    Conclusions: What conclusions can you draw from your data? (Sum-
marize your results.)

Whitman's diction is particularly good for this assignment because of the
diversity of the language that he uses; he includes words from all stages of
language (neologisms, obsolete terms, Americanisms and adaptations from
foreign terms that were becoming Americanized and other Americanisms,
and current terms); all languages (Greek and Latin, German, Spanish, Italian, French, English); all levels of languages (learned, slang, colloquial,
poetical, technical); and all subject areas (fields such as astronomy, trade
and manufacturing, music, and phrenology). In addition, it was important

to him to use words that described and expressed America and Americans, especially the American working class and the average, common American. Almost any passage from Whitman's *Leaves of Grass* is suitable for this project. By studying the vocabulary used in the following poems or sections from poems, students can find examples of terminology from scientific and technical subject areas. The lists of words that follow are representative, not exhaustive:

Anatomy ("I Sing the Body Electric," lines 129–64, sec. 9): head, neck, hair, tympan of the ears, eyes, eye-fringes, iris of the eye, eyebrows, mouth, tongue, lips, teeth, jaws, jaw-hinges, nose, cheeks, forehead, chin, throat, neck-slue, armpit, breast, elbow-socket, arm-sinews, instep, lung-sponges, heart-valves, bones, brain

Astronomy (throughout Whitman's poetry): rotate, revolve, retrograde, revolving satellite, crescent, perturbation, centripetal, centrifugal, ether, telescope, constellations, spectroscope, meridian, sun, moon, force of gravitation, comets, meteors, solar systems, asteroids

Carpentry and construction ("Song of the Broad-Axe," lines 186–217, sec. 9): shingle, rail, prop, wainscot, jamb, lath, panel, gable, cornice, trellis, pilaster, balcony, sash, turret, porch, auger, adze, bolt, line, square, gouge, bead-plane, saw, jack-plane, mallet, wedge, rounce, work-box, scaffolds

Military and war terms (selections from *Drum-Taps*): artillery, cannons, guns, bayonet, drilling, tents, army, general, sword, drum-corps, rank, war-ships, transports, soldiers, battle, regiment, batteries, bombs, veteran, brigade, flag, bullet, manoeuver, detachments, encampment, cavalry, bivouac, bugles, rifle-balls, chief-gunner, accoutrements, parley. Note that there aren't as many terms related to war and the military as one might expect, given the number of poems in this collection.

Nautical terms and terms related to the sea (selections from *Sea-Drift*): waves, seashore, sea, beach, spray, shore, ocean, sand, gale, helm, ship, sea-reefs, steersman, bows, freighted ship, brine, sea-lettuce, coral, sperm-whale, shark, sea-leopard, sting-ray, sails, gunwale, hawser, spars, foam, wake, astern, ballast, capstan. Note that there aren't as many nautical terms and terms related to the sea as one might expect.

Terms naming professions and businesses and the equipment and materials used in them ("A Song for Occupations," lines 103–21, sec. 5): house-building, blacksmithing, glass-blowing, nail-making, coopering, tin-roofing, shingle-dressing, stone-cutting, butcher, rigger, grappler, sail-maker, block-maker, confectioner, distilling, rope-twisting, sign-painting, electroplating, electrotyping, iron-works, blast-furnace, puddling-furnace, pig-iron, oil-works, silk-works, caulking-iron, brewery, wine-makers, vinegar-makers, reaping-machines, thrashing-machines, flour-works, carman, factory, cotton-picking

Terms describing the flora and the fauna of America (throughout Whitman's poetry): arbutus, cactus, calamus, chestnut, clover, corn, cotton, dandelion, gooseberries, hackamatch-roots, hickory, larkspur, lilac, magnolia, maize, mullein, onion, orange, malt, pawpaw-tree, persimmon, pitch-pine, prairie-grass, salt-lettuce, sweet-flag, tobacco; alligator, antelope, bear, blue-bird, brood-cow, butterflies, chickadee, eagle, earth-beatle, elk, fish-hawk, gnat, halibut, hawk, hermit thrush, katy-did, lark, lobster, mocking-bird, opossum, phoebebird, prairie-dog, rattlesnake, sparrow, spider, thrush, tree-toad, trout, turkey, wren

Some of Whitman's better-known poems and passages are good for demonstrating the wide range of his vocabulary: "I Hear America Singing," "O Captain! My Captain!," "When I Heard the Learn'd Astronomer," "Pioneers! O Pioneers!," "A Noiseless Patient Spider," and section 32 from "Song of Myself."

Supplemental Work

Instructors can discuss editions, describing in particular Blodgett and Bradley's definitive edition of *Leaves of Grass*, which indicates how Whitman revised and expanded his book.

If the *Oxford English Dictionary* and *Dictionary of Americanisms* are not available, students can use an unabridged dictionary or a standard collegiate dictionary.

Instructors can introduce students to usage dictionaries, thesauruses, and dictionaries of technical terms.

Instructors can provide information about defining as a rhetorical technique in writing.

Students can give short oral reports presenting the results of their research, or they can informally discuss Whitman's vocabulary in the passages that they analyzed.

Humanistic research projects such as the one I've described have broad application. Teachers can incorporate them as part of any lower-division English course in which students write.

In "Song of Myself," Walt Whitman wrote, "I am large, I contain multitudes" (sec. 51). Similarly, those in the humanities and in scientific and technical fields can contain multitudes; they do not have to limit themselves to their own subject areas.

WHITMAN ON THE UPPER LEVEL

"Scattering it freely forever": Whitman in a
Seminar on Nineteenth-Century American Culture

Ed Folsom

I have always enjoyed teaching Whitman because he is the first major American writer to have been educated as I was and as most American students now are. In a time when serious writers were expected to have classical, structured educations, Whitman had the original relativistic training. I don't mean that today's college educations are the equivalent of Whitman's six years of basic elementary school education (Whitman's actual schooling was a relatively insignificant part of his real education, which "had scarcely begun" when he left school [Allen, *Solitary Singer* 17]). Rather, I want to suggest that the unstructured, meandering course of Whitman's reading and learning anticipated the more individualized, broadly based curricula offered today. Whitman picked up information here and there, depended heavily on the media of popular culture, read widely but never systematically, had incredibly broad interests, picked up a smattering of French but never really learned any foreign language, and appropriated as his classrooms museums, daguerreotype galleries, theaters, opera houses, beer halls, and phrenology parlors. He spent his formative years immersed in American culture, and we must encourage our students—if they are to read him properly—to undergo the same immersion, to range far and wide in the odd and surprising and forgotten corners of the culture. Whitman is a poet who requires of his readers not so much a love *for* American culture as a desire to be immersed *in* that culture. He loved the chaotic mix of the culture and chose to make a poetry out of it; the challenge for the teacher is to model a class on that same energetic mix and to have faith that it will somehow form into a pattern.

To come at Whitman's work armed with systematic training and a formal approach is to miss him; we must instead come at his work unarmed, willing to roam into fields we may not have known existed. "Missing me one place search another" (*LG* 89; "Song of Myself," sec. 52), he advises, and his advice can be read as a statement of principle for American studies in general and for Whitman studies in particular. Whitman requires us to be as scattered in our interests as he was: "I will scatter myself among men and women as I go," Whitman said, emphasizing his joy in "Scattering it freely forever" (*LG* 152, 41; "Song of the Open Road," sec. 5; "Song of Myself," sec. 14). With his love of etymology, Whitman knew that the root meaning of the word *scatter* was "treasure," and the basis of his poetics was that treasure was indeed scattered and hidden everywhere; he defined the poet's duty as continually uncovering that hidden beauty: "I think ten million supple-fingered gods are perpetually employed hiding beauty in the world—burying it everywhere in everything—and most of all in spots that men and women do not think of, and never look . . ." (*Daybooks* 766).

Because Whitman sought significance in such a vast scatter of places and composed his work out of such a variety of influences, he has generated a scatter of critical approaches; commentator after commentator has discovered the treasures of approaching him from a new perspective—of medicine, of opera, of government, of French influence, of Oriental thought—and the surprise always is that Whitman was out there occupying or at least looking around those fields a century before we discovered they were an essential part of his poetry. Whitman is the poet of the grand conjunction, the singer of "and." His whole poetic fabric is woven with that conjunction; his catalogs are the formal manifestation of his incessant desire to conjoin, to sing the parts of the world into a massive juxtaposition. He forges a vision of wholeness out of disparate parts held together by his adhesive voice. The English language's sign of connection—"and"—is Whitman's poetic sign; one of his favorite concepts is "adhesiveness," a term he takes from phrenology and applies to a range of emerging democratic friendships that he would come to call "camaraderie." As he searched for and invented names for this quality of strong democratic affection, he found its grammatical equivalent in the English conjunction indicating adhesion, "and." "And" allowed the voice to bind the parts of the world together, to blend them, and it served Whitman well in creating what C. Carroll Hollis has demonstrated to be a remarkably metonymic vision, a poetry that creates its world by naming things next to each other (*Language*).

It is not surprising, then, that so many of our books and essays about Whitman echo that conjunctive impulse: *Walt Whitman and the Civil War, Walt Whitman and Opera, Walt Whitman and the Body Beautiful, Emerson, Whitman and the American Muse, Walt Whitman and Emily Dickinson,*

"Whitman and the American Idiom"[1]—the list goes on and on. The titles reflect the critical consensus that Whitman is best understood contextually, as a writer who absorbed many aspects of his culture into his work, and whom we best read by moving out from the poetry into the world that the work was woven from.

In my seminars on Whitman, I take advantage of this conjoining energy by tapping into the diversity of student interests represented in any one class. Interests in the Civil War, in American economics, in politics, in music, in medicine, in the classics, in sports, in American Indians, in fashion, in geography, in sexuality—all can serve as the focus of a fertile semester-long investigation into Whitman and his relation to American culture. When I'm able to select seminar participants from a large pool—as in an NEH summer seminar—I use diversity of interests as a criterion of selection, to bring together a group of individuals who resemble a Whitman catalog in their surprising juxtaposition and variety. But any group will do; some groups can even be assigned different areas of interest and develop diversity as they progress in their studies. The key is to have the group members heading out in different directions into the culture and its history, then converging back on Whitman's writings, which serve to organize, validate, and inter-twine their individual investigations. Whitman's work is illuminated, then, in the discussions that serve as the adhesive that joins the individual studies.

This procedure reenacts the process of Whitman's poetry—"efflux" and "influx," an expansion out into the world, a contraction back into the self, the incessant dilation between "sympathy and pride," between the many and the one, the self as infinitely expandable but also as deeply united (*LG* 50, 716; "Song of Myself," sec. 22; "Preface 1855"). So in studying Whitman's work, the seminar agrees to disperse in order to reunite, and with each reunion there is a larger self made of increasingly diverse individual inves-tigations. The seminar becomes the pedagogical equivalent of Whitman's deep sense of unity as he so often expresses it: "The diverse shall be no less diverse, but they shall flow and unite—they unite now" (*LG* 432, "The Sleepers," sec. 7). The very process of the seminar, then, lets us talk in some depth about Whitman's concept of Union, about how his "Union hold-ing all, fusing, absorbing, tolerating all" (*LG* 203; "Song of the Exposition," sec. 8) works in individual, political, aesthetic, and historical ways, and how it works in pedagogical ways as well. The seminar sessions become the arena of weaving the varied insights; the individual research time between the sessions becomes the period of casting out for new things that later will be woven into the growing unity. The goal of the seminar, I tell my students, is to enact Whitman's confident stance that "I am large, I contain multitudes" (*LG* 88; "Song of Myself," sec. 51); the participants—each with a specific slant on Whitman's text—work to discover the intertextures of the group, the odd places that their various ideas connect in *Leaves of Grass* and illuminate the text. In doing so, students verify for themselves Whitman's claim that *Leaves* was "an attempt, from first to last, to put a *Person*, a human being (myself, in the latter half of the Nineteenth Century, in America,) freely, fully and truly on record" (*LG* 573–74; "A Backward Glance")—and they see how intimately this person and his song are composed of his place and his time.

Preparatory discussions during the first several sessions lead participants to realize the essentially absorptive nature of Whitman's work:

> To absorb, and express in poetry, any thing of [the present age]—of its world—America—cities and States—the years, the events of our Nineteenth Century—the rapidity of movement—the violent contrasts, fluctuations of light and shade, of hope and fear—the entire revolution made by science in the poetic method—these great new underlying facts and new ideas rushing and spreading everywhere. . . . (*LG* 740; "Preface 1872: As a Strong Bird on Pinions Free")

He is out to incorporate *everything* into his poetry, for to leave out is to discriminate (and Whitman's *Leaves* will try to leave nothing out; ideally, there should be *no* missing leaves). To discriminate, Whitman believed, is the primordial antidemocratic act: if the self is to be as fully absorptive and expansive and united as America itself must be, then the song of that self must be open as well, willing to include whatever it encounters. So the English language, the material out of which the song will be constructed, must be an expanding, unruly, open language, welcoming experiences and feelings and people that previously were excluded from the culture's written art. The emerging American language must have a growing lexicon. Whitman's *American Primer*—an exciting, quirky, and accessible short prose piece—becomes the perfect text for opening the discussion.

Thus right at the start many students are surprised to learn that Whitman—who some have been taught to believe is a relatively careless or casual user of words—took a real interest in lexical science, in the quickly evolving art of dictionary making. A student in one seminar made Whitman's fascination with lexical science her particular interest; she traced the development of etymological studies and found what English dictionaries during Whitman's time looked like, what they included, and what theories of language they represented. She discovered that modern lexical science evolved during Whitman's lifetime, beginning with Webster's *American Dictionary of the English Language* (1828), developing with the appearance of Skeat's etymological dictionary in the 1880s, and culminating with monumental projects like the *Century Dictionary* (1889–91) and the initial work on *The Oxford English Dictionary*, which was under way at the end of Whitman's life. She was fascinated with Whitman's own aborted attempts to construct a dictionary and quickly immersed herself in Whitman's notebooks on language (*Daybooks* 664–825; *Notebooks* 1621–1710). She found not only that

Whitman had studied Webster's dictionaries very carefully in the 1850s but also that he arranged with G. and C. Merriam and Company to exchange a copy of his prose and poetry for a copy of *Webster's International Dictionary* (*Daybooks* 713–18, 595–96). When she found that Whitman answered William Michael Rossetti's query about the meaning of the word *calamus* by referring to the definition in *Webster's Dictionary*, she decided to look up key Whitman words there and see what definitions he was assuming the reader would know; she was intrigued to find that *calamus* had several suggestive definitions, including a writer's pen or quill and a wind instrument made of reed—it seemed that the image of calamus, besides signifying a phallic grass, also melded Whitman's concerns with voice, song, and writing. When I led her on to William Swinton's *Rambles among Words* with the suggestion that Whitman at least knew the book well and may indeed have written a good part of it, she was excited to discover revealing folk etymologies of many words (including *calamus*) that are idiosyncratic markers in Whitman's poetry—words like *crone* and *accoucheur* and *felon* and *comrade* (originally, *Rambles* tells us, a "chamber-fellow" [103]); *Rambles*, she found, even contains the etymology of *Whitman* (right before that of *Longfellow*). In essays like "Slang in America" (*Prose Works*), she noted Whitman's celebration of the fossillike nature of etymologies, and this led her to consider the Webster etymologies that Whitman would have known as he constructed *Leaves of Grass*. She quickly convinced the seminar that Whitman was no casual user of words.

Her work with the dictionaries and etymologies that Whitman knew and used helped another student who was probing the question of American Indians and their relation to Whitman. This student had run across Whitman's reference to some nineteenth-century linguists who worked with native languages and who had told him about the definitions of *Paumanok* and *Mannahatta*, the two native words he used to begin his effort to ground his language (and America's method of naming) in autochthonous linguistic soil. After learning that Whitman actually worked in the Indian Bureau, this student investigated Whitman's brief tenure there; of particular interest was Whitman's "An Indian Bureau Reminiscence" (*Prose Works* 577–80), with its suggestive descriptions of individual natives. Looking carefully through Whitman's poems, he found that images of Indians appear more frequently than our initial impression might suggest, beginning with Whitman's earliest pre-*Leaves* poems, continuing (perhaps surprisingly) in over half of the poems in the first edition of *Leaves*, and developing on through very late poems like "Yonnondio."

This student's work complemented that of another participant who was interested in the origin and development of the theory of evolution and its effect on Whitman. This student became concerned with Whitman's evolutionary view that put Indians in "arriere" (*LG* 27; "Starting from Paumanok," sec. 18) to the dominant white race in America, and she worked with the implications of social evolution during Whitman's lifetime to uncover the ways that he posited the evolution of one race into another.

In turn, this work fit well with the reading of another student interested in the slavery issue and Whitman's changing response to it. Initially very troubled with Whitman's nonabolitionist stance, this student began reading some of Whitman's journalism in order to understand his developing Free Soil position and to see how that position meshed with his emerging poetics of expansion and containment. For this student, Whitman's prose pastiche on slavery (*Notebooks* 2171–90) became a vital document and helped illuminate many passages of poetry.

These examples suffice to suggest how complex and tight the web of discussion can become. A productive gesture late in the semester was the risky act of entering Whitman's novel *Franklin Evans* into the discussion; all students found aspects of their special interests anticipated there, and they began to see that even this flawed and juvenile novel contains in embryo many of Whitman's key concerns. They laughed at the awkwardness of the plot and the preacherly tone, but they also saw the seeds of Whitman's later development. The student working on Indians viewed the novel as structured around the "Windfoot" story of native revenge and betrayal; the student working on slavery was amazed at the long scenes set in the South that deal with Franklin Evans marrying a slave and giving away her brother; the student working on evolution read the novel as a treatise on the possibilities of more noble human emotions eventually conquering baser ones.

The discussions became even more illuminating when we focused on "Song of Myself." The student who had worked on dictionaries and etymologies read the poem as an exploration of the physiology of speech, initiated in the opening two sections where the speaker avows that his "tongue" is "form'd from this soil, this air," and that the "atmosphere" is "for my mouth forever" as he breathes in and ingests the world so that he can exhale it in language: "The sound of the belch'd words of my voice loos'd to the eddies of the wind . . ." (*LG* 29–30). Students discovered that the words Whitman uses for *positive* expressions of voice—*belch, trill, buzz, yawp*—have no etymologies but rather are themselves a kind of sound-release, a loosing of the stop from the throat, a natural "respiration" of the poet's "inspiration" (*LG* 29; sec. 2), while the words he employs for the kinds of language usages he *rejects* have roots that suggest cutting apart and categorizing, words like *discuss* and *talk* and *lecture*. Whitman enacts in language his own theories about words as he tries to "have no mockings or arguments," as he tries to escape "the talk of the beginning or the end," as he tries to penetrate the "fog" of "linguists and contenders" (*LG* 30, 32; secs. 3, 4). The student working on American Indians argued for a reading that posited the tableau of "the marriage of the trapper" to "a red girl" as the central joining of Americans to their land, a conjoining reflected throughout the poem and all of Whitman's work in recurring images of sexual unions enacted on a geographical scale. The student exploring the slavery issue tracked the recurring imagery of the "runaway slave" in "Song of Myself," and he argued that the whole poem can be read as a slave-escape narrative. When the speaker experiences the slave's pain and humiliation ("I am the hounded slave"), he embodies the fugitive's struggle, realizing that we are all slaves to traditions and habits of thought and oppressive forms that this poem sets out to escape from (sec. 33). The student working with evolution believed the central parts of the poem were sections 31 and 44, where evolutionary theory becomes a key metaphor for the progress of the self, for the development of identity.

These are not wildly original ideas about Whitman, but a scattered approach that sends each student off on a search into some pocket of nineteenth-century American culture can produce some wild originality, some lively discussions, and some very useful insights. Each seminar will create its own juxtapositions, and the new clashes and interpenetrations at their best engender the same shock of awareness that Whitman's catalogs, at *their* best, engender. The students, by imitating on a small scale the very process of Whitman's poetry—expanding and contracting, diffusing and conjoining—come to understand Whitman's process and accomplishment more intimately than they would in a class where everyone is guided into taking a uniform approach to the same texts. The New York University Press edition of *The Collected Writings of Walt Whitman*, now available in most college libraries, opens up the vast body of supporting materials that allow for such wide-ranging investigations; students now have easy access to the roiling mass of notes Whitman made about every aspect of his culture, and they can learn to find their way around those notes and attach them to Whitman's poetry and prose. With some guidance into a few good primary and secondary sources, students can emerge from such a seminar feeling good about their increased knowledge of American culture and, by anchoring all the approaches in Whitman's work, achieving success in tying their specific areas to those of the other participants. This process encourages them to learn Whitman's most challenging lesson for any student of literature: "I round and finish little, if anything; and could not, consistently with my scheme. The reader will always have his or her part to do, just as much as I have had mine" (*LG* 570; "A Backward Glance").

NOTE

[1]The authors or editors are, respectively, Charles I. Glicksberg, Robert D. Faner, Harold Aspiz, Jerome Loving, Agnieszka Salska, and William Carlos Williams.

Teaching the Whitman Seminar

Alan Helms

In the spring of 1986, I taught a Whitman seminar for twenty advanced students at the University of Massachusetts in Boston. Ours is a young commuter campus where most students are older than the average student, work part- or full-time, come from working-class backgrounds, and bring a great diversity of educational preparation to their studies. My students were typical, and typical too of the public at large, in their initial impressions of Whitman and his work. As best I could tell, they saw him as "democratic" and "mystical," loud and crude, perhaps scandalous and even vulgar, but certainly "great" (otherwise, why this seminar?), yet on the whole a bit embarrassing. The English boasted Shakespeare, the Greeks Homer, the Italians Dante, the Germans Goethe, but we, alas, had to make do with Whitman. The disappointment in the room was perceptible. I had no doubt that a seminar in Blake or Stevens at the same hour would have winnowed the recruits who now sat with polite expressions of misgiving, waiting for me to begin that first two-and-a-half-hour class of the semester.

Our principal text was Justin Kaplan's edition in the Library of America series, the only volume containing first and last editions of *Leaves of Grass* plus all the major prose. My goals, I said, were to read with them all of Whitman's major poetry and prose, to place his work in its literary, historical, and cultural contexts, to trace his various selves and also the varying fortunes of his book and his reputation, and finally, to glance at his influence on subsequent writers. Since Whitman is an unusually difficult poet, my approach to his poetry would be formal and stylistic, but I would use biography throughout—to explain otherwise inexplicable features of his writing and, since Whitman lived his life amid the main currents of his day, to provide the historical and cultural background necessary for full understanding of his work. I admitted there was much about the poetry I didn't understand and was therefore willing for us to raise questions that we left unanswered, citing T. S. Eliot's remark that some of the poetry he loved most he didn't understand. I hoped that by the end of the semester my students would acknowledge Whitman as one of the great poets in English and would know firsthand the profound effect his writing has had on readers from his day to ours.

For the next two hours, I led the students step by step through Whitman's biography, working from an extensive handout, quoting often from Whitman's and others' writing, and closing with a couple dozen photographs of the nineteenth century's most photographed man. Initially I used biography simply to excite my students, and it worked, for Whitman's life is one of the best roadshows going: farmboy, schoolteacher, printer, reporter and editor, novelist and short-story writer, political organizer, terrible versifier, book reviewer and critic-at-large, mechanic, stagecoach driver, carpenter and contractor, author of the *Leaves*, Civil War volunteer nurse, free-lance journalist, government clerk, social critic, memoirist, public lecturer, minor celebrity, and finally, custodian of his gradually growing fame. This list amounts to a bare-bones version of one of his own catalogs; add signal scenes like the Lafayette embrace, the Emerson "No," Oscar Wilde's visit, and Tennyson's telegrams, and you have an American version of one of the grand operas he loved so much. The students thrilled to the story, and they were now eager as I read them the first five sections of "Song of Myself" and then sent them off to continue on their own—with Emerson's essay "The Poet" to prepare their way, William James's chapter on mysticism from *The Varieties of Religious Experience* to ground them, and a strong caution against reading any criticism at that early stage. I wanted them to have something of the experience Whitman's first readers had, with all its attendant joys and frustrations. Besides, it's a travesty to send students to criticism early in the semester when Whitman tells them to "no longer take things at second or third hand . . . nor feed on the spectres in books" (Kaplan 28).

With the second class, we began a slow, close reading of "Song of Myself" that lasted almost a third of the semester. I wanted my students to know Whitman's most famous poem well, and I knew I could use those weeks to guide their responses and provide background material, thus laying the groundwork for all that followed. We read always aloud and round-robin, stopping after each section to analyze and interpret, to reread, to make as many connections as possible, sometimes simply to marvel, as we moved slowly forward into the poem. For the most part, students took the lead in discussing subjects and structure; I kept raising questions about style. Many students read poetry purely for content (even advanced English majors), as if poems were riddles to be translated into prose equivalents. To frustrate that tendency, I devised exercises that obliged them to study Whitman's language. Describing a part of their bodies without naming it (an old Pound trick) helped them see the linguistic invention in Whitman's descriptions of the body; rewriting a short Longfellow poem as Whitman might have written it helped them better understand his line; and so on. I found I needed to pay special attention to prosody (I usually do)—not because Whitman's is especially difficult, but students are rarely taught prosody anymore, and in any case free-verse prosodies are harder to discern than metered ones. Repeatedly I scanned passages to show them Whitman's rhythmic patterns and the subtle variations he works on them. Metered and rhymed poems by Poe and Longfellow showed the poetic norm in mid-nineteenth-century America; together with Whitman's earliest poems, they helped my students appreciate the radical formal originality of the first *Leaves of Grass*. The students needed no help from me to appreciate how radical Whitman's themes were and are.

Biographies by Gay Wilson Allen, Roger Asselineau, Justin Kaplan, and Paul Zweig provided valuable historical and cultural information that helped

ts of the poem. Students learned of Whitman's devotion to
and animal magnetism, his enthusiasm for the technological
his day, and his avid reading about the new disciplines of geology
.... logy and discoveries in astronomy that profoundly influenced
his conceptions of time and space. His obsessive concern for health made
more sense given the history of psychic disorders in his own family and
given too the unhealthy diet and eating habits of nineteenth-century Americans. Attention to such matters meant that as we moved further into the
poem, we moved further into its period. Excerpts from early reviews showed
how vicious Whitman's first critics could be, and the differing responses of
important early readers such as Emerson, Thoreau, Arnold, Swinburne, and
Hopkins gave more sense of literary context while sanctioning the students'
own varying views. But I continued to warn them against criticism in those
first weeks, willing to risk their confusion a while longer on behalf of their
own evolving judgments.

Some were still floundering halfway through the poem, however, and no
great wonder. Whitman is, as I've said, an unusually difficult poet. His
movements are associational and unconscious rather than logical; his subjects
can be unwieldy (mystical illumination, sexual self-discovery); and though
his language at first glance seems simple, it's quite challenging and sometimes even opaque. He's alluring but elusive, frank but reticent, and his
goal is the subversive, traumatic one of changing his readers' lives. Some of
my students were baffled. A rescue operation was in order: Malcolm Cowley
performed it with the preface to his edition of the first *Leaves*, still the best
short introduction to the early poetry. For further help, I gave them Randall
Jarrell's essay "Some Lines from Whitman," less a piece of criticism than a
statement of superb appreciation from a discerning fellow reader, but one
that is perhaps more helpful later in the semester when students have become adept readers.

In the fourth class, I asked them to write a brief autobiography so
they could see what difficult decisions are involved in any written self-
presentation, and a spiritual history to get them thinking, if they weren't
already, about the place of the spiritual in their own lives. Some students
asked that I do the same exercises; unfortunately, I agreed. I came out as
a gay man in my autobiography, and two men dropped the course a short
time after, complaining of its "content." I also told too much, and thereby
troubled the class by sanctioning a move from professional to personal relationships. The move was hard to resist. Almost a third of the way through
the course now, most of us were intoxicated with Whitman and ripe to
respond to his injunctions to "Undrape" ourselves. At the time, I prided
myself on having contributed to an atmosphere in which most of my students
felt free to speak of alcoholic childhoods and failed marriages, sexual exper-
imentation and self-discovery. A lesbian came out to the class; students
sought me out to discuss personal problems; I was asked for referrals to

therapists and twelve-step programs such as Al-Anon. How wonderful, I thought at the time; how dangerous, I now think. This sense of self-discovery and release from customary restraints is one of the joys of teaching Whitman, but in my case, I learned too late that since my students were not all equally prepared to respond, the approach proved divisive.

We concluded our long reading of "Song of Myself" with a marathon session at my apartment that was full of the excitement and authentic personal response I had come to expect. The long reading had paid off. My students had for the most part become discerning readers of the poetry, aware of Whitman's craft and able to track his speaker through the rapidly fluctuating tones of his amazingly various voices. "Like Boston weather," one of them said. Much was left unexplained or half-understood, yet almost to a person they had experienced a conversion. To a jaundiced eye, we had become full-fledged Whitmaniacs, and I thought of John Burroughs's breathless remark to a fellow Whitman admirer: "Our cause gains fast" (qtd. in Kaplan 324). We now read the rest of the first edition, paying special attention to "The Sleepers" and "There Was a Child Went Forth." (Helen Vendler suggests starting the study of Whitman with this last poem, and I agree: it's short, superb, characteristic of his early manner, and it contains the clearest expression of his epistemology.) We moved on to "Crossing Brooklyn Ferry" and the excitement in the class grew greater still. The uncanny presence of the speaker in that poem is a truism, so I wasn't wholly surprised when a student began to dream of Whitman, who sent her letters to me and messages to the class. Several students began to use our text as a kind of bible, opening it at random for guidance and inspiration. Wordsworth's "Immortality" ode and passages from Blake helped us define Whitman's sense of the immortality of the soul, and I now began to assign criticism—starting with Harold Bloom's review of Paul Zweig's biography and eventually using roughly a third of the critical essays in *Walt Whitman: The Measure of His Song* (Perlman, Folsom, and Campion).

The stage was set for the major poetry of the third edition: "Out of the Cradle Endlessly Rocking," "As I Ebb'd with the Ocean of Life," and *Calamus*. Whitman's biography served me best here, since nothing explains better the drastic shift from the exuberant poet of the first two *Leaves* to the tormented one of the third. Whitman destroyed his diaries and journals from 1857–59 when he was composing these works, but he carefully copied out in a private notebook and kept close to him the rest of his life another composition from the same period, "Live Oak, with Moss," a twelve-poem sequence that he soon dispersed among the poems of *Calamus*, thereby obliterating the narrative it contains. "Live Oak" gives us the story of a love affair with a man who then abandons the speaker, leaving him full of fear and self-loathing. Internal evidence makes it clear that the experience recorded in "Live Oak" shook Whitman's faith in his original vision and prompted the doubts and fears in the major poetry of the third edition. Reassembling

Oak" proved immensely helpful and exciting. But whether I had used ц.... equence or not, to arrive at *Calamus* was of course to deal with Whitman's homosexuality.

The subject had in fact come up in the first class when a woman asked, "Was Whitman gay?" I said I preferred they arrive at their own answers on the basis of the text (a maneuver that induced some extremely close reading), adding that we would keep the question alive since it was an especially important one for a poet as sexual as Whitman, and particularly interesting in that Whitman himself would not have understood it. General confusion, which gave me a chance to point out that the words *gay* and *homosexual* didn't exist in Whitman's day in their contemporary sense. *Gay* had existed for centuries in several languages, including English (Boswell 41–45), but it was used to describe sexual acts or relationships; only since World War II has it come to designate a sexual or social identity. *Homosexual* (coined by German psychologists in the late-nineteenth century) first appears in English in 1891, a year before Whitman's death. Thus, no matter how Whitman thought of his sexual identity, he couldn't have thought of himself as either gay or homosexual. I wanted to keep us from settling into proscriptive statements at any cost, including that of my personal conviction, and also to prepare for future discussions about how definitions of sexuality are socially and culturally conditioned. Later on, I felt an obligation to keep the question open since I had declared my own homosexuality. Moreover, I trusted my students' eyes and ears. Whitman's erotic attraction to men is not some peripheral matter of his biography; it's a fact of the text, vividly present in "Song of Myself," "The Sleepers," "Live Oak," *Calamus*, and elsewhere. Since women in our society tend to be more accepting of sexual diversity than men, I was lucky that they revived the question of sexual diversity; Whitman had of course already elicited their sympathy because of his sympathy with them. Alfred Kinsey and French theorists helped with their notions of an entire range of sexualities in which most people fall somewhere between the extremes, and I confused the stereotypes even more with excerpts from *The Hite Report on Male Sexuality* in which American "straight" men recount homosexual experiences with pleasure and gratitude. Some students finally decided Whitman was gay, some that he was bisexual, some never made up their minds.

In any culture as virulently homophobic as ours, there will always be readers who deny Whitman's homosexuality, partly through Whitman's own connivance. For others, I have advice. I would decide beforehand how much or how little you will talk about sex, how you will talk about it, how open you will be about your own sexuality (whatever its nature), and how open you will encourage your students to be. Lesbian and gay students sometimes experience sexual self-discovery in response to Whitman's own, and we should be prepared to help those students—if not openly in class, then through the kind of historical contextualizing I've mentioned. As for homophobic responses from students, no responsible teacher allows students to demean anyone under any circumstances. Students will look to teachers for guidance in these matters, and we can do worse than to keep the question open, refer it to the text, let students take the lead, and bear in mind the example of Whitman's own large-minded acceptance of the whole range of human possibility. Anything less is probably incompetent.

After the third edition, we were showing signs of emotional fatigue; that and the prospect of the Civil War period just ahead prompted me to arrange a viewing of *Rigoletto* in the hope of unraveling Whitman's remark to a dinner companion in Boston in 1860 that the two greatest influences on his poetry had been Emerson and opera. We had dealt with Emerson's influence, but how had opera influenced Whitman? After reading some of Whitman's superb music reviews from the late 1840s, we met one Sunday to see an opera he recalled with great pleasure at the end of his life. The exercise clarified not only Whitman's discovery in opera of a size and range of emotion he could bring into poetry but also his formal debt to opera's freer lines and larger structural units. Specifically, the viewing helped us understand the musical structures of "Out of the Cradle" and the Lincoln elegy.

Then the Civil War period, probably the most moving episode of Whitman's life, and one in which his heroic nursing is partly accounted for by his erotic attraction to the wounded registered in *Drum-Taps* and in his letters from that period. I followed Joseph Cady's lead in treating many of the *Drum-Taps* poems as love poems disguised as elegies. We were now reading Whitman's account of the Civil War in *Specimen Days* as well as his prose recollections of Lincoln, and the cross-references between poetry and prose proved useful. The Lincoln elegy was a high point of the course, especially because it expresses Whitman's mature acceptance of death and shows his conscious appropriation of a central role in the tradition of American poetry. We concluded our study of the poetry with brief discussions of "Passage to India" and "Prayer of Columbus" and a longer look at the late, short lyrics which in their visual intensity and impersonality anticipate Pound's imagism by over thirty years. I don't prize Whitman's late poetry, but I suggested that instead of a depletion of his powers, perhaps we have a diversion of them into prose and even into his old-age conversations with Horace Traubel, his biographer. Since we had followed Whitman's revisions throughout his career, I asked my students to write about the formal and thematic differences between first and last versions of "Song of Myself." They're enormous, and ignorance of them and of his many other revisions goes far toward explaining popular misconceptions about his poetry.

In the last three weeks of the semester, we discussed the remainder of *Specimen Days, Democratic Vistas*, and "A Backward Glance o'er Travel'd Roads," and we visited Boston's Museum of Fine Arts to see if we could discover why Whitman had been so deeply moved by the paintings of Jean-François Millet to tell Traubel that "the Leaves are really only Millet in another form—they are the Millet that Walt Whitman has succeeded in putting into words" (1: 7). Slides can serve as well, and one need not be trained in art criticism to do this exercise. Millet's painting *The Sower* shows immediately what Whitman had in mind: the massive, mysterious figure of the peasant strides across the darkening fields like a force out of nature, the commonplace raised to the level of the heroic and the ideal. Whitman's old-age remark gave me a chance to review the several Whitmans we had read throughout the semester: the fresh, ebullient poet of the first two editions; the daunted older man of the third; the cautious Good Gray Poet of the fourth and fifth, obsessively revising his earlier work; and finally the old-age celebrity, insisting on the spiritual and ideal aspects of his poetry, speaking of himself in the third person now, readying the public record for posterity.

In the penultimate class, I lectured a second time—on Whitman's influence on twentieth-century writers, especially the Americans of the first half of the century and the women, black, and Latin American writers of the second half. This is a huge subject, yet something needs to be done to show Whitman's immense influence on subsequent writers. In our last class, students filled out course- and teacher-evaluation forms, and we drank champagne (Whitman's favorite old-age drink) while listening to tape recordings of the mockingbird and reading favorite passages from the poetry and prose round-robin. Then we bid one another good-bye.

Some of my students would be amazed to read this account of their experiences—certainly the two men who withdrew and the five or six who included complaints on their evaluations. Yet taken all in all, and judging from the responses of the best students, the course was a success. We had reopened the book Whitman had sought to seal, and we had discovered a greater poet than he himself was able to imagine at the end of his life. The semester had been filled with intellectual adventure and discovery, as well as a sense of deep involvement with Whitman's writing that for many had resulted in a personal awakening in their own lives. Throughout the semester and even after, students said that the course was changing their lives in fundamental ways. It certainly changed mine. It banished forever any lingering doubts I had about the quality of Whitman's accomplishment. It renewed my dedication to teaching and increased my respect for my students. And it gave me the most exhilarating experience of my fifteen years as a university teacher.

Whitman and Democratic Women
Sherry Ceniza

When I teach Whitman now, I enter the classroom early and rearrange all the chairs, including mine, in a circle. I then sit down and wait. As my students enter and find a place in the circle, we begin to talk. We begin talking about cultural space, starting with our space in the classroom. We note how it changes when we move out of the hierarchical configuration of teacher standing in front of the classroom, behind a desk, looking down at the seated students, lecturing. "Don't raise your hands," I say. "Just pitch in; let's talk."

To be truthful, at times I do go into what one of my former students fondly called my "solo performances." I go into one as I talk to my students about Abby Price. She was one of Whitman's most intimate friends for some twenty years (1855–78), and once we recognize and document her as a person, reading *Leaves of Grass* becomes a different experience. By discussing her, we do what Whitman did for the poetic line; we open up space. Space in Whitman scholarship is mostly occupied by men. We hear males talk about Whitman, and they in turn talk about Whitman's male friends. Whitman, though, talked a lot about women and to women. He addressed women as his readers. And he wrote letters to Price.

Once we find out who Price was and weave that knowledge into the fact of their friendship, we realize that for twenty years one of Whitman's best friends was a woman's-rights activist, a utopian socialist, a working woman, a writer well aware of the role words play in bringing about change and, therefore, well aware of Whitman's poetic agenda. Whitman biographers have not informed themselves about Price, who gave speeches at the first three national woman's-rights conventions and who wrote extensively for newspapers. Until now, I tell my students, she has amounted to little more than a footnote to his life, and her near absence in all the versions of his life that we have read is one sign of the politics of biography, the power of criticism. By making her (and others like her) come alive again in Whitman's life, we can reconfigure it.

Price lived for eleven years at the Hopedale Community (in Massachusetts), a Christian socialist commune that required prospective residents to sign an oath. This oath served to separate Hopedale from society at large. It erected a boundary; it defined Hopedale's cultural space. From Hopedale she moved to the Raritan Bay Union, a Fourierist commune that had no oath. She lived there for two of the commune's three years of life. She moved to Brooklyn and then across the East River to Manhattan. In time, she became part of a workers' cooperative. Her life's pattern was, in a sense, one of negotiating space—how to move out of the home into the workplace and at the same time maintain ties with friends and take care of her children and, seemingly, Mr. Price, as well.

At the time Whitman met Price, he made the following notebook entry:

"My final aim To concentrate around me the leaders of all *reforms*—transcendentalist, spiritualists, free soilers" (*Notebooks* 1: 147). Such a group had gathered around Price. When Whitman visited her home, he was surrounded not only by transcendentalists, spiritualists, and Free-Soilers but by woman's-rights activists, free lovers, bohemians, nonresisters, and abolitionists. Her circle of friends included some of the outstanding male and female reform-minded thinkers of her day. Price's female associates, but most especially Price, provide models for Whitman's images of "Woman under the 'new dispensation,' " to use his own term (Schwartz and Hanaburgh 82).

Price's circle also provides us with a possible explanation for Whitman's failure, as he saw it, to become an orator, to take his message out to the people. Off and on throughout his life—in notebooks, in letters to his mother, in talks with Horace Traubel—Whitman spoke of his intention to become a lecturer. Perhaps the two configurations—a circle of friends sharing the give-and-take of conversation and a single speaker presenting a lecture to an audience—explain why Whitman never delivered those lectures his brother George said were sitting in a barrel in Whitman's room in Brooklyn. Perhaps the practice didn't mix with the theory—with his concept of democracy, where all people would be both authors and readers, speakers and listeners, arranged more suitably in a circle of exchange than in a passive group listening to one voice. His lifelong pattern was to involve himself with circles of friends—his Brooklyn home circle, Abby Price's, Nelly and William O'Connor's, Susan Stafford's, Anne Gilchrist's, and his own Mickle Street circle. Gay Wilson Allen's biography suggests that Whitman's plan for a mausoleum grew from his desire to bring together his family circle (*Solitary Singer* 540), and so, even in death, we can see the communitarian Whitman, encircled with family in the averaging earth he so often talked about, ready to share in death in that other circle he also talked about.

The omission of Price's circle in Whitman scholarship deprives us of a rich communitarian context for Whitman, who directs our attention to community in the first *Leaves*, in the opening three lines, when he begins with "I" and moves to "you." In the preface to this edition, he describes the same movement: the soul, he says, has "measureless pride . . . but it has sympathy as measureless as its pride and the one balances the other and neither can stretch too far while it stretches in company with the other" (*LG* 716). In *Democratic Vistas*, he reiterates this concept. "Pride" becomes "Personalism"—the strong, independent individual who can never be subjugated—and "Sympathy" becomes "Democracy," or Union—the vision needed to see beyond individual self-interest. But by the time he wrote *Democratic Vistas*, 1867–71, he saw threatened the balance he had posited between the "I" and the "you."

By 1871, he had come to see sympathy as the quality most lacking in American democracy, which certainly did not seem threatened by an insufficient sense of self. By the end of the Civil War, Whitman had come to believe that the binding power needed to hold the Union together had to come from personal relationships. He looked to his culture for the kind of relationship that entailed more than personal gratification. He was looking for a kind of vision, which he found most obviously expressed in motherhood. He wanted to find it in friendships and erotic relationships. He saw it in few, if any, heterosexual marriages, which were, as so many women made clear, a form of enslavement. He wanted his words to expand the space in people's imaginations for the relationships that fulfilled both the "I" and the "you."

For people in general, Whitman in essence wanted to democratize space. For women specifically (for middle-class white women, anyway), he wanted to tear down the barrier his culture had erected between the workplace and the home. But it wasn't always easy for him; he too was part of his culture. There were tensions between what he wanted and what he knew and found comfortable and familiar. These tensions surface in instructive ways in the four images Whitman gives of the "democratic woman" in *Democratic Vistas*, as good a place as any to begin a discussion with students about nineteenth-century concepts of female democratic possibilities.

Here Whitman sketched four possible ways to see women under "the new dispensation." Judged by today's standards, these images seem bland. Carefully read in their historical context, however, they show Whitman imaging women's space as expansive, yet they show as well the poet's concern that expansion would turn out to mean, paradoxically, constriction. The basic premise Whitman indirectly dealt with in conceptualizing democratic woman dominates feminist discourse today: the *nature* of "woman."

I suggest to my students that we briefly look at the discussion going on now concerning this issue: how to theorize gender, that is, how to account for difference. The cultural feminists argue that women possess discrete qualities as a consequence of their biology, that there is an innate femaleness. The poststructuralist view holds that gender is culturally constructed. Linda Alcoff and Teresa De Lauretis, among others, stress the incompleteness of these attempts to conceptualize "woman" and offer new ways of thinking. (Alcoff opens her essay, "For many contemporary feminist theorists, the concept of woman is a problem.") This controversy within feminism brings Whitman's own contradictions home to us. The "moral superiority" view furthered in the nineteenth century by women themselves argues for biological determinism, which in essence is the cultural feminists' argument today. Whitman also stressed women's innate qualities. But his abiding belief in language as a way to *construct* rather than just *mirror* aligns him with feminists who reject the body as sole determinant of gender. I say to my students that for me Whitman's push was to offer ways out of biological determinism, though he was working within his cultural web and occasionally got stuck.

With this context in mind, we see that the woman in the first sketch of *Democratic Vistas* takes on significance as she defies the conventional role of nineteenth-century white middle-class women, a role now called the "Cult of True Womanhood." This role bound the woman to the home and demanded from her piety, purity, and subservience; preferably she was married and had many children. The woman in Whitman's first sketch, however, defies this convention by being a single working woman supporting herself but still reaching beyond self to help educate her sisters. She works in the two respectable occupations open to women—sewing and domestic service. She leaves the first because it is ruining her health; then she "boldly" tries one position after another until she finds one that suits her. This position gives her independence, time, and opportunity for "mental improvement" and self-dignity. (One of Price's main themes was that women must have relief from domestic work in order to grow.) Whitman addresses in a positive way the very things so problematic for working women—the closed-shop nature of the workplace, the stigma domestic employment held for many working women, the lack of time it gave them for self-improvement. By boldly pursuing the job market, Whitman says, a woman could get a job she liked. By treating the two professions open to women, he deals with conventional possibilities. The single most important message, however, is that this woman lives on her own, without the prop of marriage. She does not belong to the "Cult of True Womanhood."

The woman in Whitman's second sketch even more overtly denies bounded space. This woman has taken over "a mechanical business," and though she "dashes out more and more into real hardy life, is not abash'd by the coarseness of the contact . . . and will compare, any day, with superior carpenters, farmers, and even boatmen and drivers," she "has not lost the charm of the womanly nature, but preserves and bears it fully, though through such rugged presentation" (*Prose Works* 2: 400). Very possibly Price was a model here. Her daughter Helen, who was also close to Whitman, never married; she kept house for her mother and in time went to school in the afternoons to learn telegraphy, making her a model of sorts for the first sketch.

The third sketch appears innocuous to the contemporary reader if read ahistorically, but put into its cultural context, it shows Whitman once more moving against mainstream ideology. This woman, the wife of a mechanic, resists the prescribed role in two ways: she takes time away from domesticity (duty to others) for herself, and even more out of character, she has only two children. What makes this image of a mother with only two children especially significant in the context of *Leaves of Grass* is that it modifies the widespread notion of Whitman as the poet of fecundity, echoing his culture's obsession with eugenics.

Though Whitman was working against the grain of his culture in these respects, he nonetheless embraced its values. In the third sketch, the language describing this woman's joy in her "genuine womanhood" is much more eloquent than in the previous sketches. The language voices the attractiveness the domestic role still held for Whitman. Or, perhaps, he was following the lead of nineteenth-century women activists themselves who continued paying homage to "women's most important business," no matter how passionately they wanted change. But to be honest, I think not. This, I say to my students, is something for them to decide.

I suggest that Whitman feared the consequences of the new-dispensation woman because he feared that she would lose the inclusive vision he felt women had—a kind of spirituality, a going out of self. The individual citizen needed this breadth of vision, which Whitman saw expressed most often in motherhood. Whitman kept saying that it was a matter of men catching up—"The great chastity of paternity, to match the great chastity of maternity" (*LG* 105; "Spontaneous Me"). Ultimately, he did not mean that this quality was gender-bound, though he frequently voiced his idea this way, nor did he mean that it occurred only in heterosexual, homosexual, or parental relationships: in a democracy, this quality had to infuse all human relationships.

He himself experienced the binding nature of nurturing, or moving outside the boundaries of self, when he cared for the Civil War wounded. In his poetry Whitman often imaged parenting without respect to gender or age:

> O ripen'd joy of womanhood! O happiness at last!
> I am more than eighty years of age, I am the most venerable
>   mother,
> How clear is my mind—how all people draw nigh to me!   (*LG*
>   180; "A Song of Joys")

> I sit low in a straw-bottom chair and carefully darn my grandson's
>   stockings   (*LG* 427; "The Sleepers")

In an 1860 notebook entry, he explicitly depicts the mother as binder:

To Picture-Makers

Make a picture of America as an IMMORTAL MOTHER, surrounded by all her children young and old—no one rejected—all fully accepted—no one preferred to another. . . . For as to many sons and daughters the perfect mother is the one where all meet, and binds them all together, as long as she lives, so The Mother of These States binds them all together as long as she lives.   (*Notebooks* 1: 435)

Obviously, this quotation suggests to us now not only mother as binder but also the mother bound by her role. Theoretically, Whitman didn't want the latter. He wanted space democratized for women but not at the expense of their ability to see beyond the self. He wanted women's entry into public space to transform that space, to inscribe onto it the expansiveness of their inclusive vision. He wanted a poem to show "Woman under the 'new dispensation' . . . who [would] be able to ride, swim, run, resist, advance, refuse, shoot, defend herself, sail a boat, hunt, rebel,—just as much as a man," and at the same time he wanted that poem to show that "Mothers precede all"; "in Poems bring in the idea and term of Mother—the idea of the mother with numerous children—all, great and small, old and young, equal in her eyes—as the identity of America" (Schwartz and Hanaburgh 82).

The last sketch in *Democratic Vistas* portrays this Mother of All. In it we see an eighty-year-old woman whom Whitman called the Peacemaker, a mother and grandmother of many children—the Republican Mother. The same qualities she has shown in her life as "domestic regulator, judge, settler of difficulties . . . reconciler in the land" are the very qualities America needed to bind the states into a Union. Whitman spoke of his own mother as the peacemaker, and more than once he referred to her as "the greatest patriot of them all" (*Correspondence* 1: 186).

Each of Whitman's four representations of democratic women is bounded by conventions, yet each suggests new possibilities. There's a lot to talk about here, I say to the students sitting around me, and together we'll investigate the resonance of these female democratic images as we circle in and out of the poetry and prose, in and out of Whitman's biography, the familiar and unfamiliar parts.

A year and a half before Price died, in May 1878, Whitman wrote to her, "got your letter—write again—believe me, Helen and Abby dear, I appreciate the letters, & most of all your persistent & faithful friendship" (*Correspondence* 3: 62). Whitman valued that friendship. Price was, quite simply, his comrade. He wanted what he called adhesiveness—which he saw in motherhood, in friendship, and wished to see in erotic love—to form the binding element of democracy, and he came to use the word *comradeship* to express this. By comradeship he meant women and men, single and married, homosexual and heterosexual, and nongendered parents; and parenting meant caring for more than one's biological children. "I think," Whitman said, "there is nothing beyond the comrade—the man, the woman: nothing beyond: even our lovers must be comrades: even our wives, husbands: even our fathers, mothers: we can't stay together, feel satisfied, grow bigger, on any other basis" (Traubel 3: 581).

The Bard of Both Americas

Doris Sommer

Ever since Cuba's José Martí published his 1887 review in Mexican and Argentine newspapers, Walt Whitman has been admired, translated and adapted throughout the other, Latin, America. For Martí, Whitman was the model poet of New World democracy, the purveyor of an irresistible (i)deal: "Let us hear what this hardworking, contented people sings; let us hear Walt Whitman. Self-assertion raises this people to majesty, tolerance to justice, order to happiness" (8). To guide students along the multiple traces Whitman has left on Spanish American poetry, one can refer to Fernando Alegría's encyclopedic *Walt Whitman en Hispanoamérica*, where the phantom of Whitman's ubiquity is grounded in a series of concrete and weighty forms. For a more interpretative discussion, one may ask what accounts for Whitman's Pan-American democratic appeal. If the answers include the eloquence of his silences and the seductiveness of his narcissism, they will be paradoxical but not wrong.

The question of Whitman's appeal has at least three dimensions. One aspect is technical or aesthetic; it asks how Whitman produces the effect of democracy. Another is historical and explores how Whitman's poetry fits into the ideological and political framework of antebellum America and whether his work can be universally valid. A third is ethical and focuses on the consequences of Whitman's demand for an equalizing identity with the reader. A glimpse at three Spanish American poets who could not resist Whitman's invitation to write and to justify him illustrates his broad appeal and provides students with the critical and defamiliarizing distance needed to consider the dimensions at hand. This approach is appropriate for advanced undergraduates in a range of courses. Students of comparative literature should read the Latin Americans (either in Spanish or in excellent available translations) and experience these writers' fascination with Whitman. This exposure will point up the hemispheric challenge to create a legitimate American voice in a European, but domesticated, language. Whitman's successful domestication of English, as well as his ideological availability, makes him an unavoidable touchstone for the poets of both Americas. A course in United States literature or a more specialized course in poetry would logically focus on Whitman himself, using the range of his Latin American readers—or misreaders—as a symptom of his particular universalizing (perhaps neutralizing) achievement. Whether focusing on the Americas in general or on *the* American poet, teachers might begin a discussion of Whitman's contested accomplishments with the observations that follow.

Walt Whitman is claimed left, right, and center of the political spectrum in Spanish America. Octavio Paz's poetry, for example, bears (bares) the contradictions in Whitman, whose identification of self-love with the general good may have been untenable, but self-love may be what identifies us as Americans. Paz evidently recognizes the predatory tendency in Whitman's expansive democracy (a compatriot of Paz's, González de la Garza, wrote a book called *Walt Whitman: Racista, imperialista, antimexicano*), but his own loyalties to the double goal of personal and political freedom lock Paz into an anxiety of influence (see his "Whitman"). Jorge Luis Borges was less interested in Whitman's effort to produce a public sphere from private desire; instead, he read Whitman as a Schopenhauerean pessimist who might have said, "I am you, you are me, so we are neither." Rather than imagine democracy as the free exercise of multiple and discreet wills, Borges defines it as the freedom from stable or coherent identities ("La nadería de la personalidad"). In a different vein, Pablo Neruda typically "rights" what Whitman "left" out. In case the pun is too terse or its joke too surprising for students who know Neruda as the Communist poet for Latin America's masses, I should explain that the left, democratic quality of Neruda's poetry is debatable. His self-avowed rights to the Whitman patrimony allow him to write in all the gaps left open. Neruda's admiration for the master may have displaced Whitman's narcissism with love for others, but a class can see (with the help of Freud's "On Narcissism") that it did so by replacing self-love with the hierarchy-producing secondary narcissism of hero worship.

Students should consider whether Whitman's aesthetic egalitarianism needs the empty spaces between fragments of poetry and within the fragments themselves. He chose not to fix or finish them because, as he says in the 1855 preface, no living thing ever reaches the stasis of perfection. Some of his readers are annoyed by the sloppiness, notably Mark Van Doren, whose 1945 essay introduces the widely distributed *Portable Walt Whitman*:

> Whitman had the illusion, common to prophetic natures, that everything he said must be right because he said it. Poetry has a special way of exposing the error, for it demands its own kind of rightness, regardless of any other. Whitman did not regularly take the trouble to be right as a poet. He has paid the penalty. (xxiv)

But Whitman's preface isn't an excuse for the rawness and dissonance of some of his work; it's a manifesto for a new American poetry that isn't always just right. And the self-conscious rawness is taken up again in a preface of 1872 where, after several editions that added to, deleted from, and rearranged the book, Whitman finally defends the coherence of *Leaves of Grass*. Yet he insists, sounding almost like a Derridean reader of his own texts, that writing goes on, in "the surplusage forming after that volume." Of the current "supplementary volume" he confesses uncertainty, since "there is no real need of saying anything further. But what is life but an experiment? and mortality but an exercise? . . . If incomplete here, and superfluous there, n'importe—the earnest trial and persistent exploration shall at least be mine" (Broderick 9). The model of disturbance Whitman offers allows for variations that invite the student, as accomplice, to fill in the ellipses and to fit into the gaps between the fragments, so that a democratic poetry is produced every time a reader takes up Whitman's invitation to be his equal.

Ironically, students may perceive that so passionate a disciple as Neruda undoes Whitman's teaching by resuscitating older models that never even tempted the reader with a promise of equality, models Whitman had kissed off in the first paragraph of his 1855 preface. From the commanding "Heights of Macchu Picchu," part 2 of the colossal *Canto general*, Neruda writes in and closes off the spaces for the poet's interlocutor by returning America's new fragmented epic to a familiar tradition of seamless Romantic narrative. The *Canto general* sets Whitman's rawness right; it tames the earlier and more revolutionary aesthetic until what's left of Whitman is the figure of the father (see especially "Woodcutter, Awake," pt. 9), something Whitman claimed he never wanted to be. Neruda thus reaffirms the political usefulness of representative romance over what Barbara Herrnstein Smith calls a poetry of "pure possibility," and he reestablishes the hierarchy of poet over people that Whitman had managed (however briefly) to level.

This irony, not so much personal as historical, was prepared by the cultural politics of the Communist Party's Popular Front, dating from the mid-1930s. As Michel Fabre tells us, during that period the Left stopped condemning Whitman as a narrowly nationalist, even jingoist, poet and acclaimed him as the herald of an international democratic order. Americanism again became synonymous with democracy, as Whitman had always maintained, and struggles for national liberation became part of Communism's internationalism. For obvious reasons, the American Whitman attracted Spanish American Popular Frontists like Neruda. But he attracted other Spanish American heirs as well. To give an idea of the debates these Spanish Americans aroused with their partial misreadings (in Harold Bloom's double sense of being both insufficient and interested), of how contemporary Spanish American poets literarily fight over Whitman's dead body, the teacher can juxtapose two publication events. In 1969 Borges published an exquisite, but selective, translation of *Leaves of Grass* and dedicated it to Richard Nixon (Retamar). Four years later, Neruda's *Incitación al nixonicidio y alabanza de la revolución chilena* (Incitation to Nixonicide and praise for the Chilean revolution) was published posthumously. It opens the assault by invoking Walt Whitman in the following fastidiously rhymed lines:

> Es por acción de amor a mi país
> que te reclamo, hermano necesario,
> viejo Walt Whitman de la mano gris.

> From an act of love for my land
> I call on you, necessary brother,
> old Walt Whitman of the gray hand. (My trans.)

Although not all invocations are quite this dramatic, one could multiply examples of Whitman's inscription in Spanish American verse since José Martí celebrated him as the bard of both Americas. The fragmentary style that invites a coauthor produces the ideological diversity of his readings. The coauthor is further seduced by Whitman's direct appeal to a single reader, you who are reading and responding to your lover. "This hour I tell things in confidence, / I might not tell everybody, but I will tell you" ("Song of Myself," sec. 19). That Whitman will be just as available and intimate with anyone else who picks him up doesn't contradict the terms of his offer; it reinforces them. The important thing is that he calls us into the relationship as individuals, not as a compact mass who may share some characteristics. The collectivity is constructed through our particular mergings with Whitman; it doesn't precede him. In the beginning were the gift and the intimate tone of Whitman's offer. Borges noticed the intricate mechanism of Whitman's apostrophes to the reader: "We are touched by the fact that the poet was moved when he foresaw our emotion" ("Note" 70). A daring example follows from Whitman's anticipation of our surrender: "Prodigal, you have given me love—therefore I to you give love!" (sec. 21), as if it were the reader who initiated the "prodigal" gift to which Whitman obligingly responds.

One approach to Whitman's feuding heirs is to point out that his construction of a utopian plenitude ignores political conflict and social hierarchies and therefore has no need to oppose them. Instead of attempting to coordinate liberalism and democracy in his poetry (as he would in essays like *Democratic Vistas*), Whitman manages to sidestep the ideological competition by fixing the contestants in an uncannily static and perfect moment. Some readers have been coaxed into mistaking or exchanging celebration for dynamism, utopia for development, and the resonance of a single voice for the harmony of a nation. We may intuit a better future, but the promise comes in the form of an inviolable present. Something about Whitman's poetry puts conflict under erasure; it doesn't deny the conflict but neutralizes it on the page. One reason Whitman's ideal America will fuel as well as frustrate later writers is that his promise doesn't need or even admit the possibility of change. How, then, can he have any real heirs? In fact, the fragility of his static construct shatters as soon as time touches it.

Whitman's remarkable availability for other poets certainly lies in his genius for neutralizing ideological differences and thus establishing a discursive space in which all positions appear legitimate. But how is the neutrality articulated? Students may suggest a variety of thematic answers, including his limitless embrace and his protests that differences are only superficial. The teacher may have to supply an answer about Whitman's poetic practice, namely that the neutral space is really a lack of space, a tight fit between the writer and his reader that leaves no room for differences. The very first lines of "Song of Myself" insist on absolute control:

> I celebrate myself, and sing myself,
> And what I assume you shall assume,
> For every atom belonging to me as good belongs to you.

Is this an invitation or a challenge? If students refuse to be his ideal readers they are no readers at all. If they are to feel the seductive power he holds over others, they must provisionally accept his terms and read on. Then a deal is struck for nothing less than their bodies and souls. Whitman gives himself freely, claiming at times to expect nothing in return. Then the reader can ask if he really forgets that gifts are made to circulate and ultimately to return to the giver. And the profits Whitman expected were enormous:

> What is commonest, cheapest, nearest, easiest, is Me,
> Me going in for my chances, *spending for vast returns*,
> Adorning myself to bestow myself on the first that will take me,
> Not asking the sky to come down to my good will,
> Scattering it freely forever.   (Sec. 14, my emphasis)

This economic vocabulary (see also secs. 40 and 41) raises historical as well as ethical questions about the nature of Whitman's democracy. Whitman's political and erotic equality expresses itself in market metaphors, which reproduce the oxymoronic economic ideal of antebellum America: to preserve free-market trading among independent producers without promoting unequal relationships or class formation. Whitman involves each reader in a relationship that enacts the ideal of free and equal access to an American market where the best commodities are the cheapest. (Whitman, however, monopolizes the market and cancels the freedom by offering himself so cheaply, "Outbidding at the start the old cautious hucksters" ["Song of Myself," sec. 41]). Each reader is a perfectly adequate buyer, because Whitman is so "reasonable" and because we all have the resource for exchange: our selves. Thus, we affirm the Lockean, liberal ideal of political equality through equal opportunity in a free market. The same ideal will find a convincing rhythm in Whitman's apparently arbitrary catalogs, where the most extreme differences of social class, profession, origin, and gender level out through the steady and ardent incantation that melts differences into mere variation.

The broad appeal produced by these techniques gives an effect of universality, yet students should trace that appeal back to an antebellum context in which the market and capitalism were antithetical terms (Kaufman). Some critics argue that Whitman is a precursor of revolutionary poetry, others insist that his heirs are the nihilists, and yet others say that he is the father of a mystical individualism (see Wolfson). The disagreement is a contest for political stakes. But Whitman is not any one of the above. He is all of them. He cultivates their cultural space. And any attempt to read today's ideological options back into his poetry would be limiting and would probably miss the point that his democratic liberalism has no direct heirs. At most we can say that the balance Whitman manages to strike between individual freedom and social equality survives for others only as an impossible ideal. At best it suggests nonmimetic directions for future poets who may be able to construct relationships rather than imitate existing patterns. In this sense, César Vallejo's wrenching and popularizing experiments show perhaps the best Spanish American reading of Whitman (see Franco). Whitman's poetry exhibits a sensibility and an aesthetics that establish a pretext and at the same time go beyond immediate identification with any of today's ideological options. There is no mystery in this seeming paradox if we remind students that Whitman's contribution to modern poetry was to forge an aesthetics of liberal democracy that fragments into various and competing options. Later readers, including the aged Whitman, lose confidence in America's experiment to coordinate Lockean liberalism, or equal-market relationships and the natural right to personal property, with Rousseauean democracy that insists on equality of political participation (see Pennock). That is why C. B. Macpherson can eulogize America's effort in *The Life and Times of Liberal Democracy*. Some results of this loss of confidence in Whitman's twentieth-century partial misreaders will be a left-wing populist poetry, like Neruda's, a Schopenhauerean pessimism, like Borges's, and an erotic mysticism as Paz practices it to fill the void left in the wake of nineteenth-century liberalism.

The ethical hazard of dehistoricizing Whitman comes into focus once students recognize that despite the embarrassment of some fans Whitman's narcissism is the necessary origin for the equalizing intimacy he establishes with his reader. By supplying his perfect self as the ideal lover for each of us, Whitman elicits our desire for him. And if students understand that he is trying passionately to appeal to them (in both senses of *appeal*) through a laconic work that invites completion, they will feel the infectious excitement of Whitman's proposition to be his lover and coauthor. The empty and unpredictable spaces in the poem promise free and equal exchange and therefore also promise to level the traditional hierarchy of writer over reader, teacher over student. We have said that this does more than reaffirm the ideal equality of American subjects. It constructs that equality by seducing each reader into becoming Whitman's ideal lover and counterpart. The question to be raised here is whether Whitman's construction allows for the community of differences that a liberal democracy presumes or whether (in the spirit of Tocqueville's critique) it imagines democracy as a cloning process in which citizens all look suspiciously like the ideal Whitman.

Students should consider the contradiction between Whitman's apparent invitation to equality and his assumption that equality, diversity, and ultimately Americanness are embodied in him. They should ask why Whitman's disavowal of conflict in his "unfinished" pieces seems to legitimate competing political "misreadings." What does it mean for Whitman to love the American ideal by loving his ideal self, which he offers as our model too? Like Narcissus, Whitman is in love with his mirror image repeated by the reader, who has been seduced into staring back from the other side of the poems. Are Whitman's open spaces the emptiness that provides the site of real dialogue with an equal counterpart? Or are they the glassy and predictable surfaces already informed by a master poet who leaves room enough only to repeat himself and for whom equality can only mean an identity with his own infinite self, an equality that disavows any differences?

The threat of class and other social divisions, which our students probably take for granted, is so unspeakable that Whitman enthralls us in order to overcome all differences, perhaps even the ones that his ideal liberal democracy and market thrive on. On the one hand, in *Democratic Vistas* he endorses John Stuart Mill's definition of democracy as a polity with varied character and full play of differences (Van Doren 317). But, on the other hand, differences represent obstacles to be overcome by one equalizing force that Whitman in his poems calls love or sex and in *Democratic Vistas* calls the "tremendous Idea" of the true nationality, "melting everything else with resistless heat, and solving all lesser and definite distinctions in vast, indefinite spiritual, emotional power" (324). Why does Whitman assume that "distinctions" must be "solved," as if they were problems? And even if we grant that some solution or mediation is in order, what does it mean for democratic practice to equalize by "melting everything else with resistless heat"? Whitman's ardor may be burning up the very thing he celebrates, just as his generosity threatens to monopolize his free-market ideal, unless, of course, what he celebrates is only himself, the ideal American whom we can become if we but let him love each of us.

With resistless heat is precisely how Whitman comes on to his reader in "Song of Myself." He is the hottest item imaginable; we seem to enact an exchange between free and equal partners, but we cannot refuse him. How can we, when he knows that our desires are infinite (Lockean) and promises to respond to them all (à la Rousseau). Students should recognize his appeal as a seduction. We are free to look away, and some readers manage to escape him through their indifference; but those of us who hold on to the book are held in turn by Whitman's pledge that to know him, to be him, is to know and be our best possible selves. From now on the differences between curiosity and vanity, interest in others and self-interest, and ultimately between democracy and imperialism begin to blur.

Years after the Mexican War, which annexed half of Mexico's territory to the United States, and right after the Spanish-American War, known to Cubans as their War of Independence, the Uruguayan José Enrique Rodó expressed a collective worry about one thing leading to another.

> As fast as the utilitarian genius of that nation takes on a more defined character, . . . so increases the impatience of its sons to spread it abroad

166 THE BARD OF BOTH AMERICAS

by propaganda, and think it predestined for all humanity. Today they openly aspire to the primacy of the world's civilization, the direction of its ideas, and think themselves the forerunners of all culture that is to prevail. (120–21).

Passages from Whitman's *Democratic Vistas* of 1871 sound as if they were among Rodó's sources:

When the present century closes, . . . The Pacific will be ours, and the Atlantic mainly ours. There will be daily electric communication with every part of the globe. What an age! what a land! Where else-where, one so great? The individuality of one nation must then, as always, lead the world. Can there be any doubt who the leader ought to be? (Van Doren 369)

Borges's suggestion that we compare Whitman's intimacy with the tone of other poets was meant to illustrate that, unlike traditional bards, Whitman does not take the poet's superiority for granted. Whitman knows he has to conquer that advantage every time he asks, or even demands, permission to represent each of his readers. Instead of assuming that he can legitimately be his readers' collective voice by virtue of his superior sensitivity, Whitman reconstructs the bard's legitimacy by having each individual reader enlist him for the role. But he knows in advance that he can overcome us by the brute force of his love. I have said before that Whitman slyly begins by offering himself instead of claiming someone else's love; then he continues with a calculated modesty. His thoughts are not "original," he says: "If they are not yours as much as mine they are nothing, or next to nothing" ("Song of Myself," sec. 17). Later he will add more aggressively: "All this I swallow . . . it becomes mine" (sec. 33); and "I have embraced you, and henceforth possess you to myself" (sec. 40). This direct appeal is hard to resist because his self-importance is not exclusive; it's contagious. By identifying the authorial voice with the overwhelmed interlocutor, the reader cannot help enjoying some of Whitman's megalomania as if it reflected on the power of the silent partner.

José Martí responded to Whitman's erotic power despite the hint that persuasion bordered on coercion. But something about Martí's admiring language confesses his own powerlessness to refuse and a potential fear that here only heightens the awe. Whitman's poetry sometimes "sounds like a stolen kiss, *like a rape*, like the snapping of a dried-out parchment in the sun . . . his verses . . . gallop on devouring the land; at times they neigh eagerly like lustful stallions; at times covered with lather, they trample clouds with their hoofs . . ." (14–15, my emphasis). Whitman's seduction, in other words, makes real dialogue unnecessary, but it does acknowledge the poet's dependence on the reader, just as a rapist needs a partner even though he is not performing an act of love.

When we allow Whitman to give himself to us, he not only guarantees his own returns; he also seduces us into denying the value of any will but his. While the assaults, or appeals, are multiple, they are framed by the enactment of an ideal democracy in which equality is reduced to identity. If each participant identifies with the poet, we repeat at the level of political subjects the same equality that the free market affords by being available to each citizen. What contradiction can there be here between Lockean equal economic opportunity and Rousseauean equal political participation or between United States interests and South American liberty?

CONTRIBUTORS AND SURVEY PARTICIPANTS

The generous and perceptive insights provided by these respondents to the MLA's request for information on teaching *Leaves of Grass* have contributed significantly to the creation of this volume.

Robert E. Abrams, University of Washington; Gay Wilson Allen, New York University (retired); Antler, Milwaukee, Wisconsin; Denise T. Askin, Saint Anselm College; Harold Aspiz, California State University, Long Beach; Roger Asselineau, Université de Paris-Sorbonne (retired); David Baldwin, Hartwick College; W. T. Bandy, Vanderbilt University (retired); Calvin Bedient, University of California, Los Angeles; Martin Bidney, State University of New York, Binghamton; Stephen A. Black, Simon Fraser University; Harold W. Blodgett, Union College, New York (retired); Maria Clara Bonetti Paro, Faculdade de Filosofia, Ciências e Letras Santana, São Paulo; William K. Bottorff, University of Toledo; Paul A. Bové, University of Pittsburgh; Lawrence Buell, Oberlin College; E. Fred Carlisle, Miami University, Ohio; Lorelei Cederstrom, Brandon University; Sherry Ceniza, University of Iowa; V. K. Chari, Carleton University; Edward Chielens, Henry Ford Community College; Angelo Costanzo, Shippensburg University; Robert Creeley, State University of New York, Buffalo; Susan Day Dean, Bryn Mawr College; Lynn Dickerson, University of Richmond; Martin K. Doudna, University of Hawaii, Hilo; James P. Dougherty, University of Notre Dame; Victor A. Doyno, State University of New York, Buffalo; Margaret H. Duggar, Chicago State University; Walter H. Eitner, Kansas State University; Betsy Erkkila, University of Pennsylvania; Robin Riley Fast, Emerson College; Ed Folsom, University of Iowa; Florence B. Freedman, Hunter College, City University of New York (retired); Roberts W. French, University of Massachusetts, Amherst; John J. Gatta, Jr., University of Connecticut, Storrs; Scott Giantvalley, California State University, Dominguez Hills; Allen Ginsberg, New York, New York; Samuel B. Girgus, University of New Mexico; Arthur Golden, City College, City University of New York; Alan C. Golding, University of Mississippi; Barry K. Grant, Brock University; Dorothy M-T. Gregory, Princeton University; Edward F. Grier, University of Kansas; Charles S. Grippi, Suffolk County Community College; Huck Gutman, University of Vermont; Donald Hall, Danbury, New Hampshire; Alan Helms, University of Massachusetts, Boston; Milton Hindus, Brandeis University; C. Carroll Hollis, University of North Carolina, Chapel Hill (retired); Robin P. Hoople, University of Manitoba; George B. Hutchinson, University of Tennessee, Knoxville; Matthew F. Ignoffo, United States Military Academy Preparatory School; John Lee Jellicorse, University of North Carolina, Greensboro; Diane Kepner, Minneapolis, Minnesota; M. Jimmie Killingsworth, Texas A&M University; George Klawitter, Viterbo College; Maurice Kramer, Brooklyn College, City University of New York; Joann P. Krieg, Hofstra University; David Kuebrich, George Mason University; Earle Labor, Centenary College of Louisiana; Hank Lazer, University of Alabama, Tuscaloosa; Joe Lawrence Lembo, San Francisco, California; Denise Levertov, Tufts University; Herbert J. Levine, Franklin and Marshall College; Jerome Loving, Texas A&M University; William G. Lulloff, North High School, Eau Claire, Wisconsin; Janet Macaulay, The Webb Schools, Claremont, California; Ivan Marki, Hamilton College; Robert K. Martin, Concordia University, Loyola Campus; John B. Mason, Western Washington University; Eugene J. McNamara, University of Windsor; Diane Middlebrook, Stanford University; James E. Miller, Jr., University of Chicago; Joel Myerson, University of South Carolina, Columbia; Howard Nelson, Cayuga Community College; Marco A. Portales, Texas Southmost College; Kenneth M. Price, Texas A&M University; Dennis K. Renner, Hope College; Robert T. Rhode, Northern Kentucky University; Louise M. Rosenblatt, New York University; Frederik L. Rusch, John Jay College, City University of New York; Robert J. Scholnick, College of William and Mary; Alan Shucard, University of Wisconsin, Parkside; William H. Shurr, University of Tennessee, Knoxville; John R. Snyder, University of Houston, Clear Lake; Doris Sommer, Amherst College; Sherry Southard, East Carolina University; William Stafford, Lewis and Clark College (retired); Rolf Kristian Stang, New York, New York; Donald Barlow Stauffer, State University of New York, Albany; James T. F. Tanner, North Texas State University; Estelle W. Taylor, Howard University; M. Wynn Thomas, University of Wales at Swansea; George Y. Trail, University of Houston, Downtown; Helen Vendler, Harvard University; Randall H. Waldron, Ohio Wesleyan University; John S. Wannamaker, Drake University; James Perrin Warren, Washington and Lee University; Edward M. Wheat, University of Southern Mississippi; William White, Oakland University (retired); Richard Wilbur, Smith College (retired); John R. Willingham, University of Kansas; James Woodress, University of California, Davis; Arthur Wrobel, University of Kentucky.

WORKS CITED

Editions of *Leaves of Grass*

Allen, Gay Wilson, ed. *Walt Whitman:* Leaves of Grass. New York: Signet–NAL, 1955.

Blodgett, Harold W., and Sculley Bradley, eds. Leaves of Grass: *Comprehensive Reader's Edition*. New York: New York UP, 1965. (Abbrev. *LG*.)

Bradley, Sculley, and Harold W. Blodgett, eds. Leaves of Grass: *A Norton Critical Edition*. New York: Norton, 1973.

Bradley, Sculley, Harold W. Blodgett, Arthur Golden, and William White, eds. Leaves of Grass: *A Textual Variorum of the Printed Poems*. 3 vols. New York: New York UP, 1980.

Bridgman, Richard, ed. Leaves of Grass: *A Facsimile of the First Edition*. San Francisco: Chandler, 1968.

Buell, Lawrence, ed. Leaves of Grass *and Selected Prose*. New York: Modern Library–Random, 1981.

Cowley, Malcolm, ed. *Walt Whitman's* Leaves of Grass: *The First (1855) Edition*. New York: Viking, 1959.

Kaplan, Justin, ed. *Walt Whitman: Complete Poetry and Collected Prose*. New York: Library of America, 1982.

Miller, James E., Jr., ed. *Walt Whitman: Complete Poetry and Selected Prose*. Riverside Edition. Boston: Houghton, 1959.

Murphy, Francis, ed. *Walt Whitman: The Complete Poems*. Harmondsworth, Eng.: Penguin, 1975.

Pearce, Roy Harvey, ed. Leaves of Grass *by Walt Whitman: Facsimile Edition of the 1860 Text*. Ithaca: Great Seal–Cornell UP, 1961.

Van Doren, Mark, ed. *The Portable Walt Whitman*. Rev. Malcolm Cowley. New York: Viking, 1973.

Books and Articles

Aaron, Daniel. *The Unwritten War: American Writers and the Civil War*. New York: Knopf, 1973.

Alcoff, Linda. "Cultural Feminism versus Post-Structuralism: The Identity Crisis in Feminist Theory." *Signs* 13 (1988): 405–36.

Alegría, Fernando. *Walt Whitman en Hispanòamérica*. Colección Studium 5 Mexico City: Ediciones Studium, 1954.

Allen, Gay Wilson. *American Prosody*. New York: American Book, 1935.

———. "Biblical Analogies for Walt Whitman's Prosody." *Revue Anglo-Américaine* 10 (1933): 490–507.

———. *The New Walt Whitman Handbook*. New York: New York UP, 1975. Rpt., with a new introduction and selected bibliography. New York: New York UP, 1986.

———. *A Reader's Guide to Walt Whitman*. New York: Farrar, 1970.

———. *The Solitary Singer: A Critical Biography of Walt Whitman*. New York: New York UP, 1955. Rev. ed., 1967. Rpt., with a new preface. Chicago: U of Chicago P, 1985.

———. *Walt Whitman*. Rev. ed. Detroit: Wayne State UP, 1969.

———, ed. *Walt Whitman Abroad: Critical Essays from Germany, France, Scandinavia, Russia, Italy, Spain and Latin America, Israel, Japan, and India*. Syracuse: Syracuse UP, 1955.

Allen, Gay Wilson, and Charles T. Davis, eds. *Walt Whitman's Poems: Selections with Critical Aids*. New York: New York UP, 1955.

Anderson, Quentin. *The Imperial Self: An Essay in American Literary and Cultural History*. New York: Knopf, 1971.

———. "Whitman's New Man." *Walt Whitman's Autograph Revision of the Analysis of* Leaves of Grass *(For Dr. R. M. Bucke's Walt Whitman)*. Ed. Stephen Railton. New York: New York UP, 1974. 11–52.

Armistead, J. M. "Ending with Whitman." *Journal of English Teaching Techniques* 7 (1974): 14–21.

Arvin, Newton. *Whitman*. New York: Macmillan, 1938.

Aspiz, Harold. *Walt Whitman and the Body Beautiful*. Urbana: U of Illinois P, 1980.

Asselineau, Roger. *The Evolution of Walt Whitman: The Creation of a Book*. Cambridge: Belknap–Harvard UP, 1962.

———. *The Evolution of Walt Whitman: The Creation of a Personality*. Cambridge: Belknap–Harvard UP, 1960.

———. "Walt Whitman." *Eight American Authors: A Review of Research and Criticism*. Ed. James Woodress. Rev. ed. New York: Norton, 1971. 225–72.

Asselineau, Roger, and William White, eds. *Walt Whitman in Europe Today: A Collection of Essays*. Supp. to the *Walt Whitman Review*. Detroit: Wayne State UP, 1972.

Austin, John Langshaw. *How to Do Things with Words*. Cambridge: Harvard UP, 1962.

Bachelard, Gaston. *On Poetic Imagination and Reverie*. Trans. and ed. Colette Gaudin. Indianapolis: Bobbs, 1971.

———. *The Poetics of Space*. Trans. Maria Jolas. New York: Orion, 1964.

———. *The Poetics of Reverie: Childhood, Language, and the Cosmos*. Trans. Daniel Russell. New York: Orion, 1969.

———. *The Psychoanalysis of Fire*. Trans. Alan C. M. Ross. Boston: Beacon, 1964.

———. *The Right to Dream*. Trans. J. A. Underwood. New York: Grossman, 1971.

Bakhtin, M. M. *The Dialogic Imagination*. Ed. Michael Holquist. Austin: U of Texas P, 1981.

Barker-Benfield, G. J. *The Horrors of the Half-Known Life: Male Attitudes toward Women and Sexuality in Nineteenth-Century America*. New York: Harper, 1976.

Barthes, Roland. *The Pleasure of the Text*. Trans. Richard Howard. New York: Hill, 1975.

———. *S/Z*. Trans. Richard Miller. New York: Hill, 1974.

Bartlett, Irving H. *The American Mind in the Mid-Nineteenth Century*. New York: Crowell, 1967.

Bauerlein, Mark. "The Written Orator in 'Song of Myself': A Recent Trend in Whitman Criticism." *Walt Whitman Quarterly Review* 3 (1986): 1–14.

Baym, Nina, et al., eds. *The Norton Anthology of American Literature*. 3rd ed. Vol 1. New York: Norton, 1989.

Beaver, Harold. "Homosexual Signs." *Critical Inquiry* 8 (1981): 99–119.

Beaver, Joseph. *Walt Whitman: Poet of Science*. New York: King's Crown, 1951.

Benveniste, Emile. *Problems in General Linguistics*. Trans. Mary Elizabeth Meek. Coral Gables: U of Miami P, 1971.

Bercovitch, Sacvan. *The American Jeremiad*. Madison: U of Wisconsin P, 1978.

———. *The Puritan Origins of the American Self*. New Haven: Yale UP, 1975.

Bergman, Herbert. "Ezra Pound and Walt Whitman." *American Literature* 27 (1955): 56–61.

Berthold, Dennis, and Kenneth M. Price, eds. *Dear Brother Walt: The Letters of Thomas Jefferson Whitman*. Kent: Kent State UP, 1984.

Bickman, Martin. *The Unsounded Centre: Jungian Studies in American Romanticism*. Chapel Hill: U of North Carolina P, 1980.

Bidney, Martin. "Structures of Perception in Blake and Whitman: Creative Contraries, Cosmic Body, Fourfold Vision." *ESQ: A Journal of the American Renaissance* 28 (1982): 36–47.

Black, Stephen A. *Whitman's Journeys into Chaos: A Psychoanalytic Study of the Poetic Process*. Princeton: Princeton UP, 1975.

Blake, William. *The Complete Poetry and Prose of William Blake*. Rev. ed. Ed. David V. Erdman. Commentary by Harold Bloom. Berkeley: U of California P, 1982.

Blodgett, Harold W. "*Democratic Vistas*—One Hundred Years After." *Geschichte und Gesellschaft in der amerikanischen Literatur*. Ed. Karl Schubert and Ursula Müller-Richter. Heidelberg: Quelle, 1975. 114–31.

———. "Teaching 'Song of Myself.'" *Emerson Society Quarterly* 22 (1961): 2–3.

———. *Walt Whitman in England*. Ithaca: Cornell UP, 1934.

Bloom, Harold. *Agon: Towards a Theory of Revisionism*. New York: Oxford UP, 1982.

———. *A Map of Misreading*. New York: Oxford UP, 1975.

———. Rev. of *Walt Whitman: The Making of the Poet*, by Paul Zweig. *New York Review of Books* 26 Apr. 1984: 3–7.

Bly, Robert. "What Whitman Did Not Give Us." Perlman, Folsom, and Campion 321–34.

Borges, Jorge Luis. "La naderia de la personalidad." *Inquisiciones.* Buenos Aires: Proa, 1925. 84–95.

———. "Note on Walt Whitman." *Other Inquisitions: 1937–1952.* Trans. Ruth L. C. Simms. Austin: U of Texas P, 1964. 66–72.

———. *Selected Poems, 1923–1967.* Ed. Norman Thomas Di Giovanni. New York: Delta-Dell, 1973.

Boswell, John. *Christianity, Social Tolerance, and Homosexuality.* Chicago: U of Chicago P, 1980.

Bowers, Fredson, ed. *Whitman's Manuscripts:* Leaves of Grass *(1860), A Parallel Text.* Chicago: U of Chicago P, 1955.

Bradley, Sculley. "The Fundamental Metrical Principle in Whitman's Poetry." *American Literature* 10 (1939): 437–59. Rpt. in Cady and Budd 49–71.

———. "The Teaching of Whitman." *College English* 23 (1962): 618–22.

Brasher, Thomas L. *Whitman as Editor of the* Brooklyn Daily Eagle. Detroit: Wayne State UP, 1970.

Broderick, John C., ed. *Whitman the Poet: Materials for Study.* Belmont: Wadsworth, 1962.

Brooks, Van Wyck. "On Creating a Usable Past." *Dial* 11 Apr. 1918: 337–41.

———. *The Times of Melville and Whitman.* New York: Dutton, 1947.

Brown, Calvin S. *Tones into Words: Musical Compositions as Subjects of Poetry.* Athens: U of Georgia P, 1953.

Brown, Gillian, and George Yule. *Discourse Analysis.* Cambridge: Cambridge UP, 1983.

Brown, Norman O. *Life against Death: The Psychoanalytical Meaning of History.* Middletown: Wesleyan UP, 1959.

Bruffee, Kenneth. "Social Construction, Language, and the Authority of Knowledge: A Bibliographical Essay." *College English* 48 (1986): 773–90.

Bucke, Richard Maurice. *Cosmic Consciousness: A Study in the Evolution of the Human Mind.* 1901. New York: Causeway Books, 1974.

Buell, Lawrence. *Literary Transcendentalism: Style and Vision in the American Renaissance.* Ithaca: Cornell UP, 1973.

Burgess, Anthony. "The Answerer." *Urgent Copy.* By Burgess. New York: Norton, 1968. 48–53. Rpt. in Bradley and Blodgett 972–76.

Burke, Kenneth. *A Grammar of Motives.* 1945. Berkeley: U of California P, 1969.

———. "Policy Made Personal: Whitman's Verse and Prose-Salient Traits." Hindus, Leaves 74–108.

Cady, Edwin H., and Louis J. Budd, eds. *On Whitman: The Best from American Literature.* Durham: Duke UP, 1987.

Cady, Joseph. "*Drum-Taps* and Nineteenth-Century Male Homosexual Literature." Krieg 49–59.

Canby, Henry Seidel. *Walt Whitman: An American.* Boston: Houghton, 1943.

———. "Walt Whitman." Spiller et al. 1: 472–98.

Carlisle, E. Fred. *The Uncertain Self: Whitman's Drama of Identity.* East Lansing: Michigan State UP, 1973.

Cavitch, David. *My Soul and I: The Inner Life of Walt Whitman.* Boston: Beacon, 1985.

Chapnick, Howard, ed. *The Illustrated* Leaves of Grass, *by Walt Whitman.* New York: Madison Square, 1971.

Chari, V. K. *Whitman in the Light of Vedantic Mysticism: An Interpretation.* Lincoln: U of Nebraska P, 1964.

Charvat, William. *The Origins of American Critical Thought, 1810–1835.* Philadelphia: U of Pennsylvania P, 1936.

———. *The Profession of Authorship in America, 1800–1870.* Ed. Matthew J. Bruccoli. Columbus: Ohio State UP, 1968.

Chase, Richard. " 'Out of the Cradle' as a Romance." Lewis, *Presence* 52–71.

———. *Walt Whitman.* University of Minnesota Pamphlets on American Writers 9. Minneapolis: U of Minnesota P, 1961.

———. *Walt Whitman Reconsidered.* New York: Sloane, 1955.

Cherry, Conrad, ed. *God's New Israel: Religious Interpretations of American Destiny.* Englewood Cliffs: Prentice, 1971.

Claudel, Paul. *Cinq grandes odes; La cantate à trois voix.* Preface by Jean Grosjean. Paris: Gallimard, 1957.

Coffman, Stanley. " 'Crossing Brooklyn Ferry': A Note on the Catalogue Technique in Whitman's Poetry." *Modern Philology* 51 (1954): 225–32.

Consolo, Dominick P. ed. *Walt Whitman: "Out of the Cradle Endlessly Rocking."* Merrill Literary Casebook Series. Columbus: Merrill, 1971.

Coyle, William, ed. *The Poet and the President: Whitman's Lincoln Poems.* New York: Odyssey, 1962.

Crawley, Thomas Edward. *The Structure of* Leaves of Grass. Austin: U of Texas P, 1970.

Curti, Merle. *The Growth of American Thought.* 3rd ed. New York: Harper, 1964.

Davis, William C., ed. *Shadows of the Storm.* Vol. 1 of *The Image of War, 1861–1865.* Project of the National Historical Society. New York: Doubleday, 1981.

De Lauretis, Teresa. "Feminist Studies/Critical Studies: Issues, Terms, and Contexts." *Feminist Studies/Critical Studies.* Ed. De Lauretis. Bloomington: Indiana UP, 1986. 1–19.

D'Emilio, John, and Estelle B. Freedman. *Intimate Matters: A History of Sexuality in America.* New York: Harper, 1988.

Denny, Margaret, and William H. Gilman, eds. *The American Writer and the European Tradition.* Minneapolis: U of Minnesota P, 1950.

Derrida, Jacques. *Dissemination.* Trans. Barbara Johnson. Chicago: U of Chicago P, 1981.

———. *Of Grammatology.* Trans. Gayatri Chakravorty Spivak. Baltimore: Johns Hopkins UP, 1974.

Dickinson, Emily. *The Poems of Emily Dickinson.* 3 vols. Ed. Thomas H. Johnson. Cambridge: Belknap–Harvard UP, 1955.

Ditsky, John. " 'Retrievements out of the Night': Approaching Whitman through the 'Lilacs' Elegy." *Calamus: Walt Whitman Quarterly: International* 7 (1973): 28–37.

Douglas, Ann. *The Feminization of American Culture*. New York: Knopf, 1977.

Duffey, Bernard. *Poetry in America: Expression and Its Values in the Times of Bryant, Whitman, and Pound*. Durham: Duke UP, 1978.

Eby, Edwin Harold. *A Concordance of Walt Whitman's Leaves of Grass and Selected Prose Writings*. Seattle: U of Washington P, 1949–54. New York: Greenwood, 1969.

Edinger, Edward F. *Ego and Archetype: Individuation and the Religious Function of the Psyche*. New York: Putnam's, 1972.

Eliot, T. S. *The Use of Poetry and the Use of Criticism*. 1933. London: Faber, 1970.

Elliott, Robert C. *The Literary Persona*. Chicago: U of Chicago P, 1982.

Emerson, Ralph Waldo. *Essays and Lectures*. Ed. Joel Porte. New York: Library of America, 1983.

Engell, James, and David Perkins, eds. *Teaching Literature: What Is Needed Now*. Harvard English Studies 15. Cambridge: Harvard UP, 1988.

Erkkila, Betsy. *Walt Whitman among the French: Poet and Myth*. Princeton: Princeton UP, 1980.

———. *Whitman the Political Poet*. New York: Oxford UP, 1989.

Everson, William. *American Bard, by Walt Whitman: The Original Preface to Leaves of Grass*. New York: Viking, 1982.

Fabre, Michel. "Walt Whitman and the Rebel Poets: A Note on Whitman's Reputation among Radical Writers during the Depression." *Walt Whitman Review* 12 (1966): 88–93.

Faner, Robert D. "The Use of Primary Source Materials in Whitman Study." *Emerson Society Quarterly* 22 (1961): 10–12.

———. *Walt Whitman and Opera*. Philadelphia: U of Pennsylvania P, 1951.

Feidelson, Charles, Jr. *Symbolism and American Literature*. Chicago: U of Chicago P, 1953.

Folsom, Ed. "The Poets Respond: A Bibliographic Chronology." Perlman, Folsom, and Campion 359–81.

———. "The Poets Continue to Respond: More Citations of Whitman as Poetic Subject." *Walt Whitman Quarterly Review* 5 (1988): 35–40.

———, ed. "*This Heart's Geography's Map*": The Photographs of Walt Whitman. Spec. issue of *Walt Whitman Quarterly Review* 4.2, 3 (1986–87): 1–76.

———. "The Whitman Project: A Review Essay." *Philological Quarterly* 61 (1982): 369–94.

Forgie, George B. *Patricide in the House Divided: A Psychological Interpretation of Lincoln and His Age*. New York: Norton, 1979.

Foucault, Michel. "What Is an Author?" *Language, Counter-Memory, Practice*. By Foucault. Trans. Donald F. Bouchard and Sherry Simon. Ithaca: Cornell UP, 1977. 113–38.

Franco, Jean. *César Vallejo: The Dialectics of Poetry and Silence*. Cambridge: Cambridge UP, 1976.

Fredrickson, George M. *The Inner Civil War: Northern Intellectuals and the Crisis of the Union*. New York: Harper, 1965.

Freed, Richard. "Teaching Whitman to College Freshmen." *English Record* 1 (1978): 9–12.

French, Roberts W. "Whitman as Poetic Subject." *Walt Whitman Review* 26 (1980): 69–70.

Freud, Sigmund. "On Narcissism: An Introduction." 1914. *A General Selection from the Works of Sigmund Freud*. Ed. John Rickman. New York: Anchor-Doubleday, 1957. 104–23.

Fussell, Edwin S. *Frontier: American Literature and the American West*. Princeton: Princeton UP, 1965.

———. *Lucifer in Harness: American Meter, Metaphor, and Diction*. Princeton: Princeton UP, 1973.

Fussell, Paul, Jr. "Whitman's Curious Warble: Reminiscence and Reconciliation." Lewis, *Presence* 28–51.

Gabriel, Ralph Henry. *The Course of American Democratic Thought*. 2nd ed. New York: Ronald, 1956.

Gardner, Alexander. *Gardner's Photographic Sketch Book of the Civil War*. Washington: Philip, 1866. New York: Dover, 1959.

Gay, Peter. *The Bourgeois Experience: Victoria to Freud*. Vol. 1. *Education of the Senses*. New York: Oxford UP, 1984. Vol. 2. *The Tender Passion*. New York: Oxford UP, 1986.

Gelpi, Albert. *The Tenth Muse: The Psyche of the American Poet*. Cambridge: Harvard UP, 1975.

Gerber, John C. "Varied Approaches to 'When Lilacs Last in the Dooryard Bloom'd.' " *Reflections on High School English*. NDEA Institute Lectures 1965. Ed. Gary Tate. Tulsa: U of Tulsa, 1966. 214–30.

Giantvalley, Scott. *Walt Whitman, 1838–1939: A Reference Guide*. Boston: Hall, 1981.

———. "*Walt Whitman, 1838–1939: A Reference Guide*: Additional Annotations." *Walt Whitman Quarterly Review* 4 (1986): 24–40.

Gide, André. *Journal 1889–1939*. Paris: Pléiade-Gallimard, 1940.

Gilbert, Sandra M. "The American Sexual Poetics of Walt Whitman and Emily Dickinson." *Reconstructing American Literary History*. Ed. Sacvan Bercovitch. Cambridge: Harvard UP, 1986. 123–54.

Gilbert, Sandra M., and Susan Gubar. *The Madwoman in the Attic: The Woman Writer and the Nineteenth-Century Literary Imagination*. New Haven: Yale UP, 1979.

Golden, Arthur, ed. *Walt Whitman: A Collection of Criticism*. Contemporary Studies in Literature. New York: McGraw, 1974.

———., ed. *Walt Whitman's Blue Book: The 1860–61 Leaves of Grass Containing His Manuscript Additions and Revisions*. 2 vols. New York: New York Public Library, 1968.

González de la Garza, Mauricio. *Walt Whitman: Racista, imperialista, antimexicano*. Mexico: Colección Malaga, 1971.

Gross, Harvey. *Sound and Form in Modern Poetry: A Study of Prosody from Thomas Hardy to Robert Lowell*. Ann Arbor: U of Michigan P, 1964.

Guillén, Claudio. *Literature as System: Essays toward the Theory of Literary History.* Princeton: Princeton UP, 1971.

Gura, Philip F., and Joel Myerson, eds. *Critical Essays on American Transcendentalism.* Boston: Hall, 1982.

Gutman, Herbert G. *Work, Culture, and Society in Industrializing America: Essays in American Working-Class and Social History.* New York: Knopf, 1976.

Harding, Brian. *American Literature in Context, II: 1830–1865.* New York: Methuen, 1982.

Harris, Elizabeth. "In Defense of the Liberal-Arts Approach to Technical Writing." *College English* 44 (1982): 628–36.

Helms, Alan. " 'Hints . . . Faint Clews and Indirections': Whitman's Homosexual Disguises." Krieg 61–67.

Hindus, Milton, ed. Leaves of Grass *One Hundred Years After: Essays by William Carlos Williams, Richard Chase, Leslie A. Fiedler, Kenneth Burke, David Daiches, and J. Middleton Murry.* Stanford: Stanford UP, 1955.

———., ed. *Walt Whitman: The Critical Heritage.* London: Routledge, 1971.

Hite, Shere. *The Hite Report on Male Sexuality.* New York: Knopf, 1981.

Hollis, C. Carroll. "Is There a Text in This *Grass?*" *Walt Whitman Quarterly Review* 3 (1986): 15–22.

———. *Language and Style in* Leaves of Grass. Baton Rouge: Louisiana State UP, 1983.

———. "Rhetoric, Elocution, and Voice in *Leaves of Grass.*" *Walt Whitman Quarterly Review* 2 (1984): 1–21.

Holloway, Emory. *Whitman: An Interpretation in Narrative.* New York: Knopf, 1926.

Hoople, Robin C. " 'Chants Democratic and Native American': A Neglected Sequence in the Growth of *Leaves of Grass.*" *American Literature* 42 (1970): 181–96. Rpt. in Cady and Budd 145–60.

Howe, Irving. *The American Newness: Culture and Politics in the Age of Emerson.* Cambridge: Harvard UP, 1986.

Hubbell, Jay B. *Who Are the Major American Writers? A Study of the Changing Literary Canon.* Durham: Duke UP, 1972.

Hutchinson, George B. *The Ecstatic Whitman: Literary Shamanism and the Crisis of the Union.* Columbus: Ohio State UP, 1986.

Hyde, Lewis. *The Gift: Imagination and the Erotic Life of Property.* New York: Random, 1983.

Irwin, John T. *American Hieroglyphics: The Symbol of the Egyptian Hieroglyphics in the American Renaissance.* New Haven: Yale UP, 1980.

Jackson, Carl T. *The Oriental Religions and American Thought: Nineteenth-Century Explorations.* Westport: Greenwood, 1981.

James, William. *The Varieties of Religious Experience.* London: Longsman, 1902. New York: NAL, 1958.

Jannacone, Pasquale. *Walt Whitman's Poetry and the Evolution of Rhythmic Forms and Walt Whitman's Thought and Art.* Trans. Peter Mitilineos. Washington: NCR Microcard Editions, 1973.

Jarrell, Randall. "Walt Whitman: He Had His Nerve." *Kenyon Review* 14 (1952): 63–79. Rpt. as "Some Lines from Whitman." *Poetry and the Age.* By Jarrell. New York: Knopf, 1953. 101–20.

Judine, Sister M. "Whitman and Dickinson: Implications for School Programs." *The Teacher and American Literature: Papers Presented at the 1964 Convention of the National Council of Teachers of English.* Ed. Lewis Leary. Champaign: NCTE, 1965. 128–33.

Jung, Carl Gustav. *C. G. Jung: Psychological Reflections: A New Anthology of His Writings 1905–1961.* Ed. Jolande Jacobi with R. F. C. Hull. Princeton: Princeton UP, 1970.

Kaplan, Justin. *Walt Whitman: A Life.* New York: Simon, 1980.

Kasson, John F. *Civilizing the Machine: Technology and Republican Values in America, 1776–1900.* New York: Grossman, 1976.

Katz, Sandra L. "A Reconsideration of Walt Whitman: A Teaching Approach." *Walt Whitman Review* 27 (1981): 70–74.

Kaufman, Allen. *Capitalism, Slavery, and Republican Values: Antebellum Political Economists, 1819–1848.* Austin: U of Texas P, 1982.

Kazin, Alfred. *An American Procession: The Major American Writers from 1830 to 1930—The Crucial Century.* New York: Knopf, 1984.

Kern, Alexander. "The Rise of Transcendentalism, 1815–1860." *Transitions in American Literary History.* Ed. Harry Hayden Clark. Durham: Duke UP, 1953. 245–314.

Khlebnikov, Velimir. *The King of Time: Selected Writings of the Russian Futurian.* Trans. Paul Schmidt. Ed. Charlotte Douglas. Cambridge: Harvard UP, 1985.

Killingsworth, Myrth Jimmie. "Whitman's Love-Spendings." *Walt Whitman Review* 26 (1980): 145–53.

——. *Whitman's Poetry of the Body: Sexuality, Politics, and the Text.* Chapel Hill: U of North Carolina P, 1989.

Kinnell, Galway. "Whitman's Indicative Words." Perlman, Folsom, and Campion 215–27.

Kolodny, Annette. *The Lay of the Land: Metaphor as Experience and History in American Life and Letters.* Chapel Hill: U of North Carolina P, 1975.

Krieg, Joann P., ed. *Walt Whitman: Here and Now.* Westport: Greenwood, 1985.

Kristeva, Julia. *Revolution in Poetic Language.* Trans. Margaret Waller. New York: Columbia UP, 1984.

Kuebrich, David. *Minor Prophecy: Walt Whitman's New American Religion.* Bloomington: Indiana UP, 1989.

Kummings, Donald D. "Walt Whitman Bibliographies: A Chronological Listing, 1897–1982." *Walt Whitman Quarterly Review* 1 (1984): 38–45.

——. *Walt Whitman, 1940–1975: A Reference Guide.* Boston: Hall, 1982.

Lauter, Paul, ed. *Reconstructing American Literature: Courses, Syllabi, Issues.* Old Westbury: Feminist, 1983.

Lawrence, D. H. "Whitman." *Studies in Classic American Literature.* By Lawrence. New York: Seltzer, 1923. New York: Anchor-Doubleday, 1951. 174–91.

Lease, Benjamin. *Anglo-American Encounters: England and the Rise of American Literature.* New York: Cambridge UP, 1981.

Lewis, R. W. B. *The American Adam: Innocence, Tragedy and Tradition in the Nineteenth Century.* Chicago: U of Chicago P, 1955.

———., ed. *The Presence of Walt Whitman: Selected Papers from the English Institute.* New York: Columbia UP, 1962.

Loving, Jerome M., ed. *Civil War Letters of George Washington Whitman.* Durham: Duke UP, 1975.

———. *Emerson, Whitman, and the American Muse.* Chapel Hill: U of North Carolina P, 1982.

———. "Walt Whitman." *Columbia Literary History of the United States.* Ed. Emory Elliott. New York: Columbia UP, 1988. 448–62.

———. "Walt Whitman." *The Transcendentalists: A Review of Research and Criticism.* Ed. Joel Myerson. New York: MLA, 1984. 375–83.

Lowance, Mason I. *The Language of Canaan: Metaphor and Symbol in New England from the Puritans to the Transcendentalists.* Cambridge: Harvard UP, 1980.

Lozynsky, Artem, ed. *The Letters of Dr. Richard Maurice Bucke to Walt Whitman.* Detroit: Wayne State UP, 1977.

Lucas, Dolores Dyer. *Emily Dickinson and Riddle.* De Kalb: Northern Illinois UP, 1969.

Lynch, Michael. " 'Here Is Adhesiveness': From Friendship to Homosexuality." *Victorian Studies* 29 (1985): 67–96.

Lynch, Robert, and Thomas Swanzey. *The Example of Science: An Anthology for College Composition.* Englewood Cliffs: Prentice, 1981.

Lynen, John F. *The Design of the Present: Essays on Time and Form in American Literature.* New Haven: Yale UP, 1969.

Lyons, John. *Semantics.* 2 vols. Cambridge: Cambridge UP, 1977.

Macpherson, C. B. *The Life and Times of Liberal Democracy.* New York: Oxford UP, 1977.

Malone, Edward A. "Whitman as Poetic Subject: Additional Citations." *Walt Whitman Quarterly Review* 5 (1988): 34–35.

Marki, Ivan. *The Trial of the Poet: An Interpretation of the First Edition of Leaves of Grass.* New York: Columbia UP, 1976.

Marks, Elaine, and Isabelle de Courtivron, eds. *New French Feminisms.* New York: Schocken, 1981.

Martí, José. "Walt Whitman." *Martí on the U.S.A.* Trans. Luis Baralt. Carbondale: Southern Illinois UP, 1966. 3–16.

Martin, Jay. *Harvests of Change: American Literature, 1865–1914.* Englewood Cliffs: Prentice, 1967.

Martin, Robert K. *The Homosexual Tradition in American Poetry.* Austin: U of Texas P, 1979.

Marx, Leo. "*Democratic Vistas:* Notes for a Discussion." *Emerson Society Quarterly* 22 (1961): 12–15.

────. *The Machine in the Garden: Technology and the Pastoral Ideal in America.* New York: Oxford UP, 1964.

────. *The Pilot and the Passenger: Essays on Literature, Technology, and Culture in the United States.* New York: Oxford UP, 1988.

Mason, John B. "Questions and Answers in Whitman's 'Confab.'" *American Literature* 51 (1980): 493–506.

────. "Walt Whitman's Catalogues: Rhetorical Means for Two Journeys in 'Song of Myself.'" *American Literature* 45 (1973): 33–49. Rpt. in Cady and Budd 187–202.

Masters, Edgar Lee. *Invisible Landscapes.* New York: Macmillan, 1935.

Mathews, Mitford M. *A Dictionary of Americanisms on Historical Principles.* 2 vols. Chicago: U of Chicago P, 1951.

Matthiessen, F. O. *American Renaissance: Art and Expression in the Age of Emerson and Whitman.* New York: Oxford UP, 1941.

Mayakovsky, Vladimir. *The Bedbug and Selected Poetry.* Trans. Max Hayward and George Reavey. Ed. Patricia Blake. Cleveland: World, 1960.

McElderry, Bruce R., Jr. "Personae in Whitman (1855–1860)." *American Transcendental Quarterly* 12 (1971): 25–32.

McMichael, George, gen. ed. *Anthology of American Literature.* 4th ed. 2 vols. New York: Macmillan, 1989.

Mead, George H. *Mind, Self and Society from the Standpoint of the Social Behaviorist.* Ed. Charles W. Morris. Chicago: U of Chicago P, 1934.

Michaels, Walter Benn, and Donald E. Pease, eds. *The American Renaissance Reconsidered: Selected Papers from the English Institute, 1982–83.* Baltimore: Johns Hopkins UP, 1985.

Middlebrook, Diane Wood. *Walt Whitman and Wallace Stevens.* Ithaca and London: Cornell UP, 1974.

Miller, Carolyn. "A Humanistic Rationale for Technical Writing." *College English* 40 (1979): 610–17.

Miller, Douglas T. *The Birth of Modern America, 1820–1850.* New York: Pegasus, 1970.

Miller, Edwin Haviland, ed. *The Artistic Legacy of Walt Whitman: A Tribute to Gay Wilson Allen.* New York: New York UP, 1970.

────., ed. *A Century of Whitman Criticism.* Bloomington: Indiana UP, 1969.

────. *Walt Whitman's Poetry: A Psychological Journey.* Boston: Houghton, 1968.

────. *Walt Whitman's "Song of Myself": A Mosaic of Interpretations.* Iowa City: U of Iowa P, 1989.

Miller, James E., Jr. *The American Quest for a Supreme Fiction: Whitman's Legacy in the Personal Epic.* Chicago: U of Chicago P, 1979.

────. *A Critical Guide to* Leaves of Grass. Chicago: U of Chicago P, 1957.

────. "The Mysticism of Whitman: Suggestions for a Seminar Discussion." *Emerson Society Quarterly* 22 (1961): 15–18.

────. *Walt Whitman.* New York: Twayne, 1962.

————. "Walt Whitman's Omnisexual Vision." *The Chief Glory of Every People: Essays on Classic American Writers*. Ed. Matthew J. Bruccoli. Carbondale: Southern Illinois UP, 1973. 231–59.

————, ed. *Whitman's "Song of Myself": Origin, Growth, Meaning*. New York: Dodd, 1964.

Miller, James E., Jr., Karl Shapiro, and Bernice Slote. *Start with the Sun: Studies in Cosmic Poetry*. Lincoln: U of Nebraska P, 1960.

Muccigrosso, Robert M. "Whitman and the Adolescent Mind." *English Journal* 57 (1968): 982–84.

Murphy, Francis, ed. *Walt Whitman: A Critical Anthology*. Baltimore: Penguin, 1969.

Musgrove, S[ydney]. *T. S. Eliot and Walt Whitman*. Wellington: New Zealand UP, 1952.

Myerson, Joel, ed. *The American Renaissance in New England*. Vol. 1 of *Dictionary of Literary Biography*. Detroit: Gale, 1978.

Nabokov, Vladimir. *Notes on Prosody; Abram Gannibal*. Princeton: Princeton UP, 1964.

Nagel, Paul C. *This Sacred Trust: American Nationality, 1798–1898*. New York: Oxford UP, 1971.

Nash, Roderick. *Wilderness and the American Mind*. New Haven: Yale UP, 1967.

Neilson, Kenneth P. *The World of Walt Whitman Music: A Bibliographical Study*. Hollis: Neilson, 1963.

Neruda, Pablo. *Canto general*. Buenos Aires: Losada, 1955.

————. "Comienzo por invocar a Walt Whitman." *Incitación al nixonicidio y alabanza de la revolución chilena*. Santiago: Editora Nacional Quimantu, 1973. 17–21.

————. *Selected Poems: A Bilingual Edition*. Ed. Nathaniel Tarn. New York: Delta-Dell, 1970.

————. "We Live in a Whitmanesque Age." *New York Times* 14 Apr. 1972: 37. Rpt. in Perlman, Folsom, and Campion 139–41.

Neumann, Erich. *Depth Psychology and a New Ethic*. Trans. Eugene Rolfe. New York: Putnam's, 1969.

Nye, Russel Blaine. *Society and Culture in America, 1830–1860*. New York: Harper, 1974.

Ong, Walter J. *The Barbarian Within*. New York: Macmillan, 1962.

Papini, Giovanni. "Walt Whitman." 1908. *Ritratti Stranieri 1908–1921*. Florence: Vallecchi, 1942. 199–239.

Parrington, Vernon Louis. *Main Currents in American Thought: An Interpretation of American Literature from the Beginnings to 1920*. 3 vols. New York: Harcourt, 1927–30.

Paz, Octavio. "Whitman, Poet of America." *The Bow and the Lyre*. By Paz. Trans. Ruth L. C. Simms. Texas Pan-American Series. Austin: U of Texas P, 1973. 271–74.

Pearce, Roy Harvey. *The Continuity of American Poetry*. Princeton: Princeton UP, 1961.

———., ed. *Whitman: A Collection of Critical Essays*. Englewood Cliffs: Prentice, 1962.

Pease, Donald E. *Visionary Compacts: American Renaissance Writings in Cultural Context*. Madison: U of Wisconsin P, 1987.

Peirce, Charles Sanders. "Some Consequences of Four Incapacities." *Pragmatism and Pragmaticism*. Vol. 5 of *Collected Papers*. Ed. Charles Hartshorne and Paul Weiss. Cambridge: Belknap–Harvard UP, 1965. 156–189.

Pennock, J. Roland. *Democratic Political Theory*. Princeton: Princeton UP, 1979.

Perkins, George, et al., eds. *The American Tradition in Literature*. 7th ed. 2 vols. New York: McGraw, 1990.

Perlman, Jim, Ed Folsom, and Dan Campion, eds. *Walt Whitman: The Measure of His Song*. Minneapolis: Holy Cow!, 1981.

Perry, Bliss. *Walt Whitman: His Life and Work*. Boston: Houghton, 1906.

Pound, Ezra. *Selected Poems of Ezra Pound*. New York: New Directions, 1957.

Pratt, Mary Louise. *Toward a Speech Act Theory of Literary Discourse*. Bloomington: Indiana UP, 1977.

Renner, Dennis K. "Walt Whitman's Religion of the Republic." Diss. U of Iowa, 1975.

Retamar, Roberto Fernández. "Caliban: Notes towards a Discussion of Culture in Our America." Trans. Lynn Garafola, David Arthur McMurray, and Robert Marquez. *Massachusetts Review* 15 (1974): 7–72.

Rexroth, Kenneth. "Walt Whitman." *Saturday Review* 3 Sept. 1966: 43. Rpt. in Bradley and Blodgett 976–79.

Reynolds, David S. *Beneath the American Renaissance: The Subversive Imagination in the Age of Emerson and Melville*. New York: Knopf, 1988.

Reynolds, Larry J. *European Revolutions and the American Literary Renaissance*. New Haven: Yale UP, 1988.

Richardson, Robert D. *Myth and Literature in the American Renaissance*. Bloomington: Indiana UP, 1978.

Richey, Russell E., and Donald G. Jones, eds. *American Civil Religion*. New York: Harper, 1974.

Rodó, José Enrique. *Ariel*. Trans. F. J. Stimson. Boston: Houghton, 1922.

Rubens, Philip M. "Technical and Scientific Writing and the Humanities." *Research in Technical Communication: A Bibliographic Sourcebook*. Ed. Michael G. Moran and Debra Journet. Westport: Greenwood, 1985. 3–23.

Rubin, Joseph Jay. *The Historic Whitman*. University Park: Pennsylvania State UP, 1973.

Salska, Agnieszka. *Walt Whitman and Emily Dickinson: Poetry of the Central Consciousness*. Philadelphia: U of Pennsylvania P, 1985.

Salzman, Jack, ed. *American Studies: An Annotated Bibliography*. 3 vols. Cambridge: Cambridge UP, 1986.

Sandburg, Carl. Introduction. *Leaves of Grass*. By Walt Whitman. Modern Library. New York: Boni, 1921. iii–xi.

Saunders, Henry Scholey. *Parodies on Walt Whitman*. New York: AMS, 1970.

Schiller, Andrew. "An Approach to Whitman's Metrics." *Emerson Society Quarterly* 22 (1961): 23–25.

Schwartz, Arthur. "The Each and All of Whitman's Verse." *Emerson Society Quarterly* 22 (1961): 25–26.

Schwartz, Jacob, and E. F. Hanaburgh, eds. *Manuscripts, Autograph Letters, First Editions, and Portraits of Walt Whitman Formerly the Property of the Late Dr. Richard Maurice Bucke*. New York: American Art Assn., Anderson Galleries, 1936.

Schyberg, Frederik. *Walt Whitman*. Trans. Evie Allison Allen. New York: Columbia UP, 1951.

Sealts, Merton M., Jr. "Melville and Whitman." *Melville Society Extracts* 50 (1982): 10–12.

Shively, Charley, ed. *Calamus Lovers: Walt Whitman's Working-Class Camerados*. San Francisco: Gay Sunshine, 1987.

Shucard, Alan. *American Poetry: The Puritans through Walt Whitman*. Boston: Twayne, 1988.

Shulman, Robert. *Social Criticism and Nineteenth-Century American Fictions*. Columbia: U of Missouri P, 1987.

Simon, Myron. " 'Self' in Whitman and Dickinson." *CEA Critic* 30 (1967): 8.

Smart, Christopher. *Jubilate Agno*. Ed. W. H. Bond. London: Hart-Davis, 1954.

Smith, Barbara Herrnstein. "Licensing the Unspeakable." *On the Margins of Discourse: The Relation of Literature to Language*. By Smith. Chicago: U of Chicago P, 1978. 107–24.

Smith, Henry Nash. *Virgin Land: The American West as Symbol and Myth*. Cambridge: Harvard UP, 1950.

Smith-Rosenberg, Carroll. *Disorderly Conduct: Visions of Gender in Victorian America*. New York: Knopf, 1985.

Smuts, Jan Christian. *Walt Whitman: A Study in the Evolution of Personality*. Detroit: Wayne State UP, 1973.

Snyder, John. *The Dear Love of Man: Tragic and Lyric Communion in Walt Whitman*. Studies in American Literature 28. The Hague: Mouton, 1975.

Soule, George H., Jr. "Walt Whitman's 'Pictures': An Alternative to Tennyson's 'Palace of Art.' " *ESQ: A Journal of the American Renaissance* 22 (1976): 39–47.

Southard, Sherry G. "Whitman and Language: An Annotated Bibliography." *Walt Whitman Quarterly Review* 2 (1984): 31–49.

Spann, Edward K. *The New Metropolis: New York City, 1840–1857*. New York: Columbia UP, 1981.

Spencer, Benjamin T. *The Quest for Nationality: An American Literary Campaign*. Syracuse: Syracuse UP, 1957.

Spiller, Robert E., et al., eds. *Literary History of the United States*. 3 vols. 1948. 4th ed. 2 vols. New York: Macmillan, 1974.

Spitzer, Leo. "*Explication de Texte* Applied to Walt Whitman's 'Out of the Cradle Endlessly Rocking.' " Woodress 218–27.

Stauffer, Donald Barlow. *A Short History of American Poetry*. New York: Dutton, 1974.

Steele, Jeffrey. *The Representation of the Self in the American Renaissance*. Chapel Hill: U of North Carolina P, 1987.

Stovall, Floyd. *The Foreground of* Leaves of Grass. Charlottesville: UP of Virginia, 1974.

———. "Main Drifts in Whitman's Poetry." *American Literature* 4 (1932): 3–22. Rpt. in Cady and Budd 1–19.

Swinton, William. *Rambles among Words: Their Poetry, History and Wisdom*. New York: Scribner's, 1859.

Tanner, James T. F. "Walt Whitman Bibliographies: A Chronological Listing, 1902–1964." *Bulletin of Bibliography* 25 (1968): 131–32.

Tanner, Tony. *The Reign of Wonder: Naivety and Reality in American Literature*. Cambridge: Cambridge UP, 1965.

Tapscott, Stephen. *American Beauty: William Carlos Williams and the Modernist Whitman*. New York: Columbia UP, 1984.

Thomas, M. Wynn. *The Lunar Light of Whitman's Poetry*. Cambridge: Harvard UP, 1987.

Thoreau, Henry David. *The Portable Thoreau*. Rev. ed. Ed. Carl Bode. New York: Viking, 1964.

Tichi, Cecilia. *New World, New Earth: Environmental Reform in American Literature from the Puritans through Whitman*. New Haven: Yale UP, 1979.

Tocqueville, Alexis de. *Democracy in America*. Paris: C. Gosselin, 1835–40. New York: Knopf, 1945.

Trachtenberg, Alan. *The Incorporation of America: Culture and Society in the Gilded Age*. New York: Hill, 1982.

Traherne, Thomas. *Poems, Centuries and Three Thanksgivings*. Ed. Anne Ridler. London: Oxford UP, 1966.

Traubel, Horace. *With Walt Whitman in Camden*. Vol. 1. Boston: Small, 1906. Vol. 2. New York: Appleton, 1908. Vol. 3. New York: Kennerly, 1914. Vol. 4. Ed. Sculley Bradley. Philadelphia: U of Pennsylvania P, 1953. Vol. 5. Ed. Gertrude Traubel. Carbondale: Southern Illinois UP, 1964. Vol. 6. Ed. Gertrude Traubel and William White. Carbondale: Southern Illinois UP, 1982.

Traubel, Horace, Richard Maurice Bucke, and Thomas B. Harned, eds. *In Re Walt Whitman*. Philadelphia: McKay, 1893.

Tuveson, Ernest Lee. *Redeemer Nation: The Idea of America's Millennial Role*. Chicago: U of Chicago P, 1968.

Tyler, Alice Felt. *Freedom's Ferment: Phases of American Social History to 1860*. Minneapolis: U of Minnesota P, 1944.

Vendler, Helen. "Body Language: *Leaves of Grass* and the Articulation of Sexual Awareness." *Harper's* Oct. 1986: 62–66.

Waggoner, Hyatt H. *American Poets: From the Puritans to the Present.* Boston: Houghton, 1968.

Waldron, Randall H., ed. *Mattie: The Letters of Martha Mitchell Whitman.* New York: New York UP, 1977.

Walters, Ronald G. *American Reformers, 1815–1860.* New York: Hill, 1978.

Warfel, Harry R. "A Seminar in *Leaves of Grass.*" *Emerson Society Quarterly* 22 (1961): 27–28.

Warren, James Perrin. " 'The Free Growth of Metrical Laws': Syntactical Parallelism in 'Song of Myself.' " *Style* 18 (1984): 27–42.

Waskow, Howard J. *Whitman: Explorations in Form.* Chicago: U of Chicago P, 1966.

Weisbuch, Robert. *Atlantic Double-Cross: American Literature and British Influence in the Age of Emerson.* Chicago: U of Chicago P, 1986.

Welter, Rush. *The Mind of America, 1820–1860.* New York: Columbia UP, 1975.

Whicher, Stephen E. "Whitman's Awakening to Death: Toward a Biographical Reading of 'Out of the Cradle Endlessly Rocking.' " Lewis, *Presence* 1–27.

Whitman, Walt. *An American Primer.* Ed. Horace Traubel. 1904. Stevens Point: Holy Cow!, 1987.

———. *The Correspondence of Walt Whitman.* Ed. Edwin Haviland Miller. 6 vols. New York: New York UP, 1961–77.

———. *Daybooks and Notebooks.* Ed. William White. 3 vols. New York: New York UP, 1978.

———. *The Early Poems and the Fiction.* Ed. Thomas L. Brasher. New York: New York UP, 1963.

———. *The Gathering of the Forces.* Ed. Cleveland Rodgers and John Black. 2 vols. New York: Putnam's, 1920.

———. *I Sit and Look Out: Editorials from the* Brooklyn Daily Times. Ed. Emory Holloway and Vernolian Schwarz. New York: Columbia UP, 1932.

———. *Notebooks and Unpublished Prose Manuscripts.* Ed. Edward F. Grier. 6 vols. New York: New York UP, 1984.

———. *Prose Works 1892.* Ed. Floyd Stovall. Vol. 1. *Specimen Days.* New York: New York UP, 1963. Vol. 2. *Collect and Other Prose.* New York: New York UP, 1964.

———. *Specimen Days.* Ed. Lance Hidy. Boston: Godine, 1971.

———. *Uncollected Poetry and Prose of Walt Whitman.* Ed. Emory Holloway. 2 vols. Garden City: Doubleday, 1921.

———. *Walt Whitman of the New York 'Aurora,' Editor at Twenty-Two: A Collection of Recently Discovered Writings.* Ed. Joseph J. Rubin and Charles H. Brown. State College: Bald Eagle, 1950.

———. *Walt Whitman's Memoranda during the War and Death of Abraham Lincoln.* Ed. Roy P. Basler. Reproduced in facsimile. Bloomington: Indiana UP, 1962.

Wiebe, Robert H. *The Opening of American Society: From the Adoption of the Constitution to the Eve of Disunion.* New York: Knopf, 1984.

Wilentz, Sean. *Chants Democratic: New York City and the Rise of the American Working Class, 1788–1850.* New York: Oxford UP, 1984.

Willard, Charles B. *Whitman's American Fame: The Growth of His Reputation in America after 1892.* Providence: Brown UP, 1950.

Wilson, Edmund. *Patriotic Gore: Studies in the Literature of the American Civil War.* New York: Oxford UP, 1962.

Wolfson, Leandro. "The Other Whitman in Spanish America." *Walt Whitman Review* 24 (1978): 61–72.

Woodress, James, ed. *Critical Essays on Walt Whitman.* Boston: Hall, 1983.

Wright, George T. *The Poet in the Poem: The Personae of Eliot, Yeats, and Pound.* Berkeley: U of California P, 1960.

Wright, James. "The Delicacy of Walt Whitman." Lewis, *Presence* 164–88.

Ziff, Larzer. *Literary Democracy: The Declaration of Cultural Independence in America.* New York: Viking, 1981.

Zweig, Paul. *Walt Whitman: The Making of the Poet.* New York: Basic, 1984.

Audiocassettes and Records

Readings

Allen, David. *Walt Whitman's* Leaves of Grass. CMS Records, 543, 1968.

Begley, Ed. *Walt Whitman: Eyewitness to the Civil War.* 2 cassettes. Caedmon, SWC 2040, 1969.

———. *Walt Whitman's* Leaves of Grass. 2 cassettes. Caedmon, SWC 1037, SWC 1154, 1960.

Kerr, Anita. *In the Soul.* GAIA Records, 1988.

O'Herlihy, Dan. *Walt Whitman's* Leaves of Grass. 2 cassettes. Pasadena: Cassette Book Co., 848, 1982.

Scourby, Alexander. *Treasury of Walt Whitman: Leaves of Grass.* 2 cassettes. Spoken Arts, 7133, 7134, 1983.

Welles, Orson. *Orson Welles Reads "Song of Myself."* Audio-Forum, ECN 207, 1987.

Lectures

Allen, Gay Wilson, and Arthur Golden. *Walt Whitman.* Mount Vernon, NY: Gould Media, AL3, 1971.

Cady, Edwin, and Louis Budd. *Walt Whitman and the Democratic Epic.* Madison, WI: Annenberg/CPB Audio Collection, 1987.

Davis, Charles T. *Works of Walt Whitman.* 2 cassettes. Deland, FL: Everett/Edwards, 836, 837, 1972.

Randel, William Pierce. *Drum-Taps*. Deland, FL: Everett/Edwards, 538, 1974.

————. *Leaves of Grass*. Deland, FL: Everett/Edwards, 539, 1974.

————. *Whitman as a Disciple of Emerson*. Deland, FL: Everett/Edwards, 537, 1974.

Films, Filmstrips, and Videocassettes

The Living Tradition. Film. Boulder, CO: Centre Productions, 1983. (For information, write Centre Productions Inc., 1800 30th St., Boulder, CO 80301.)

Song of Myself. Film. American Parade series. New York: Columbia Broadcasting System (National News Department), 1976. (Information on rental is available from Indiana Univ., Audio Visual Center, Bloomington, IN 47405, 812 335–2853.)

Voices and Visions: Walt Whitman. Videocassette. Washington: Annenberg/CPB Project, 1987. (Information is available from Annenberg/CPB Project, 1111 16th St. NW, Washington, DC 20036, 202 955–5251.)

Walt Whitman's Civil War. Sound filmstrip. Los Angeles: Magus Films, 1969.

Walt Whitman: Poet For a New Age. Sound filmstrip. Chicago: Encyclopedia Britannica Educational Corp., 1971.

INDEX